EveryDay Leadership
Crossing Gorges on Tightropes to Success

By
Bill Clement

Dream BIG & DARE to fail,

Bill Clement '10

EveryDay Leadership
Crossing Gorges on Tightropes to Success

By
Bill Clement

Self-Published by WHC Enterprises

ISBN: 978-0-9787809-7-5

Photos courtesy of: Bill Clement family, Philadelphia Flyers, Washington Capitals, Atlanta Flames, Calgary Flames, Ottawa 67s, ESPN

Front Cover Photo: Dan Naylor Photography
Back Cover Photo: Ned Redway Photography

Printed proudly in the USA
Printing Enterprises, New Brighton, MN

A portion of the proceeds from the sale of this book will benefit the Bill Clement Foundation. Thank you for your support!

www.BillClementSpeaking.com

This book is dedicated to my magnificent family and friends. Your love represents the true meaning of life.

On the left, my brother Pete and his family - daughter Karin, wife Nora and sons Kris and Mike (both kneeling). In the middle - my dearest mom, Lorine (standing), sister, Barby (seated). On the right, my wife Cissie, me, daughter Savannah leaning on daughter Regan's shoulders and son, Chase.

ACKNOWLEDGEMENTS

I learned through the process of creating this book that many deserving people end up owning part of the written words. It is never just the subject of the book or the author - it is so many more. This book would not have been possible without the following people, to whom I am forever grateful.

Ross Bernstein, this book wouldn't have come close to happening without you. Your contributions and guidance with the writing, your counsel when I wasn't sure, your creativity with the title as well as your idea for the cover — all you! Thank-you my friend!

My dad, who left us more than a decade ago. You influenced the fabric of who I am more than anyone in my life.

My mom, who truly is part sunshine. You have supported everything I have ever tried and always been there when I needed you. You leave every situation better than you find it.

My incredible wife, Cissie, who encourages me in everything I do. Without your love and your presence in my life, smiles would seem meaningless.

My four dynamic children — Christa, Regan, Savannah and Chase. You are made of such goodness and you inspire me every day.

My 'sis, Barby. I am always so proud to say you are my sister.

My brother, Pete and sister-in-law, Nora. The way you have raised your three beautiful young adults is a model for everyone to follow.

Mike Porcaro. Even though you live thousands of miles away my friend, I have always drawn strength from our relationship and always felt you beside me as I worked on the book.

TABLE OF CONTENTS

THE BILL CLEMENT FOUNDATION

I'm thrilled to announce that a portion of the proceeds from the sale of my book, as well as my speaking engagements, will benefit the Bill Clement Foundation. I've been involved with dozens and dozens of wonderful charitable organizations in my life and am very proud of the fact that I've played a small part in helping to raise millions of dollars for those causes.

When I finally decided to write this book, I wanted to focus on a couple of causes that are extremely near and dear to me and my family. As such, the Bill Clement Foundation's mission will be to help find a cure for Multiple Sclerosis and to serve those born with Down Syndrome, each of which touches two of my three daughters — Christa and Regan.

Christa has been afflicted with MS for more than 10 years now. She lives with it and in addition to being a very successful CPA accountant (CGA in Canada) in Ottawa, she's an incredible mother to our adorable grandchildren. Part of my foundation proceeds will go to the National Multiple Sclerosis Society (U.S.) whose mission is to mobilize people and resources to drive research for a cure and to address the challenges of everyone affected by MS.

Regan, like Christa, is one of the greatest lights in our lives. She was born with Down Syndrome and we couldn't be more proud of her. I like to refer to her as the "Pied Piper" of New Hope, our adopted hometown in Pennsylvania. Regan bags groceries at the local supermarket and EVERYBODY knows her and just adores her. She's like a local celebrity, always smiling and making others feel good about themselves. What a gift. Part of my foundation proceeds will go to NDSS (National Down Syndrome Society) whose mission is to be the national advocate for the value, acceptance and inclusion of people with Down syndrome.

All of our kids, including our New York actress, Savannah, and my soccer playing son, Chase, are amazing, beautiful people and I feel so blessed to be their father. As such, I'm determined to make a difference in all of their lives and truly appreciate your support.

If you would like to learn more about the Bill Clement Foundation, or about how you can help us with our mission, please visit my website www.BillClementSpeaking.com.

Thank you from the bottom of my heart!

Sincerely, Bill Clement

Savannah, Chase and Regan
at Christa's wedding (2001)

INTRODUCTION

The subject of leadership has been a passion of mine for as long as I can remember. I started by studying the great leaders and soon realized that because of their titles they represented only a tiny percentile of humans. Presidents, Generals, CEO's - really elite categories. What about the rest of us? I came to the conclusion that regardless of our job titles we are all in the position to influence other people's attitudes and behaviors. We therefore possess the power to impact their contributions, their decisions and their dedication to helping group endeavors succeed. EveryDay Leadership is not about our job titles, but our abilities to influence others - something that is in our grasp 24-7.

This book is as much about my failures as an EveryDay Leader as it is successes. My ego, my emotions and my mouth have all helped me fall short. Instead of writing a "how to" book on leadership, I decided to create a balance by including examples and stories that explain "how not to." I found material in my own life everywhere I turned, from failed marriages to personal bankruptcy. And regardless of where I was career-wise - hockey player, restaurateur, actor, broadcaster, professional speaker - the metaphor involving the gorge and the tightrope was always there.

In each career there were critical junctures where forces started to push back against my attempts to succeed. As a kid, I had a hard time processing these obstacles and always felt as if I was standing at the edge of a gorge that contained the things that were acting as resistors to my success. Some of the resistors were created by circumstances I couldn't control but most were internal. Fear, self-doubt, anxiety, intimidation.

I could always see performance success very clearly on the other side of the gorge. I knew where I wanted to end up, but the only visible way across was a tightrope. The tightrope was my level of courage and my willingness to attempt something I wasn't sure I could do. Years ago I would search for an easier way across, only to end up back at the tightrope. Today I know that life will always present another gorge and that EveryDay Leadership can never be mastered unless we promise ourselves to always step out onto the tightrope. Only then will people follow.

I am delighted to share my ongoing journey as an EveryDay Leader with you and hope you see at least part of yourself in these pages.

FOREWORD BY WAYNE GRETZKY

I recently shared the stage with Bill Clement at a speaking event in Palm Springs, California, and the subject of leadership came up, as it often does. I had known Bill for many years and knew who he was long before we met. As a kid I immersed myself in NHL knowledge and knew just about every player on every team. By the time I was 18 I was wearing an NHL uniform in Edmonton, playing against Bill and the Atlanta Flames. He was tenacious and determined and I was always impressed with his work ethic and that he tried to lead by example. There was definitely a competitive spirit driving him.

The Flames soon became our biggest rival when they moved to Calgary, Alberta, which was just down the road. We had some epic battles and I noticed that regardless of what the score was or where the game was being played, Bill's game didn't change. He just kept coming.

I met Bill when he retired and became a broadcaster. During my great fortune of winning Four Stanley Cups in Edmonton, all of the top TV networks covered us from top to bottom. After I was traded to L.A., Bill was there to broadcast the game in which I broke Gordie Howe's career goal-scoring record. It was almost like every time I turned around, there was Bill! I enjoyed listening to him because he was always prepared and really quick on his feet during spontaneous moments.

When Bill asked me if I would contribute a forward for this book, I wanted to know what it was about. When I was told it was a book centered on leadership, I wanted to hear more. Leadership has been a part of my life for as long as I can remember. Captaining NHL teams was something that I did in three different cities, and I always knew there were other players in the room who were great leaders, as well. I have heard so many captains playing professional team sports say in interviews, "It not just me. There are 20 other guys in this room leading as well." You know what? They're right. That's why the concept of everyday leadership intrigued me and why I believed in it right away. As a father of five kids, I am in a seat of influence 365 days per year and my title isn't CEO or Captain. It's "dad," and it's one of the most prestigious leadership titles in the world.

I sincerely hope there is something in this book for everyone, because we can all be leaders if we want to be.

1) GROWING UP IN QUEBEC...

I was born on December 20, 1950, at the regional hospital in Buckingham, Quebec, the second of three children to Adrian and Lorine Clement, and mostly raised in Thurso, Quebec, a small paper mill town about 30 miles outside of Ottawa. My father spoke both English and French and before we moved to Thurso he worked as a wheelman in a power house at a big dam on the Lievre River in Quebec. We lived in a community of just eight houses, all in a circle, and each resident worked at the dam.

His name was Adrian but everybody knew dad as "Rip." He got that nickname because he was a fast, powerful athlete. He loved football, he ran track and he dominated in tennis. He was born and raised in Buckingham and seemed content living there. Dad had a lot of opportunities to leave home as a young man but he never did. One year he was offered a tryout with the Toronto Argonauts of the Canadian Football League but never left home to pursue it. He could have done so many different things. He also had an incredible singing voice and played multiple instruments to boot. He was remarkably gifted, winning talent shows in the area with ease. Several talent scouts tried to get him to go to New York but he never wanted to leave home. A loving, compassionate dad who I think, deep down inside, wasn't able to see himself taking chances and making it across some of life's gorges on the tightropes of success.

My mom is wonderful, so sweet, and like my father also very musically gifted. She and my father met while in the Air Force during the second World War, stationed in Trenton, Ontario. At night during the Winter, for fun, everybody at the base would go skating on frozen edges of Lake Ontario. They would

11

build a big bonfire and skate around it to keep warm. Well, one night my mom was skating around the bonfire singing when all of a sudden, through the darkness, she heard someone across the way singing harmony to her song. Sure enough, it turned out to be my father. It was love at first sight, er… sound, I suppose. Funny, that was probably the last time my mother has skated! Mom was Irish, grew up in British Columbia and didn't speak any French. They fell in love though and she wound up moving to be with my dad. They eventually settled down in Buckingham, after a few years in Ottawa, and started a family. Mom fully embraced the French culture and was always proud to say she lived in Quebec.

I have an older sister, Barby and a younger brother, Peter. Pete's a wonderful person and an even better dad. Great guy. I was three and half years older than he was so whatever I did, he wanted to do better. He was a good hockey player as a kid and we got along well. Just a high quality human. Barby, meanwhile, is two years older than me and is an inspiration to everyone - just the salt of the earth.

My sister was born with congenital leg deformities and

With my sister, Barby, looking for a parade.

she only has two fingers on her right hand. Her lower legs, ankles and feet are misshapen and one leg is considerably shorter than the other. She could walk, but it was often tough for her to get around. Her attitude was one of her top assets so her exaggerated limp didn't seem to slow her down much. Barby even entered some races at the little school track meet we had every year. In spite of the obstacles posed by her anatomy, she is infinitely talented musically and plays keyboard like a concert pianist. She plays in the key of F-sharp, which is mostly black notes because her two right hand fingers can cover more ground that way. Remarkable! Any people she has asked to help her with writing or transposing music always ask her the same question over the phone, "Why in the world do you play in the key of F-sharp?", and she always says, "You'll know when you meet me."

Barby had multiple surgeries as an infant to try and correct some of the deformities and it was rough on her, but she's a very resilient person. Dad had to work, so mom would pack up Barby and make the six hour train ride to the Toronto Hospital for Sick Children. They would be gone for weeks at a time. This was in the days before health insurance and the cost of the surgeries stretched our family pretty thin. One month dad was unable to make the regular payment and he wrote a note to Barby's surgeon, Dr. Wansbrough, explaining he was a bit short of funds and asked if it could wait a few weeks. He got a note back saying, "Please consider your account paid in full." It was an act of kindness mom and dad never forgot.

I remember people always staring at Barby when I was a kid and I felt so bad for her. Later, when I got older, I would get angry and yell at those kids who stared at her. I would shield her with my body, to protect her. If they couldn't see her then they couldn't stare at her. Her exterior was different, yes, but inside she was the same as everybody else. Even better. Being around that as a child certainly made me a much more understanding person today, that's for sure. That anger and those emotions of feeling sorry for her eventually turned into a tolerance and an understanding for those less fortunate. I also realized it was only because people didn't understand and didn't know, that's why they stared. She was different and out of the norm. I couldn't comprehend all of that back then, but later when I finally grasped the whole thing, I think it made me a better person. You know, my parents never treated her any differently than Pete or me and I think that's why she is the way that she is today. She's fantastic and so talented. She's crippled and in a wheel chair now living in Ottawa, but she's OK with who she is as a person. She's a star.

When I was six we moved about 20 miles south to the little town of Thurso, nestled along the Ottawa River. My dad got a better job there as an electrical supervisor at a paper mill. It was in Thurso where I really spent my formidable years growing up. We lived in a small, three bedroom track home. Very modest. It was interesting in that I was a very pronounced English minority in a French speaking town. There were three thousand people who lived there and less than five percent were English. My dad was bilingual so it worked out great for him in his new job, but for my brother and sister and me, it was a tough transition. The schools weren't integrated either. The French were all Catholics and they all went to a big, newer school. The English people, meanwhile, we were all pretty much Protestants. Our little school was nothing more than five classrooms and a gymnasium, and that was after the expansion. First grade to seventh grade, in five rooms. You didn't have to be a math major to figure out there was more than one grade in each room. Pretty intimate.

The stench from the mill carried all the way to Ottawa with an easterly wind. When westerly winds blew, the smell would suffocate visitors but town kids never seemed to mind it. We got used to it I suppose. Perhaps we realized that without the mill our dads wouldn't be able to buy shoes for us. I used to joke and say, "That's dad's paycheck we smell."

My childhood recollections of life at home are filled with warmth and love. Outside the home was a different story though. Our neighborhood was somewhat segregated and could be a pretty lonely place to hang out sometimes, especially if you were a kid. There was a lot of animosity which led to some epic neighborhood battles, French kids versus English kids. Even today, when I meet people and they realize that I'm from Quebec, it shocks them. They always wonder why I don't have a thick French accent. Well, it's because I was raised English. I was a minority, and that's how I was educated and brought up. I learned to love the French culture though and it was a great childhood. I have so many wonderful memories and most of them involve my family.

My parents were bright, worldly, caring people. The best. They were both givers - just very giving souls. As I look back I can see certain characteristics that I got from each of them. My father's work ethic was so strong, I definitely got that from him. I used to love cutting and chopping pulpwood with dad. In that sense, I became a weekend lumberjack starting at age ten. Dad had purchased a densely wooded chunk of forest near Thurso, and we generated extra family money in that bush.

I grew up in an era when horses were still used to skid wood. When we felled a tree, we had to get it close to the road so the trucks could pick it up and haul it to the mill. My job was

Holding baby brother, Pete, with Barby looking on. She always liked being the supervisor.

to drive our Belgian mare, Lady, by holding the reins and walking beside her while she skidded the logs - often uphill. She was huge and at my age, resembled the Trojan Horse in size. When she bogged down, seemingly unable to continue up the hill with a thousand pound log behind her, I would urge her on, flicking the reins, whistling at her and shouting "C'mon Lady! Pull Lady!" Standing right beside her wasn't really the safest place and she stepped on me so many times, I still wonder why my feet didn't break. Scared me half to death and hurt like hell.

I will never forget the day my dad bought this old, beat up vehicle called a Power Wagon to replace Lady. We had graduated from skidding wood with a large animal to doing it with a big cable and a winch on the back of the wagon. Life got a lot better from that moment on. So did my feet.

Dad had such a positive attitude. He would always say to us, "Something's going to be better tomorrow if it's not very good today." He tried to put a positive spin on everything. As a result he was really good at influencing us in our moods and

Mom and dad were very affectionate and Barby, Pete and I followed closely in their footsteps.

our attitudes. I remember the ritual of him waking me up before dawn when I was seven years old and taking me out to pick raspberries. The berries came in June after my school year had ended, so I could have slept in. Dad had to be at work at the mill by 7:45 am, so we would get up really early, before sunrise, and drive up to this huge gravel pit about three miles out of town. Raspberries grew like crazy in there and when they were ripe, we were there picking as many as we could get our hands on.

He wanted to go during the week, before all the weekend pickers could get there and pick over the best stuff. I really didn't want to get up and pick raspberries in the dark, but that time alone with dad was pretty special. He was always so uplifting and so positive. He was also a master at painting that final picture. Dad helped me understand the importance of starting with the end in mind, and creating that perfect vision in your head of what it's going to turn into — if you invest in it now. When I complained about how cold and dark it was, he would talk about how warm and bright it was going to be in just a few minutes when the beautiful sunrise began. Then he would describe how wonderful the jam was going to taste that winter, so that's what I focused on. He was just a fantastic influence on me and I realized he had the ability to modify people's behaviors, simply with his positive energy.

If he found a really good patch of berries, he would revel in that discovery, but often they weren't easy to find. Sometimes you had to really get in there and dig for them because they were hidden or buried. Well, dad was so good at finding them. He was so patient. There were times when we would arrive at the pit only to discover that bushes had been pretty picked over and for me, it was discouraging. I didn't want to work that hard and get all scraped up digging in those prickly bushes. Most of the bushes would be bent over and appeared to be picked clean by the weekenders and dad would go right for them. I used to think he was wasting his time, searching for berries on a cleanly picked bush. But he would gently get into the middle of that bush, lifting and pushing the branches aside and invariably out he would come with a big clump of beautiful, luscious raspberries that all those other people had overlooked. I couldn't wait to get home to show the family the fruits of our labor, literally, like a proud fisherman. Mom would be there waiting for us, so approving and thankful and supportive. We did OK financially, I suppose, but we never had a lot of money for extra things. So stuff like this was a big deal.

Dad always reminded me that even when you may think there's nothing in front of your eyes, there was an incredible opportunity just waiting for you if you were willing to dig deep enough. Those seeds of opportunity and the concept of the payoff always being there if you are willing to work hard and willing to look where others might not, are the lessons I learned from dad out on those early mornings.

It was my introduction to two of the many concepts I live by today. The first is thinking outside the box. It seemed counter-intuitive to dive into raspberry bushes that, on the surface looked barren. They weren't.

The second, was visualizing the future as I want it to be. To this day, in almost every demanding situation I encounter, I create the "ultimate video" in my mind of how I would like a situation to be resolved. If I don't have time to visualize a video of even a few seconds in length, I go for the "ultimate snapshot." If nothing else, this technique helps me govern my behavior and demeanor most of the time. Behavioral consistency is central to successful EveryDay Leadership and our emotions can often twist our behavior and derail our goals. Visually reminding ourselves what our optimal result would be, by using the "ultimate video" or "ultimate snapshot" helps us stay on point and on track. Does it always work? As you will read on these pages, I have taken my share of swan dives off the tightrope and into the gorge.

Since we mold and shape the lives of our children from the moment they are born, the classic position of leadership is that of parent. From age zero on, we sculpt and influence our children and my dad had a profound influence on me. I feel lucky and privileged for that. I really do.

My Father was also creative and inventive. He could build or fix just about anything. He had even devised an efficient berry picking system. He would take three big apple juice cans, which were empty and had the labels peeled off, and he would cut the lids off of them. He would then punch holes on either side of the open end and attach wire loops to each. We would then loosen our belts and run them through the loops so the cans hung in front of us. Dad would get two cans, I would get one. That way you could pick with two hands and not have to hold the container in the other hand. Then he would have a big turkey roasting pan out there, like a big holding tank, so we could just walk over and dump our load of raspberries into it without having to do any extra work. He had it down to a science, let me tell you. I mean the guy was always thinking of stuff like that, little things that would make our lives easier. I can still see that big grin on his face in the dead of winter, eating a big piece of bread with raspberry jam on it. So proud, so happy. He would look at me, as if to toast me, and say, "You see, all those early mornings out there, it's all worth it now." That was the payoff to the investment. What a man. I miss him.

In my speaking programs I often ask people how they

Getting our strength up with glasses of juice
before opening presents on Christmas morning.

want to be remembered when it's all said and done. I ask them how they want their tombstones to read. It's quite profound to think about that, if not a little scary. Of course, you get the odd curveball thrown your way that can be quite humorous. During one workshop I was hosting we went around the room with people sharing what they had written as their desired epitaph. When we got to Greg for his, he said, "I told you I was sick!" Talk about cracking the room up.

Early on, I always said that mine would read: "He was a good neighbor." I got that from my dad too, no question, because he was the best neighbor. I will always remember how he enjoyed helping people who needed it. By virtue of this desire to help, he was truly a good neighbor. Whether it was somebody who didn't have a ladder and needed to borrow ours, or maybe someone who was having car troubles. I once watched dad work on my neighbor's car engine for more than a half hour in sub-zero weather with his bare hands. I remember years later, when I could fully appreciate what he had done, thinking, "How in the hell did he do that?" He never even took a break - the guy was just so tough. My hands would

Pete, Barby and me wading in the Lievre River in front of our house in High Falls, Quebec.

have been frozen solid. The tools themselves looked like they were going to freeze to his hands. But he didn't stop until he got that motor running, because he knew that our neighbor had someplace important to be. So whenever anybody needed help, my dad was THE guy in the neighborhood everybody turned to — whatever it was. He was the definition of dependable. No matter what. He just harkened back to a different era and it's hard to find people like that today. I learned so much from him just by observing him.

Simply put, dad was a giver. He went to his grave understanding that he gave more than he took. I think that's why he's very peaceful where he is now — and I look forward to reuniting with him at some point — not any time soon, but eventually. Sadly, we lost him in 2000. He was in a home for a number of years before eventually dying of complications due to Super-Parkinson's disease. It was so tough to see him go that way. In a sense, he left mentally, before he actually physically left us.

So as I've become older and hopefully wiser over all these years, I've revised my tombstone to now read: "He gave more than he took." Just like dad, that's how I want to be remembered, as a giver and not as a taker. Sure, being a good neighbor is part of that, but this just goes above and beyond that a little bit. Even now, as I look at the universe around me, I find it harder and harder to turn somebody down when they say, "Can you please help me?" It has become my nature - or was it always?

I remember visiting with my mom not too long ago and her telling me that I had been like this ever since I was a little kid. She told me one time when I was in the first grade that I came home very upset and asked if I could take a pair of my mittens and give them to one of my classmates at school. His name was Réal Levert. She asked me why and I told her it was because he didn't have any and that it was really cold outside. The poor kid was freezing whenever he had to walk anywhere outside and I figured I could help.

Now, I didn't remember the story, but it's enlightening to think that even as a kid, I was a product of my history - of my parents' influence - of my environment. I truly believe you can teach compassion and the leaders in the most powerful positions to do so, are parents. Luckily I learned that from mine and it's still a big part of who I am to this day. What's great about the mittens story though, is that my mom took it a step further. Once she heard about Réal, she knew there must be others just like him. Well, she was a member of the school board, so she organized a day where all the kids' parents sent in their old jackets and mittens and hats and scarves for those who were less fortunate. This was back in the '60s, when this sort of thing was almost nonexistent. Today it's commonplace, where every school does something like this, but back then it was almost unheard of. That was mom though. She got involved and decided to take good and then make it great.

Everybody thinks that their mom is a saint and I'm no exception. She was a stay-at-home mom. She did the cooking and the cleaning, and she did so much of the rearing of us kids. Mom just had a positive attitude about everything. When I think about EveryDay Leadership and about the power of positive energy, I can't help but think of my mom. You know,

The couch wasn't big enough for all of us. I worked at getting our family dog, Cheesecake, to smile for the camera.

energy sources always leave situations better than they found them. That was mom to a tee. Conversely, energy vampires leave situations worse off than they found them. Mom had a keen interest in almost everything, from geography to history to current events, to whatever was going on in a person's life — and she always had time to listen to them. As a result, she was able to leave situations better than she found them. She's been such a ray of sunshine for so many people who had darkness in their lives.

Mom and dad were amazing influences on me. They made do with whatever they had and just went with it, always staying positive. They were also very musical and loved singing together and playing duets on our piano. Dad even used to organize a glee club wherever we lived and the group would all come over and practice at our house. He and mom would arrange the four-part harmonies. They would perform barber shop quartet pieces and other ensemble arrangements at church and school functions. They loved it.

Mom played multiple instruments and was an accomplished pianist, so they used to fill our house with some pretty amazing music. Mom even used to teach piano lessons to some of the neighbor kids for a little extra money. She was so patient. To me it sounded like fingernails on a chalkboard, but she would just sit there and smile, praising her pupils. Music was a huge part of my childhood because it was always around in one way or another. Always. We were constantly singing something, whatever we were doing. Dad and Barby loved to perform but brother Pete just flat out refused. Mom and I were both really shy but we would get dragged out to sing as the Clement quartet, even when I didn't want to. Oh, I loved singing - just not with an audience. Halfway through our first song it always got easier and singing really brought us closer as a family.

I think music provided some of the glue that bonded our family together. I can still remember falling asleep to the sounds of the glee club practicing and harmonizing. It was soothing and comforting to me.

2) ENTER HOCKEY...

Growing up, sports was everything to me - my absolute passion. In school I played whatever was offered. We had an empty lot behind our home where us kids would all play and we also had this big wooded area, maybe 30 acres, on the other side of a long field at the edge of town near our home — we called it the "bush." We had so much fun in the summers, either in the bush or behind our house or in the street - playing games, hiking, just running around playing tag or touch football or baseball or whatever. We'd spend all day out there. Nothing was organized though, just made up by us as we went along. We didn't have any coaches or practices or anything like that. Our town was too small to have a recreation department and we didn't know any better. There was no organized

I could have stayed in the driveway shooting pucks and balls all day and often did. If the weather got nasty, I took my game inside.

football, or basketball, or baseball, so if we wanted to play anything we'd make it up or just head off to the bush. We were on our own.

There was, however, a tiny arena and organized travel hockey. I would've loved to play on the town team, but the English kids weren't invited to even try out. So, I played wherever I could and just made the best of it.

There was also a little outdoor rink behind our school that was only a block and a half away from my house, so I would be over there all day and all night playing with my friends. It was so much fun, old kids, young kids, it didn't matter — we would all play pick-up together. Heck, we would even play on the streets when they froze too. We didn't care, we just wanted to play. We'd be out there on that rink well after dark with only a few nearby street lights helping us see the puck, until dad whistled at us to come home for dinner. It was wonderful.

I was a goalie at first and loved it. I thought those big pads looked pretty neat, despite the fact that they were so old

Baseball was my second love but there were no teams in our hometown.

and rickety — probably dangerous too. I will never forget the goalie mask that I used; it was this Lucite see-thru contraption that was all scratched up. It was just scary and I could hardly see through it. I was OK as a goalie, nothing spectacular, but decent. What it did though was it made me realize pretty quickly that I was much better as a skater. Even though I was new to the sport, it turned out I was really fast. So I moved out to play forward and never looked back.

Every Saturday night we would gather around the TV and watch "Hockey Night in Canada." We never missed it. I would watch and dream of one day hoisting that beautiful Stanley Cup above my head like my heroes on TV. That show was like religion for so many people throughout Canada - more important than going to church - it was just an institution. Once we would watch it, then we couldn't wait to get outside the next day and play.

Hockey became my purpose, my main passion, and before long my childhood dream quickly turned into an obsession to one day play in the National Hockey League. I loved the

A weekend relaxing at the cottage. If we weren't felling trees and skidding wood we loved a good card game.

Toronto Maple Leafs, they were my team. Kid brother, Pete, his favorite color was red, so he rooted for the Montreal Canadiens. We couldn't wait to watch "Hockey Night in Canada" on TV and see who would have bragging rights for the week.

Pete and I practically lived out on that little rink during the Winter, playing whenever we could. We would come home for dinner and then after we did our homework we would go out and shoot tennis balls in the garage. We pretty much destroyed everything in there. Dad would park the car outside for us and we would go crazy. It was so simple but exhilarating. We would go outside and shoot pucks at the garage door when it warmed up and we trashed that too. It got really ugly - the house that is - and poor mom would just cringe because her poor home looked like a war zone with black puck marks and shattered shingles with tar paper exposed all over them. She knew we loved to play though and always put our needs and desires over hers.

Little did we know at the time, but throughout my childhood, I was honing the skills necessary to one day play professional hockey. I even hollowed out a puck and filled the middle with lead, to make it really heavy, and would then shoot at a big piece of plywood that I had hung on the basement wall. I needed the plywood because I had wrecked the poured concrete foundation. I wound up with one helluva improved wrist shot though, because I would shoot down there for hours on end.

Pete, even though he was younger than I was, could shoot a puck way harder than I could — but he was wild. So that kid did some serious damage to the outside of our house — let me tell you! When I turned 14 dad brought home two bundles of composite shingles that matched those on the front of the house and made me fix all the shingles that we had either damaged or completely crushed. It was brutal.

****

Even though I made it to the NHL, I never played regular organized hockey until I was 12, which is pretty amazing when I think back on it. It was at that age that the English speaking kids were finally invited to try out for the town team. That first season, I lined up beside a player I had been watching for five years by the name of Guy Lafleur, who would go on to become a Hall of Famer with the Montreal Canadiens. Guy wasn't just good, he was the most dominant player for his age in the history of the province. I was in awe of him. He was a year younger than I was but he played up a level and was the king there too.

When Guy first started skating there wasn't ANY organized youth hockey in Thurso, so he went across the river to Ontario to play for the Rockland Boomers. Before long he was a household name in Quebec and everybody was talking about this kid. The Boomers once beat a team 21-0 and Guy scored all 21 goals. By the time he was eight years old he had a slap shot that was comparable to a 17 year old's. Honest truth. The poor little peewee goalies that had to try and stop him were defenseless and scared to death. Some of them just moved out of the way when he unloaded that cannon of a shot because they didn't want to get hurt. They were terrified. By the time he played for the Canadiens, he had reached the status of sports hero and when Montreal was winning all those Stanley Cups in the 70s, six to be exact, Guy became a sports icon throughout North America. "The Flower," as he is known, remains a legendary beloved figure in Canada to this day.

My school in Thurso only went through the seventh grade, so when I started the eighth grade I had to take the bus back to my birth town of Buckingham every day for high school. It was a long trip but it was great to get out of that tiny little school. The world really opened up for me in Buckingham. They had organized team sports there too, which was totally foreign to me. Luckily, I had a wonderful gym teacher who taught us how to play all the different sports. One of my favorites was badminton. What a great game, I loved it. I actually went on to win the Western Quebec High School Championship, believe it or not. I also ran track and played basketball too. I quickly fell in love with basketball and at one point thought I might want to play that over hockey. But by now I was playing hockey on the Thurso town team, since they finally integrated and let the English kids play, and my coach threatened to kick me off the team if I kept missing hockey practices for basketball practices. I was bummed out about it but realized that there weren't too many Canadian basketball stars in the NBA in those days, so hockey it was.

At 15 I left home to try out with the Sorel Blackhawks of the Quebec Junior League. The NHL still had ownership interests in the junior teams in those days, so we were the farm team of the Chicago Blackhawks. I was the youngest player in the league at the time and this was a scary new world for me. It was lonely too. They threw us into a motel for my first week of tryouts and then moved me to a boarding house with a French billet (host) family that had five kids of their own. I wasn't fluent in French yet either, so it was tough. Sorel was probably a 95% French speaking town but luckily there was an English speaking high school there that I was able to attend.

I remember calling mom and dad near the end of train-

Our Thurso midget team. Dad was manager, back row, left.
That's me, front row second from left. The great Guy
Lafleur is back row, second player from the right.

ing camp, completely depressed, and telling them I wanted to come home. They said, "You know what, you've made all the cuts this far, hang in there. You have a good chance of making it."

John Choyce was the general manager of the team at the time. He was a grizzled hockey veteran of many, many years. I will never forget the first real team meeting we had. He gathered everybody around and with his head tilted forward, almost looking through his eyebrows said, "OK, anybody who wants to wear a helmet, go home." He proceeded to tell us that it was his job to prepare us to play in the NHL, and that men in the NHL did not wear helmets. Period. Most of these guys were 18, 19 and 20, and here I was at 15. Those were like dog years and it was complete culture shock for me. 65 guys tried out and there were only four openings on the team. I was really lucky to make it.

My brother also later made the team in Sorel, but he wanted to live closer to home so he tried out with the Ottawa 67s. He was a big guy, pretty strong. He was physical but

Making my first junior team in Sorel had a lot to do with my size. At 15 I was over six feet tall and weighed 185 pounds.

didn't drop the gloves to fight that much. He just didn't have it in his heart to be a tough guy. Anyway, he had gotten sent down to Ottawa's junior B team at one point and during a game one night he got into it with a guy on the other team. When Pete turned around the guy swung his stick across his face like a baseball bat and knocked out seven of his teeth. I remember him telling me the story. He said he was in the dentist's chair for hours that night and when he went to spit water out of his mouth after rinsing, it all came out the side of his cheek. Turned out there was a big hole in it. Pretty bad.

That injury, the way it happened, it really set him back emotionally. He returned to the ice but he was never the same after that. His heart just wasn't in it. A little over a year later he hung em' up for good. He decided to go to school and wound up getting his Master's degree in public administration at Carleton University in Ottawa. He played some college hockey but the fire that burned to play NHL hockey slowly disappeared. Today he runs a large non-profit organization owned by philanthropists in Montreal. I couldn't be happier for his success

At age 16 I was named captain of the expansion Ottawa 67's of the Ontario Hockey Association.

- he's a terrific guy and my best friend.

After my first season away from home, I returned to continue my summer job as a farmhand on a dairy farm. It was only a few miles from town and I stayed out there six days a week. Throwing bales of hay all day really helped me build muscle which would come in pretty handy in the career I was pursuing.

That summer I was drafted by the Ontario league expansion team, Ottawa 67's who ended up having to send three players to Sorel to get my rights. Ottawa was English speaking and closer to home so I adjusted quickly to my new surroundings. The OHA (Ontario Hockey Association) was considered a step up in caliber from the Quebec league which meant I was trending in the right direction.

During my three years with Ottawa I began working at my hometown paper mill in the off-seasons to earn my spending money. I had to speak French regularly for my job so I picked it up pretty quickly at that point. I enrolled at Carleton University at age 17 but found it almost impossible to focus on

Skating with my head up was a concept I was still trying to master.

school work as I approached my final years in Junior hockey. I wound up going to school in the summers and I always wanted to get my college degree. Unfortunately I never would.

I was a pretty shy kid in those days and didn't do a whole lot of dating, but I did get pretty serious with my first girlfriend when I was 17. Cathie was her name and she was from Ottawa. I saw her in the crowd at one of my games and we just happened to meet afterward when I was out with some of my teammates. We immediately hit it off. I thought it was love at first sight.

3) ONE STEP CLOSER...

When I was 19 years old, I was drafted by the NHL's Philadelphia Flyers. I barely missed out on playing another year of juniors because of my birth date and as a result was pretty young to turn professional. I remember going to the draft at the Queen Elizabeth Hotel in Montreal. Each team had a table in the ballroom and it was pretty low-key, nothing like the two-day spectacle that it is now with all of the TV cameras interviewing the draftees and then following them as they go up on stage to be introduced. Hardly any players were even there, but since we were close by, our coach encouraged us to go and try to meet as many big shots as we could. Three teammates of mine from the 67's and I got all dressed up in our suits and headed in, trying to look important. We all had decent size, so we wanted to meet as many general managers and scouts as possible, so they could see us up close and personal. I had big hands so I was trying to shake as many hands as I could, to give them all a firm grip so they would think I was really strong.

Sitting there as then-NHL Commissioner Clarence Campbell announced each team's picks was torture. Buffalo and Vancouver were expansion teams so they got to go No. 1 and 2, and they took Gilbert Perreault and Dale Tallon, respectively. Boston then took Reggie Leach at No. 3, and so it went, with each team making its selection. The anxiety was palpable. There were only 14 teams in those years and Philadelphia had traded away its first round pick. So, their first pick was the 18th overall, which was technically the second round. I'll never forget the feeling I had when Mr. Campbell called my name. To that point, it was the best moment of my life.

I was the first to go of the four of us and the first thought that raced through my head was, "Who the hell plays center for the Flyers?" I didn't know anything about them at the time

34

and I immediately wanted to know who my competition was going to be. It wasn't long before the coach of the Flyers at the time, Vic Stasiuk, and Keith Allen, the general manager, came over to say hello and to congratulate me. We took some publicity photos, shook hands, and that was about it. They wished me luck and I left. No free jersey, nothing.

I had wondered before the draft if my chances of being taken high would be diminished at all because of something that happened that final year in Junior hockey. It would be my first time taking a major tumble off the tightrope.

When I went to the Ottawa 67's our coach, Bill Long, gave me my first crack at being an official leader - a captain. That draft year - my third and final year in Ottawa - we were playing in Niagara Falls and late in the game I got in an argument on the bench with coach Long. My emotions revved so high that I stood up and walked directly to the locker room and took my gear off. I had no thoughts of quitting the team, just getting away from the bench at that moment.

Not much was said after the game but by the time the next game rolled around I pulled on my jersey and the captain's "C" was gone. I had been demoted and I knew Bill Long didn't really have a choice. I had allowed a lack of emotional control to override my obligations as a leader and in doing so, I quit on my team.

I haven't done many things in my life that I have regretted. This was one. I vowed to never, ever quit on my fellow warriors again. Never.

****

My dad negotiated my first contract for me and it turned out to be a pretty fair and equitable deal, comparable to what other players who were drafted where I was were making. I remember mom, dad and me driving down to the Jersey shore to meet Flyers GM, Keith Allen, to hammer out a contract. Once we got there I just kept my mouth shut and let my dad do all the talking. I got $9,500 bucks, plus a $5,000 signing bonus.

I had never felt so rich.

I immediately took the bonus and spent it on a brand spanking new bright yellow four-speed Plymouth Road Runner. Oh, it was so sweet. I loved winding that sucker out and she'd just howl. It had a black spoiler, a black strobe stripe on the roof, tie-down pins, a pistol-grip Hurst shifter, and a four barrel carburetor — it was the quintessential muscle car. All the players had big-time hot-rods. Everybody was totally muscled-up.

Unbeknownst to me, however, my car had a faulty carburetor and as a result it got just four miles to the gallon. So I wound up burning through all my cash on gas. Insane. I would jokingly say that I got four gallons to the mile! I ran out of cash before the end of the summer and I will never forget my dad taking me to the Thurso Bank of Commerce where I had to borrow $600 bucks just to make it through to my first paycheck when the season started. He didn't say much to me, he just gave me that "look." I couldn't even afford new snow tires, so I had to keep my summer tires on the winter ice — I was slipping and sliding everywhere. I was living the dream though,

Mom and dad were there when I signed my first pro contract with Flyers' GM, Keith Allen.

no doubt about it.

I trained hard that off-season and then reported to my first training camp with the Flyers. I played all right but was sent down to their top minor league team in Quebec City, the Quebec Aces, in the American League. I knew that I needed to develop my game and get some ice time at the minor pro level, so I was looking forward to soaking it all in.

My coach there was a man by the name of Eddie Bush. Bushie was an old, crusty guy and I really liked him. He had been a longtime player and then got into coaching at the junior level with the Hamilton Red Wings. He had just come to Quebec that year, so we were both newbies. When we met he told me that he had been a big fan of mine for a long time. In fact, he said that he had tried to trade for me on numerous occasions while I was playing junior. He liked my work ethic and that I played with a dogged determination. Throw in a healthy dose of skating speed and Bushie was sold. He told me that Ottawa would never agree to trade me, so now he was pretty happy that he was finally going to have me on his team. I was

At my first Flyers training camp as a 19 year old I got to pose in a real, orange and black Flyers jersey, just in case I made the team.

blown away. I mean this was pretty flattering stuff for a 19 year old kid.

I played well that 1970-71 season, scoring 58 points in 69 games - more points than in any of my years in juniors. I even scored five goals in a home-and-home series against future Hall of Fame goalie Ken Dryden, who was with the Montreal Voyageurs - the Montreal Canadiens farm team at the time. I remember saying afterward to nobody in particular, "There's no way that kid's going to make it to the NHL if I got five on him." Little did I know, he would get called up later that season and wind up winning the Conn Smythe Trophy as the MVP of the Stanley Cup Playoffs. In fact, he remains the only player in NHL history to ever win the Conn Smythe BEFORE winning the rookie of the year award. That would come the following season, due to the fact that he had been called up by the Canadiens with only six games to go before the playoffs — and didn't lose his rookie eligibility. Talk about a coming out party - the kid gets called up and simply leads the Canadiens to the Stanley Cup title. Unbelievable. Ken would go on to win a total of six Stanley Cups in the next eight seasons. Needless to say, it shows you what a good judge of talent I was!

I figured I was a good bet to get called up during the year at some point, even for a few games, but it never happened. Following the season I returned home where Cathie and I continued dating. We had been doing the long distance relationship thing and it was tough. I missed her and was anxious to have some time to spend with her. I worked hard that off-season, both on and off the ice, and felt good about my chances of making the Flyers in September.

****

The most stressful part of that next training camp, without question, was having to negotiate a new contract for myself. Little did I know...I was about to be taken to school. I figured I could negotiate my own deal this time too, without daddy.

After all I was now 20 years old with a healthy ego. I knew it all.

So I came to training camp, worked hard, and just waited until Keith Allen asked to meet with me. I was going to play hard-to-get. Now, Keith was a tough negotiator. In fact, his nickname was "Keith the Thief" because of all the good trades that he had made. He really knew how to play the game. He would make the guys who needed new contracts wait right up until the end of camp before he would even start talking to them. It was stressful. The young players all had one-year deals too, which was a tactic management used to keep you hungry and always working towards that next contract. I can remember during warm-ups in practice, talking to the other guys who were between contracts like myself and asking them, "Did you talk to Keith yet? Did you talk to Keith yet?" None of the guys coming off good seasons had talked to him and we were all starting to freak out a little bit. Finally, two days before camp ends, I get a message that Keith wants me to meet him at eight o'clock the next the morning at his office in the Class of '23 Arena, near the University of Pennsylvania, where camp was being held.

I headed over to the rink half asleep, trying to convince myself I wasn't as nervous as the herd of butterflies in my stomach was indicating, and knocked on the door. He told me to come in and sit down. There he was - my opponent...my adversary in the wrestling match that was about to begin, sitting behind his desk. Keith was this charismatic, dynamic, intimidating figure - always tan, well groomed, with a deep, resonant voice. I kept telling myself these things mattered little, because I had prepared to take him down.

He was holding a No. 2 pencil while working on something that seemed far more important than talking to me. So I sat there, patiently waiting for him to finish whatever it was that had relegated my presence to the category of "afterthought." It seemed like an eternity but eventually he looked up at me and said, very matter-of-factly, "So, what's on your mind?"

A little confused, I said, "What do you mean?", and he replied "What do you want?"

Now, I had thought about this long and hard and felt more than prepared to really stand my ground on this deal. I mean I knew how negotiations went - I'd start out high, he'd counter low, and we would saw it off somewhere in the middle. I figured that's how businessmen do it. So, I swallowed hard and said, "I'd like $16,500 for the minors and $22,500 for the NHL."

I looked over at him and I could see his eyes starting to grow in size, getting bigger and bigger and bigger, until I thought he was going to explode. He took his pencil and whipped it up into the air as hard as he could. It clicked off the ceiling and came crashing right back down onto his desk. It sounded like a telephone pole landing.

By now he was at full gallop - completely amped up. His face had turned all red and he screamed at me, "You want what?! Let me tell you something! There's you and a couple other guys on this team that think you're worth the moon and stars, and you know what?! I'm not even going to negotiate with you! I'm going to send you straight to arbitration! Now, get the hell out of my office!"

This was my introduction to negotiating. I walked out of his office thinking to myself, "Well then. This didn't go exactly as I had planned." Actually I felt as if I had just been hit over the head with a sledge hammer. I started to panic. Hell, I didn't even know what arbitration was! I honestly didn't know what I was going to do.

The next morning our trainer came up to me and said that Keith wanted to see me in his hotel room after practice. Not knowing what to expect at this point, I went to meet with him. He had a make-shift office set up in his room and I sat down in front of this little round table. On it was a contract. He looked over at me, glanced down at the contract, and said, "There it is, that's all I'm going to do. That's it. So take it or leave it."

I looked at it and it was a two-way deal: $12,500 for the minors and $16,500 if I made it in the NHL. I said to myself, "OK, this is your big opportunity to either be a man or a mouse." So I picked up the pen, signed it, said thank you, and walked out of the room squeaking like a mouse all the way down the hall. "Squeak, Squeak, Squeak!" I was so relieved just to have a contract at that point, I probably would have signed anything! Truth be told, those were the numbers I figured I would wind up with in the end — I just didn't get to them the way I thought we would.

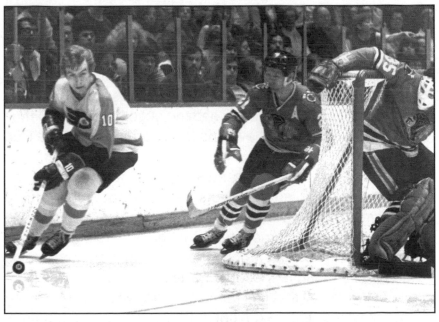

Still trying to close in on a Philadelphia Flyers roster spot with Blackhawk greats Stan Makita in pursuit and goalie Tony Esposito looking on.

4) THE "SHOW"...

Sure enough, I had a great training camp with the Flyers and actually wound up leading the team in preseason scoring. I figured I was a cinch to make the club but they thought otherwise and sent me back to the minors again. It was a big letdown. Instead of going back to Quebec though, I went to Richmond, Virginia, because that's where our Aces team was relocated to that off-season. We were renamed as the Richmond Robins and we played in a beautiful, brand new arena. The fans were hockey novices but they brought a fresh passion for the sport to every game so our new home was an exciting place to play. We actually shared the building with the ABA's Virginia Squires, whose star player that year was none other than "Dr. J," Julius Erving — the future NBA Hall of Famer with the Philadelphia 76ers.

I kept working hard and finally, after 26 games, I got called up to play with the Flyers. I will never forget it. December 9th, and it came right after a game in which Keith Allen and the Flyers Director of Player Personnel, Marcel Pelletier, had come down to watch to check on my progress. They saw me play that night and immediately had me get on a flight to Detroit to join the Flyers the next evening for a game against the Red Wings.

I remember being so nervous and so excited at the same time. As I pulled the Flyers' sweater on over my head for the first time it was as if a current of electricity shot through my body. I will never forget putting on that Flyers logo and just soaking it all in. Looking around the dressing room and seeing guys I had so much respect for, I was now about to play with.

I played well that first game and followed it up by getting the game-winner the next night in Philly against the Montreal Canadiens with Ken Dryden in goal. By then I was on autopilot though - three games in three nights in three cities. Looking back, most of it was just a blur. I was holding my own though and after my first four games I had tallied two goals and two assists. Safe to say I was not going to be headed back to the minors any time soon.

You know, I had always wondered why it took so long that second season to make my NHL debut and it wasn't until a few years ago that I finally figured out why — when Keith Allen told me a rather interesting story. As it turned out, Keith had called Eddie (Bush) a number of times to check on my progress and to see how I was doing. They didn't have video via the internet in those days, so they had to rely on phone calls for player evaluations. Well, despite the fact that I was playing really good hockey, just tearing it up, Eddie would tell Keith that I was struggling and that I wasn't ready. Incredibly, Eddie didn't want to let me go! How crazy is that? He had been lying about my progress all year so that I could stick around and NOT get called up. So when Keith and Marcel finally came down and saw me, and saw where I was as a player, they knew I was ready.

Finally in an NHL jersey to stay.

People often ask me if I was mad about having to spend that extra time in the minors and the truth is, I never knew about it until many years later — so I was oblivious to it. Heck, I was just happy to finally make it to the "show." Truth be told, those extra games in the minors probably worked to my advantage, allowing me to develop at a slower pace and really gain some confidence.

THE FOG

The Flyers' new coach was Fred Shero, but all of the players called him Freddie. He was the son of immigrants who fled Russia and moved to Canada to escape religious persecution. As a hockey player, Freddie was good enough to spend a couple of seasons with the New York Rangers in the late forties, but most of his sixteen years as a pro were spent in the minor leagues. Freddie wasn't a big man, and during his playing career opponents who assumed that his lack of size left him vulnerable paid a hefty price to learn the truth. Freddie was tough. During his stint in the Canadian Navy he boxed in the

Intensely loyal to his players, Fred Shero was an enigma to those who didn't know him. I learned more about leadership from The Fog than any other coach.

lightweight and middleweight categories, and was a champion who rejected a $10,000 offer to turn professional, choosing to play hockey instead.

Freddie had a penchant for seeming intellectually lost. When he pierced his lips and squared up his Fu Manchu moustache, he appeared to be groping for a thought. Anyone trying to read his eyes through his glasses, which often needed cleaning, swore he seemed confused. Simple questions appeared difficult for him to answer and he often came at situations from an angle that could only be called obtuse. After a game in which our No. 1 goalie, Bernie Parent, gave way after 35 consecutive starts to our No. 2 guy, Bobby Taylor, Freddie was asked by a reporter why he had started Taylor. Very matter-of-factly he replied, "It was his turn." A beat-writer covering the Flyers had nicknamed Freddie, "The Fog", and it stuck.

To those of us who went into hockey battles with The Fog as our general, he was anything but intellectually lost. He had a keen grasp of everything going on around him and of every player in our locker room, and seemed to enjoy the fact that outsiders had trouble getting a handle on the "real" Freddie. I always felt that Freddie "The Chameleon" would have been a better nickname because his leadership style, his strategy, his approach to the situations our team faced, changed depending on the circumstances. He was creative and inventive and intensely aware of the relationship between success and enjoyment.

Our practices were always fun. Freddie would often break out the tennis balls and have us do drills with them instead of pucks. We laughed at, and mocked one another as we struggled to control the bounces when the balls came alive. If we worked hard in practice, which we usually did, we would finish with a shoot-out, occasionally with the tennis balls, but mostly with pucks. One at a time we would skate in from center ice on the goalie. Single elimination — if you missed, you were out. When one shooter was left he would get two chances to score on the goalie. If the goalie stopped both, he was the winner.

What made the shoot-outs unusually entertaining, in

fact more fun than they should have been, was the cash prize that Freddie threw in for the winner. It was usually just a dollar, but on days that he felt extravagant, he upped the ante to five bucks. The amount really wasn't important. It was the fact that there was a prize to be won and Freddie knew we were just kids trapped in men's bodies. As long as we were Philadelphia Flyers and he was behind our bench, we were his kids.

Freddie wasn't a speech maker. That's not to say he didn't communicate verbally with us, but he never aspired to be a Knute Rockne. We often arrived at the rink to find a message written on our chalkboard. Rather than containing explicit directives, the messages were delivered in the form of quotes. One read: "Success is not the result of spontaneous combustion. You must first set yourself on fire." Another read: "Be more concerned with your character than your reputation. For your character is what you really are, while your reputation is merely what others think you are."

Some were easier to understand than others, and some of them left us wondering if we weren't missing a much deeper meaning. A lot of times I would read Freddie's quote and quietly ponder whether it was meant to be specific to the game we were about to play, or if it was just supposed to be "take-home" knowledge. If I couldn't decide, I would ask a teammate for his interpretation which generally led to more confusion.

When it came to specific on-ice direction, Freddie often handed out sheets of paper which rarely contained X's and O's or diagrams of plays. More often they were Freddie's philosophy on what to do and when to do it. One handout was Freddie's 10 Commandments. Things like: "Never be outnumbered in any zone. If you carry the puck to the offensive blue line and you don't have a 3-on-2 or a 2-on-1, dump the puck into the corner. Eight feet inside your blue line, get the puck out and eight feet outside their blue line, get the puck in." We were expected to commit the 10 Commandments to memory and Freddie was big on pop quizzes.

Freddie truly worked hard to treat us like adults. I'm sure on some days it was a challenge, but we could tell he wanted to respect us. All coaches had curfews on the eve of

games when their teams were on the road and most were en-
forced with a bed-check which came in the form of a phone
call or knock at the door. Typical of Freddie, his method was
different. He scheduled meetings in his hotel room at 11 o'clock
on the nights before games. This way he didn't have to treat
us like kids by phoning our rooms or walking the halls. He assumed that we would head to our rooms after the meeting
rather than go back out to the smoke-filled bars. Most of the
time, he was right.

That rookie season, Freddie handed out copies of
Bobby Orr's "Four T's of Success" to all of us. It was a maga-
zine article featuring wisdom from the Boston Bruins' great defenseman. His four T's were: Talent, Teamwork, Time
Utilization and Tenacity. We were told to learn the four T's.
The week after Freddie handed out Orr's Four T's, we left
Philadelphia on a three game road trip. The first stop was St.
Louis and on that night I got to attend my first 11 o'clock meeting. Considering these meetings were poorly disguised curfews, the content was generally fluffy. Twenty-one of us
squeezed into Freddie's room as he reviewed a couple of
scheduling items for the next day. He then said, "I'm going to

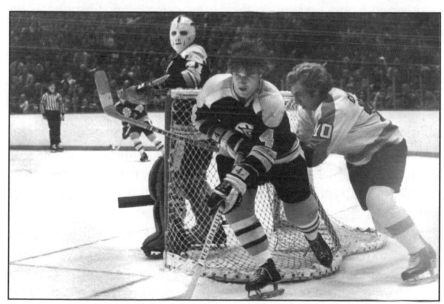

The legendary Bobby Orr left everyone
in the rearview mirror, including me.

pick one of you to tell us what the Four T's of Success are, and we're not going to leave the room until he gets all four." Gulp!

I mentally raced through my recall banks and was pretty sure I had them, but luckily Freddie tapped Jimmy Johnson. Jimmy was a grizzled veteran from western Canada who was quiet and never aspired to be the center of attention. This particular night he had also consumed his share of beers. "Talent", Jimmy slurred. We gave him a loud cheer and why not? We knew we weren't leaving until he got them all right and he already looked like he could use some help.

The room quieted. "Time," Jimmy half burped. He had forgotten Time Utilization, but Freddie gave it to him. Two down. With very little delay, Jimmy uttered "T" number three, "Teamwork." A roar went up. Our boy Jimmy was mowin' 'em down with one to go. No sooner had he nailed the third "T", however, than a puzzled look came to his face. A minute went by and Jimmy was clearly struggling. Between encouragements of, "C'mon Jimmy, you can do it," we whispered "Tenacity" to one another. After what seemed like an eternity Freddie said, "Well, Jimmy? Do you know the fourth T?" As Freddie was posing the question, the pained look on Jimmy's face gave way to one of confidence. A light had obviously gone off in his head. With great pride and a posture of certainty, Jimmy shouted, "Tennessee!" The entire room disintegrated into deafening laughter, including Freddie. Meeting adjourned.

Fred Shero taught me a lot about EveryDay Leadership. More than anything he was a consistent example of what can be accomplished if you respect your subjects - your constituents. Unlike any coach I had ever had, Freddie never embarrassed anyone. All the others regularly chose group settings to chastise and berate but Freddie left you with your dignity. If he was upset between periods he would let you know but would never leave you on an island. He would say, "First it's MacLeish, then it's Clement, then it's Crisp." Always a list, never one name. Oh, you knew when you were the target but you always had company.

In that sense, The Fog helped launch my understanding

of the concept of pulling people, rather than pushing them. The great 5-Star General and 34th President of the United States, Dwight Eisenhower used to use a simple but profound illustration he spoke of leadership. He'd take a piece of string and he would put it on a table and he'd say, "Watch, when you pull it, it will follow you wherever you go, but when you push it, it will go nowhere at all." He said, "It's the same way when you're leading people as well." A sure way to slip off the tightrope as a leader is to push to the point of embarrassment. People who use this style of leadership are soon branded as dictators and have expiration dates tattooed on the middle of their foreheads.

****

I felt an immediate bond with my mates in Philadelphia. We finished 26-38-14 that first year I was there, 1971-72, and missed the playoffs with four seconds to go in our final game

Dropping the gloves was part of staking your claim to an NHL roster spot.

of the regular season when the Buffalo Sabres scored to beat us. I got a decent amount of ice time and tallied 23 points in 49 games, and overall had a good rookie season. It was a thrill to play the game at its highest level and I was really enjoying being a major league athlete. Despite our team missing the playoffs, I could see that we had some outstanding talent and that we were one of the league's up-and-coming teams.

Something interesting happened during my rookie season that I will never forget. I was asked to do my very first speaking engagement. My agent said he had gotten me a paid gig - turned out it was for a hundred bucks. I told him to keep the money and that I didn't want to do it. I was deathly afraid of public speaking at that time. Deathly afraid. He talked me into it though and assured me that it would just be a Q & A session where I would get up and they would ask me a few questions. He reminded me that this kind of stuff was all a part of being a professional athlete, so I agreed. He told me that it was a father-son breakfast at nearby Father Judge High School. I figured it would be a bunch of kids and their dads milling around a little gymnasium eating pancakes. No

Winning this fight left the fans wanting more, which was probably a mistake. It beat the alternative though.

problem. Well, when I got there I quickly learned that Father Judge was the largest all-male school in the state of Pennsylvania. There must have been 400 fathers and sons there and it was a really big deal. I walked in and saw the head table, elevated up on a platform at the front of the room, and immediately I had an anxiety attack. I was terrified. I thought, "Oh my God, I have to speak here!" I had nothing planned. I had nothing prepared. Nothing.

I looked at the lineup of speakers and realized that I was No. 2 on the list. I figured the first guy would say a few words and then I would get up, the big celebrity hockey player, thank them for having me and answer a few questions. Ok, I was a bit relieved, I had a plan. So speaker number one is introduced and heads to the podium. His name was Tom Woodeshick and he was a fullback for the Philadelphia Eagles. I figured, how good could this guy be? He didn't look that bright or articulate - at least that was the idea I was trying to sell myself on. Well this oaf, Tom, proceeds to hit a tape-measure home run - I mean he knocked it right out of the park. No kidding, from the second he opened his mouth until the second he sat down, people laughed, people cried and they spontaneously applauded over and over again. He was amazing.

The more they laughed and applauded, the more I tried to slink down off the front edge of my chair so I could hide under the head table. I was now officially petrified that I had to follow this guy. When my name was announced to come up and speak it was as if a loud voice was echoing, "Bill Clement, the electric chair is now ready for you!"

I lumbered up to the podium microphone, took one look at that huge crowd and proceeded to hyperventilate. Sweat started dripping off my nose - it was right out of a movie. The room then got real quiet and real cloudy. I started mumbling incoherently and luckily the MC, who was sitting right beside the podium, could see that I needed some help so he started feeding some really easy questions. At one point not only was he feeding me these softball questions, he was also feeding me the answers. I was in that much trouble.

It was the most humiliating experience of my life. As I

drove away after the function, I vowed never to let something like that happen again. Next time, and I knew that there was going to be a next time, I was going to be prepared. I learned a big lesson the hard way that day, but it was such a valuable learning experience for me.

Hard to believe that I now make a good portion of my living as a professional speaker, having spoken to thousands of people all over the world.

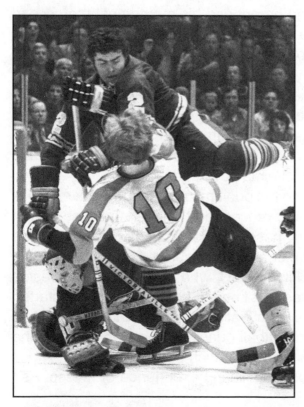

I developed an immediate understanding of what being "eliminated from the play" meant when Buffalo Sabres' defenseman Jim Watson landed a straight left to my jaw.

5) SETTLING IN...

As soon as the season ended I headed back to Ottawa to see Cathie. I really missed her. All my travel and time away had gotten to her and she wound up giving me an ultimatum: "We get married or I move on." I wasn't ready to settle down but I didn't want to lose her, so I agreed. The big issue was the fact that we couldn't have any kids due to the fact that Cathie was a genetic carrier of a strain of Muscular Dystrophy. Her brother, Tony, suffered from MD and the doctors told us that if we ever had kids it was a 50/50 chance that it would be passed on to them — nearly 100% chance if it was a boy.

Tragically, Tony died just three days before our wedding. He was only 17 years old and such a great kid too. He had been in a wheel chair since he was seven years old and he just loved life. He especially loved it when I took him out in my muscle car. I would lift him up into the seat and strap him in and away we would go. When I nailed the gas to wind that thing out, his head would press back against the seat and his broad smile would turn into a giggle.

I will never forget the week he died. I took him and his buddies out to watch the jet boat races on the Ottawa river on a Sunday. I was kind of a big brother to both he and his buddies. Tony got too much sun that day and when we went home he got his pals to park him in front of the air conditioner to cool off. He wound up catching a cold. By Tuesday he was admitted to the hospital with congestion in his lungs and we all started taking short shifts staying with Tony, fully expecting him to be back with us - being his usual charming and funny self by Saturday - our wedding day.

On Wednesday evening my father-in-law-to-be called the house and through his choking sobs communicated that Tony was gone. He had died of lung failure. We were all absolutely devastated and it immediately became a tumultuous time in our lives. Tony died on a Wednesday and we buried him that Friday in the specially made tuxedo that he was to wear at the wedding. Incredibly, we got married that Saturday. That decision was not an easy one, but Cathie's family felt strongly that Tony wouldn't have wanted us to postpone it. I agreed, so we went through with it in his honor. It was so tough on everybody. He was Cathie's only sibling and his parents' only son so I couldn't even imagine how they were feeling.

I think I knew deep down that it was the wrong decision to get married. Not because of Tony's death but because I was an immature 21 year old. I'm sure I didn't really know what I wanted at that stage of my life. I was playing in the NHL and I think the notion of me never meeting anybody who knew me before I was a professional athlete really scared me. It was comforting knowing that Cathie knew me before I had any money or fame, if that makes any sense.

I will never forget the day I told my parents that we were going to get married. They looked at me and I could just tell they were torn. Their mouths said, "We wish you all the happiness in the world", but their eyes were saying, "We don't think you're ready for this." I could see the sadness in their eyes because they sensed our marriage most likely wasn't going to last. They just knew. And in the end, they were right. I have always said that the greatest gift my parents ever gave me was the ability to make decisions on my own, and to ultimately fail. I don't think I ever would have grown into who I am today without that gift of failure.

****

I was looking forward to my first full season with the Flyers and was anxious to get settled, so Cathie and I drove down to the East Coast and wound up getting an apartment in Maple Shade, New Jersey. A bunch of my Flyers teammates lived in the same complex, including Billy Barber, Bob Kelly, Gary Dornhoefer and Dave Schultz. We would carpool to practice and games together and our wives all hung out together too, which was great. Cathie and I were soaking up life with our new social circle in and around Philadelphia. We were all a bunch of kids and we acted like it — drinking and partying — we were a very tightly knit group.

Our entire team was close, wives and girlfriends included, and after home games we'd often congregate and party together. After games when the guys were on the road we'd all go out and tear it up, often seeing the lights flash for "last call" in the wee hours of the morning. It was the '70s and we wore our checkered suits and platform shoes. Damn straight we were cool. Yeah buddy! It was a fast lifestyle - just a part of the pro-sports culture back then.

Believe it or not, like many of my teammates at the time, I even smoked cigarettes. Nowadays you would never see a professional athlete lighting up, no way. Let me qualify that... maybe the odd Russian. Many of the players lit up in those days though, that's just the way it was. Moose Dupont and I liked Kents. That was our brand of choice. We were young and

Some players had bad hair days. I had a bad hair career.

dumb and all suffered from invincibility complexes. What the heck did we know?

Some guys were closet smokers - or should I call them denial smokers. They didn't admit to having the habit because they never actually bought their own packs. Instead they would always just bum from us.

We even smoked between periods! We'd go in the bathroom and light up, thinking we were being all sneaky about it. Like nobody could smell it, right? Coach Shero was a heavy smoker and he didn't really care what we did as long as we worked hard. Inside the fake fog cloud he was really a subtly funny guy with a keenly dry sense of humor. I remember him once walking in between periods and stopping in the middle of the locker room, then raising his nose and sniffing as if he were discovering something upwind. We could see him through a crack in the door and he bellowed, "Ahhh, you guys! Come on! You don't think I know you're in the bathroom lighting up?!" We were school kids caught red-handed. "What the

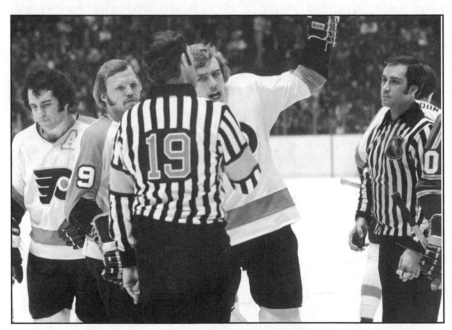

With teammate Bob "The Hound" Kelly looking on and Joe "Thunder Mouth" Watson waiting patiently in the background, I attempted to win a debate with a referee - something that to this day has never been done.

hell are you guys doing?", he continued. "You're going to nick up your skate blades on the bathroom tile! For God sakes, go in the other room where the bumper-pool table is. At least there's carpeting in there!" He was a riot. He didn't care what we did as long as we produced on the ice and dedicated ourselves to one another.

Fred Shero's multi-faceted leadership style was one that I respected and tried to emulate. I still do, but often to no avail because of my intensity level. He was dead serious about winning but chose not to take himself too seriously. In key, pressure situations his demeanor as our leader behind the bench was invaluable. He seemed to have an innate feel for when the pressure valve needed to be opened in order to keep everybody from exploding.

****

Playing in the NHL was better than great. I was literally living the dream. We had a great young nucleus of talent on our team and we were feeling pretty good about ourselves. Management had made some changes and brought in some new players that off-season and we could just feel the surge building. We were getting stronger. We went 37-30-11 that 1972-73 season and made it back to the post-season.

I wound up scoring 28 points that year as well, which was just okay. It wasn't good enough to keep me in the line-up as a regular and as a result, every now and then I became a dreaded "healthy scratch." The dream I was living suddenly became cloudy. Rosters were set at 22 players but only 19 could suit up for the playoffs. If I was going to play, my level of persistence and determination had to rise. A couple of guys had been called up from Richmond and they also became part of the healthy scratch rotation - the taxi-squad boys. As we all jockeyed for what we hoped was a "starting" assignment, I was able to acquire one of the most valuable lessons on the importance of behavioral consistency and avoiding becoming an energy vampire.

After games when the call-ups had been scratched, one of them developed a habit of complaining about his situation and the injustice of being held out of the line-up. These complaints - ok they were really bitching sessions - were often voiced to other players in group settings, usually after games and it just didn't sound right. First of all, we didn't make the decisions about one another's playing time, the coach did. Secondly, we were all in this thing together and at some point we would all need one another. I watched as my teammates, who were the intended listeners, one by one tuned the "woe is me" guy out. I vowed to never complain to my teammates. They didn't want to hear it or need to hear it, and they couldn't do anything about it anyway. I didn't realize it at the time but it would have labeled me as an energy vampire - a persona in direct conflict with being an EveryDay Leader.

****

Our team was tough and intimidating - a collection of people

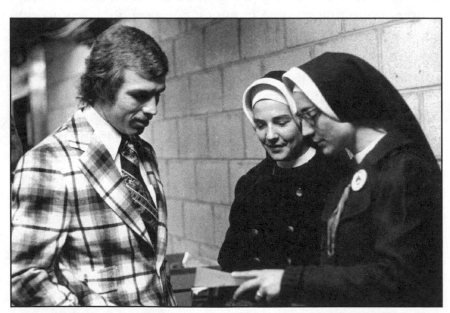

*Wearing that suit I **should** have been looking for religion!*

58

who could really mix it up - all dedicated to the group goal of winning the Stanley Cup. The rest of the hockey world felt that our pictures deserved to be on post office walls, but the organization was in its sixth season by now and really wanted to lose its mediocre "expansion team" label.

In January, after a huge brawl in a 3-1 victory over Atlanta, one of the local writers referred to us as the "Broad Street Bullies." Our arena, the Spectrum, was on Broad Street, hence the name. In 2010 HBO would produce a documentary by the same name that was critically acclaimed - even by Flyers haters.

We were led in every aspect of the game by our young captain, Bobby Clarke, who won the NHL's MVP award that year, and Rick MacLeish, who became the first Flyer to score 50 goals in a season. We were really good. In the first round of the playoffs we came from behind and beat Minnesota, four games to two. The big momentum swinger for us came in Game Five, when Gary Dornhoefer notched a spectacular overtime game-winning goal. It would become the franchise's first ever playoff series win. It was a big deal for everybody, in fact Dorny's goal was later immortalized as a bronze statue outside of the Spectrum.

We ran into a reality check in the next round though, losing to Montreal in five games. Yet there was a glowing ember hidden in the rubble of our post-season loss. We started to truly believe we could be a force in the league.

****

With the season over, Cathie and I headed up to Canada to live with her parents in Ottawa. They had a small house but we would just bunk up with them and make the best of it. I didn't own a home at that point and certainly couldn't afford one either. Hardly any of the players owned homes in those days, it just wasn't financially feasible. Based on current salaries it's hard to believe, but most of us simply couldn't come up with the down-payment or afford the mortgage payments.

Cathie and I did a lot of soul searching that summer. We knew that we could never have any children of our own and that really weighed heavily on us. It was impossible to wrap our heads around the thought of having a son and watching him die when he got to be 16 or 17 years old as Tony had. We really wanted kids though and we were able to adopt a beautiful little six-day old girl, just two years after we got married. We named her Christa Lorine and she was our instant pride and joy. Life changed in a heartbeat for us, but it was all good. I grew up in a hurry after that. We both did.

6) A STANLEY CUP CHAMPION...

By the time the 1973-74 season rolled around, we knew we were on the verge of something special. You could just tell. We had the best goalie, Bernie Parent, we had scoring, we had toughness, and we had leadership. The chemistry was also right, the camaraderie amongst the guys and with the coaches was right, so everything was lining up. We were a tightly knit team and whatever we did, we did together. We won together and we lost together. We laughed and cried together and most of all, we fought together. With Dave "The Hammer" Schultz and Bob "The Hound" Kelly leading the way, we terrorized teams, especially those that lacked toughness. There were 18 of us together, as a team, and we always had one another's backs. Freddie's caring, yet diverse style had turned us into a family. We were "one."

We finished up the regular season strong and then went on to defeat the Atlanta Flames and New York Rangers in the playoffs to advance to the Stanley Cup Finals. In practice during the conference finals against the Rangers, I got hung up and tore some ligaments in my left knee. It was bad enough that the team doctor put me in a cast and said I had to wear it for three weeks. "Depressed" couldn't even begin to describe how I was feeling at that point. As a cheerleader, I rooted on my teammates as they would now face our biggest rivals, the Boston Bruins, for the right to hoist Lord Stanley's holy grail.

Every member of our Flyers team was Canadian and we had all grown up dreaming of winning the Stanley Cup. If we won, it would be the first Cup for ALL of us. We had, however, a slight problem in taking on the Bruins. We did not have home ice advantage, which meant we would have to win at least one game in the Boston Garden in our best-of-seven series. That was going to be easier said than done though, considering that we had not won at the Garden in our last 31 meetings — a hideous streak which spanned seven years.

The first two games were in Boston and we came into their house determined to leave with the split we had come for. Game One was close, right up until the end. With 22 seconds to go, however, Bobby Orr raced into our zone, took a pass in the slot and ripped a high shot past Bernie Parent to win it by the final score of 3-2. That really took the wind out of our sails and I could sense that we were already at an emotional crossroads.

That night, after the game, Freddie gathered the team together at our hotel. What he said shocked us all. "Because we don't have a game tomorrow you have a choice," he said. "You can all go downtown to Boston Garden and practice for an hour, or you can play nine holes of golf." We looked at one another as if we had just been spoken to by someone insane. But he was not only sane, he was serious, so we took a quick vote and asked what time he wanted us to tee off.

The stipulation was that if we played golf we had to each turn in our scorecards to him. That was Freddie the chameleon, always throwing in odd little things like that which made no sense whatsoever - unless you thought about it for a second. I mean what difference would it have made whether we turned in our scorecards or not? He wanted to make sure we were all together, whatever we did. Well, we all chose to go golfing and clear our heads, although my head didn't need much clearing since I was in the cast. Ironically, it actually helped correct my slice.

Game Two was an uphill struggle. In spite of the loss two nights before, we had outplayed the Bruins and they knew it, so they came out flying and opened up a two goal lead. We clawed our way back though and ended it in dramatic fashion. Moose Dupont tied it up with 52 seconds left in regulation then Bobby Clarke got the game-winner in overtime to even up the series with it now shifting back to Philly. We still had a mountain to climb but this win was a huge lift for us. Our dream could never have come true without it.

I always wondered why Freddie let us go golfing that day instead of making us practice like every other coach would have done. I knew he wanted us to hang together but I also knew if we lost Game Two the next night he would have been vilified for his decision. The entire hockey world would have laughed at him and it would have, most certainly, damaged his credibility and reputation. And what if, God forbid, we got smoked - like 9-2. Then what?

I had a chance to spend some time with Freddie in 1990 just before he died after a long battle with lung cancer. I decided to ask him. He just looked at me and started to explain his reasoning. He knew we were in good enough shape and he knew we needed to let our hair down a little bit to continue exhibiting the quality that made our team special - the bond that held us together. He wanted us to forget about the pressure of the moment and have some fun. That's why he let us golf.

The answer confirmed Fred Shero's inner strength - his courage. He let us make that decision and then he had the courage to live with the ramifications, one way or the other.

Just as it seemed counter-intuitive for my dad to dive into raspberry bushes that, on the surface looked barren, Freddie had taken his thought process outside the box - way outside the box and onto the tightrope. Sure enough, it worked brilliantly. The lesson was the same but the stakes were a little higher than raspberry jam.

****

With that victory we had the win we needed in Boston. Now all we had to do was win our home games back at the Spectrum. As soon as we got home I went to our team doctor, John Wolf, and said "Doc, you've got to take the cast off, I want to see if I can play." He said, "It's only been nine days, you're not ready — you're going to jeopardize your career."

I said "I want to give it a shot, I want to see if I can play." He said "no." I then looked at him, got real serious, and said

"Please take it off." He said, "OK, but you're on your own." So he took the cast off and I immediately hopped off the medical table as if getting the cast off meant I was all healed. I almost fell on my face and had to grab a set of crutches just to make it to my car. Undaunted, I went down to the arena and managed to lace my skates up to go for a spin. Maybe skating would be easier than walking. Wrong! I could barely stand up on it. What was I thinking?

The following night I watched as we won Game Three. We then had a day off before Game Four so I tried skating again. Still no good.

Feeling hopeless the night of Game Four, I went and sat in the hot whirlpool before the game to get some treatment and to loosen up my leg. I still couldn't bend it to 90 degrees. As I sat in the Jacuzzi feeling sorry for myself our captain, Bobby Clarke, pulled up a chair and sat down beside me. He was in his hockey underwear and already had a big chew of gum on the go. His curly sandy-blond hair always gave him an angelic look but when he took out the plate that housed his four front teeth, he was all hockey player.

"How is it?" he said very calmly and with a genuine concern.

"Not very good," I replied. "I tried to skate again this morning and I can't seem to put any weight on it."

"That's too bad," he said, "because we really need you." We had lost other soldiers along the way as Barry Ashbee, Gary Dornhoefer and Bob Kelly all had injuries more serious than mine.

Clarke continued, "Ashcan, Dorny and The Hound have no chance of making it back in time and the guys that we've called up from the minors, they can't do what you can do out there. You do so much for us, I'm not sure we can win this without you. Even if you could just kill penalties, that would mean so much to the guys. We need you, but at the same time we all understand you're hurt. When you're ready to come back, we're sure ready for you."

As Bobby walked out my head started to spin. Over the years, people have suggested he was just trying to peer-pressure me into playing hurt. I've never seen it that way because it wasn't the case at all. What Bobby did was to make me feel important and to let me know that I had value to him and to the rest of the team. He didn't come in and say, "What are you, faking it? You're not really hurt. Come on, get out there and play!" Instead, he made me feel that they could not do it without me. I would have felt pressure had he been trying to apply it. He was understanding, supportive and genuine and instead of pressure, I felt inspired. But could I really do this?

I got out of the whirlpool and I said to our trainer, Frank Lewis, "Frank, shave my leg and tape me up, I'm going to take the warm-up." We had no ready-made braces or anything like that, so he improvised. By the time I was all taped up, my knee looked like a bowling ball in a sock. I didn't care. I got my gear on and headed out for warm-ups.

My top asset as a player was my skating. I was both strong and fast and as I hobbled around I wondered if I could contribute anything if my best attribute was so diminished. I truly felt as if I had a 40-foot neon sign on my back that said, "One-Legged Man." The stabbing pain with each stride reminded me why I was still supposed to be in a cast. Yet I felt exhilaration.

I limped up the tunnel to our locker room and there stood trainer, Frank, waiting for the verdict. "Well, can you go?" he asked.

My brain immediately reacted and screamed, "Not a chance!". My lips and my voice, however, said, "Yes."

I played and survived that night and behind 17,000 delirious fans rocking the Spectrum, we won Game Four and sent the series back to Boston for Game Five, up three games to one. Afterward, my knee felt no better or worse than it had before the game. But I felt like a million bucks. Bobby thanked me and told me I had done a great job. It meant a lot.

I learned so much about leadership that night. I learned about it firsthand from a guy who was one of the greatest leaders in the history of pro sports. As captain, Clarke was without equal and he had complete grasp of the art of pulling people. People are pulled - motivated and inspired - when they feel that they are important to achieving the group goal. I believe we all want to feel that we are vital to the outcome, that we're important to the bank branch we work in, the department store we toil for or whatever we do in life? It's more than a human want, it's a human need. And if you feel important or feel vital - I am living proof - you'll play important and accomplish things you otherwise might not have considered possible.

Like all great leaders, Bobby inspired me. He was able to do it in less than two minutes and get me to do something I simply did not believe I was capable of doing. This simple principal of leadership has never changed: If you want people to do important work, convince them that their work is important.

****

In Game Five we came out flat. The Bruins won easily and it didn't take long for Bobby to once again impress me as a leader. During the third period, Rick MacLeish came off from his shift and sat down beside me to my left. Bobby was directly to my right.

Rick was our most talented and skilled player but his motor didn't always run at high speeds. At times he seemed disinterested, almost as if he were someplace else. This was one of those nights. Bobby let Rick catch his breath for a few seconds then leaned in front of me with his jaw clenched and in a level but stern voice said, "Ricky? I sure hope you're saving it for Game Six, you son-of-a-bitch!", then sat back upright.

Over the years people have suggested to me that Bobby was "pushing" and not "pulling" as a leader and that this is in complete contradiction with my philosophy on EveryDay Leadership - and I explain that there is more. Leaders are obligated to hold their constituents to a certain standard of performance and when expectations are not met, leaders MUST stand up and speak. When the window of time available for results is small, such as game five of a seven game series, the tone and the choice of words need to match the situation's urgency.

Yes, he knew when to pull, but he also knew when to challenge people to meet expectations. And he was never afraid to vocalize the challenge, sometimes aggressively.

One of the most debilitating "resistors" that lives in the gorge, pushing back against our success as EveryDay Leaders is the fear of the consequences of saying the difficult things. The ability to step out onto the tightrope and have the tough conversation and hold people accountable to a championship standard remains one of the hardest things for people to do.

****

Back to Philly we went, still ahead three games to two. When I arrived for Game Six my butterflies almost had me airborne, and I imagined my teammates were feeling about the same. I walked into the locker room and there on the chalk board was another one of Freddie's quotes, except this one stopped me in my tracks. I realized reading it that it was an absolute truth, as well as a definition of our futures.

"Win today, and we will walk together forever," it read. That night we did, and we were able to beat the Big-Bad-Bruins 1-0 to be crowned Stanley Cup Champions. Rick MacLeish scored the only goal of the game and was dynamic all night long. The seconds of the last five minutes of the third period seemed to tick off like a 5,000 pound pendulum. Tick.........Tock.........Tick.........Tock.

To say that both literal and figurative chaos erupted when the final buzzer sounded would be a gross understatement. Their was an explosion of emotions in realizing we had done it. It was surreal to the point that I wondered if it had really happened. Could our lifelong dreams have been realized or was I about to be awakened from this crazy scene? There was also physical mayhem on the ice as hundreds of fans scaled the glass and joined the celebratory pandemonium. For the first time in my life I was able to touch the Stanley Cup, which I did. Nothing will ever compare.

We eventually made it to our locker room where champagne waited. People I didn't even know were everywhere and typical of the era, they were all male. Women didn't belong in the warriors' man-cave in those days. I decided quickly that this wouldn't do - that something was missing and it was the wives and girlfriends. I trudged out the door and down the hall to the wive's lounge and grabbed Cathie by the hand. I hadn't even taken my skates or my jersey off. Other wives followed and within moments the locker room was complete. As we took turns drinking champagne from the Cup, I never wanted the night to end. Come to think of it...it didn't.

Yes, today my teammates and I still walk together, bonded by time, circumstance, talent, friendship and Freddie. It's a bond, as he predicted, that will never be broken. Freddie no longer walks among us, but I know he's still walking with us. And beyond wonderful mentoring and metaphors, Fred Shero left me with a great understanding of leadership. He never strayed from his core values or changed the way he communicated with us and he addressed each situation with fresh ideas and bold solutions. To play for Freddie was to fol-

Winning the Stanley Cup is something I wish everyone could experience.

low him into battle. He was never in a fog, he was a chameleon — always adjusting, always sensing when something new and out-of-the-norm was appropriate. His legacy as a leader is that he cared about each game and about excellence. Most of all, he cared about us.

Looking back, I am extremely proud of my contribution that post-season because I know that I played a role in helping our team win the Stanley Cup. I might not have even dreamed of trying to play in those last games though, unless I had been made to feel that I was vital to the outcome. Bobby Clarke re-assured me that I was and encouraged me to dig deep. Luckily I did.

After we won the Cup we had a parade through the streets of Philly that drew over a million spectators. It was utterly insane. As a city, Philly seemed to be suffering from a confidence crisis, craving a championship in the worst way. We were the spark that ignited the town in so many ways. The economy was poor and people were struggling. What a thrill to be a part of the resurgence of such an amazing city.

The parade consisted of a procession of cars driving through the streets and none of us could see a damn thing. It was actually pretty scary. People were hanging out of trees and off of buildings and on street lights, just to get a glimpse of us. We were literally moving masses of humanity because fans jumped all over our cars. Cathie and I had about 15 people stuck to our vehicle at one point and it got very claustrophobic. We were hanging on for dear life. While I thought we had it bad, the cars driving Clarke and Bernie Parent were in so much trouble they just ditched the parade.

I was a smoker at the time and I remember taking my lit cigarettes and burning the fingers of the fans who were trying to reach in through the small crack in the sun roof. We thought we were going to die, we really did. So much anxiety for something that was supposed to be a relaxing celebration. I just cracked open another beer.

7) TWO IN A ROW...

Going to back to Ottawa that off-season I felt really good about where I was in life. I was a Stanley Cup champion, I had a loving wife and a beautiful daughter, I was making some money, and overall I was happy. Living the dream.

I worked hard that off-season to rehab my knee and came back to training camp ready to go. I knew that we were going to have a big target on our backs as the defending champs, which meant teams would be coming for us. We had terrorized the opposition the year before. In fact, they had even come up with a term to describe an "ailment" that opposing players used to come down with just before they had to play us: "The Philly Flu." Guys were mysteriously getting sick and sitting out on nights they had to play us. They didn't want to lose any teeth, I suppose. Anyway, to counter our pugilistic tactics, many of those teams decided to bring in a herd of tough guys of their own that off-season. The arms race was on. They were going to fight muscle with muscle.

Our top heavyweight was Dave Schultz and The Hammer, as he was appropriately nicknamed, was an intimidating human. If an opposing player misbehaved by taking physical liberties with one of our scorers or skilled players, they knew that they might as well have clanged a big bell that announced round one with The Hammer. We had a healthy crop of nasty players so few teams took cheap shots at us, especially because Schultzie was so feared.

It seemed like an awful job but he was world class at it and was the single baddest animal in the hockey jungle back in the early '70s. It was his job to fight all the toughest guys from all the other teams, sometimes on a nightly basis. He was as feared as any player in the league and boy, could he throw hands. Interestingly, Dave Schultz was also (and still is) the nicest guy off the ice - just a total Jekyll and Hyde persona

- like most tough guys in hockey. He actually wound up setting an NHL record for penalty minutes that season, with 472. It was unbelievable. That's almost eight hours - the equivalent of eight complete games. The penalty box was his home away from home.

I would often be on the ice standing next to him while he beat the crap out of some guy and I would just watch in awe. Afterward, I would be the guy who went around and picked up his gloves and elbow pads and stick. Since I wasn't much of a fighter that's pretty much all I did for Schultzie and the other tough guys. Then I would deliver them in armfuls to the penalty box. "Hey, Schultzie, good job, here's your stuff." "Thanks, Bill."

I just didn't have the stomach or the guts for it - never did. I've realized over the years that I am highly competitive but not necessarily confrontational. Luckily we had a lot of guys on our roster who either enjoyed it or were just willing to do it, which allowed me to stay in the shadows of the brawls — which was where I wanted to be. I really lacked the courage to get out on the fighting tightrope. While I did drop the gloves occasionally it didn't happen often. They were too scary. Getting punched in the face by a guy like Dave Schultz wasn't my idea of a good time.

We used to have bench-emptying brawls in those days and there were only three officials back then. Three. So, 20 guys on one team plus 20 guys on the other team, all fighting, with only three refs to break it all up. Do the math - it's not enough officials. But I had to show up - we all did - and I couldn't run and hide. When my teammates all jumped over the boards to join in I was right there with them. Truth be told, I just wanted to find another non-fighter that I could handle, just in case all hell broke loose. At least then my odds of survival would be greater. I would have a fighting chance. I certainly didn't want to have to pair up with a guy like Schultzie, that was for sure! Luckily the tough guys usually found one another but you didn't want to get to the party late in case all of the pacifist dance partners were taken.

Courage is a huge part of being a hockey player, no

question. In varying proportions it's just as important in every-day life and it's something that a lot of people wish they had more of - kind of like the cowardly lion in the Wizard of Oz. And you can't talk about courage without talking about fear. There's fear of failure, fear of the unknown, fear of change, fear of criticism, fear of poverty, fear of rejection, fear of public speaking and many, many more. I felt fear in certain situations when I played in the National Hockey League and I can openly admit that now, but it was extremely tough for me to admit when I was playing. The person who I credit the most in help-ing me put things in perspective in those days was Schultzie.

I thought I was the only gutless guy in the NHL and I was always worried that somebody would find out that I had these fears. That all changed when I had a conversation with Schultzie one night when we went out for a couple of beers after a game. No, check that, we had a lot of beers. Eventu-ally the truth serum went to work and I said to him, "Davey, are you ever afraid out on the ice?" He just looked at me like I had three heads. I mean, hockey players were macho. We weren't supposed to be talking about stuff like this, right? You don't sit down and have your morning coffee and say, "Let's talk about what we're scared of today everybody."

He kind of mumbled and said, "Yeah."

I said, "You are?"

Glancing around to make sure no one was eavesdrop-ping on our conversation he said, "Yeah, I am. And just think how scared I am - I have to fight the toughest guys on the other team." He then described how he hated playing our biggest rival at the time, the Boston Bruins. He hated playing them because he knew that every time he stepped out onto the ice, Terry O'Reilly, their tough guy, would be waiting for him. They had fought many, many times over the years — epic, bloody battles.

To make things even riskier, Schultz was a righty, mean-ing he punched with his right hand and O'Reilly was a lefty - punching with his left. Fighters seldom used both hands back then. What that meant was every time they would lock-up, or grab onto each other and start throwing haymakers, each was pounding away with his dominant free hand. No defense, no protection - just knuckles on faces.

In most cases, both fighters are righties so they can pretty easily tie each other up and not take too many blows to the head. With O'Reilly, Schultzie knew that there was going to be some major head-banging going on. That stress weighed on him. A lot. Schultzie told me that he wouldn't even look at the schedule because he didn't want to know when we were going to play the Bruins. If he knew, it meant he wouldn't sleep for two weeks before we played them. He even told me that on more than one occasion, he felt like picking up the phone and calling Terry to say, "Hey, Terry, we've got to stop this, man, somebody's really going to get hurt." But he never did.

That night I realized that courage isn't an absence of fear. Courage is simply how we deal with fear. What saddens me about our culture is that we are quick to recognize and crit-

My good friend, Dave "The Hammer" Schultz was every opponent's nightmare - the toughest animal in the hockey jungle.

icize fear, yet slow to recognize and applaud courage, even if it only exists in small portions. I'm not talking about the fireman carrying a child out of a burning building - just the everyday things people have to do that may be foreign to their natures or out of their comfort zones.

Every sane person on earth is afraid of something. Every one! The fears lurk in the gorges waiting to knock us off the tightropes to success - or worse, preventing us from even taking that first step. Every sane person also possesses a quantity of courage and the amount is always greater than they think.

That night I discovered that just as Schultzie had enough courage to step out on his tightropes, in many ways I was stepping out on mine. That conversation changed my life and changed the way I approached the sport that I loved - for the better.

****

Back on the ice, my Flyers tore it up that 1974–75 season – going 51-18-11, and finishing with the best record in the league. After a first-round bye, we swept the Toronto Maple Leafs in our first round of the playoffs. From there, we hosted the New York Islanders and after going up three games to none, we figured we would sweep them too. The Islanders, however, fought back by winning the next three games, setting up a dramatic Game Seven.

Our top guys stepped up that night and we held them off, winning the game, 4–1. Amazingly, it was the ninth game that playoff year that the Islanders played facing elimination. They had been the team that wouldn't die, until we finally drove the stake through their hearts. The prize for knocking them out was another ticket back to the Finals. We were now just four wins away from being back-to-back Stanley Cup champions.

The Buffalo Sabres would present our final challenge and they were led by the "French Connection" of Gilbert Perreault, Richard Martin and René Robert. They were a good team but the thought of playing them didn't intimidate us the way the Bruins had the year before.

Full of confidence, we came out and won Games One and Two at home. Bernie was incredible in net, allowing a total of just two goals over both games. We were feeling really good about our chances at that point and knew that we had all the momentum on our side. We also knew that if we could just win one up in Buffalo, we could clinch it back home.

Game Three would prove a memorable spectacle and ultimately go down in hockey lore as "The Fog Game." Due to an unusual May heat wave in Buffalo — temperatures rose into the upper 80's with high humidity — an interesting mete-orological phenomenon occurred that actually cost us the win. The old Buffalo Auditorium lacked air conditioning and as such, waves of fog rolled onto the ice during the game. It was unlike anything anybody had ever seen before. Visibility was so bad you literally couldn't see from one blue line to the other, or even one side of the ice to the other. Hardly anybody could see the puck and that included fans, officials and players. We could only see it if we were looking down at it on our stick. It was truly bizarre.

Eventually, just a few minutes into the game, the Audi-torium management had no choice but to attempt to engineer some type of solution. The first attempt to solve the problem involved the players. The officials asked both teams to come off the benches and skate in unison as fast as we could around our respective ends of the ice. We started to do this whenever it got bad, to sort of create a vortex of wind that would lift the fog up into the air and off the ice.

Now, the ice at the Aud was bad enough under perfect conditions, but with 20 guys zooming around at high speeds the surface was being converted to a moon-scape of ruts, gouges and potholes, especially behind the nets. Our defensemen needed to control pucks back there so they soon put a stop to that route and yelled at the guys to start skating through the crease, in front of the net. Needless to say, Bernie Parent wasn't pleased with that either.

The Sabres were mirroring what we were doing and both teams realized we were rapidly sabotaging our respective defensive zones with each "fog lifting" carousel of skaters. So we boycotted and told the referee to tell the Auditorium bosses to find "another way." And that they did.

Their attempt to solve the problem was so bizarre, if not primitive, it seemed surrealistic to everyone - right out of a B-movie. The game was halted, the doors along the end boards were opened, and out skated eight teenagers working in pairs. Each skater carried a twelve foot bamboo pole and between each pair of poles was stretched a large white bed sheet. The kids looked like a cross between Cirque du Soleil rejects and Cuban refugees trying to sail their way to Miami without a boat. Around and around they skated, showing no sign of wilting under the tremendous burden they shared — to alter an entire weather pattern and thus ensure the continuation of the Stanley Cup Finals — all with only their skates, their bamboo poles, and their sheets. Lo and behold, much of the fog lifted and the bamboo boys instantly became cult heroes in Buffalo.

Just when we thought things couldn't get any crazier, a bat descended from the rafters and proceeded to fly around the ice surface. It started dive-bombing a face-off circle where Rick MacLeish was preparing to face-off against the Sabres' Jimmy Lorentz. Lorentz waited for the bat to make another pass and picked it out of mid-air with a precise flick of his stick. It was a helluva swat and he would earn the dubious distinction of becoming the first and only player to kill an animal during an NHL game. He told me years later that he got tons of hate mail from animal rights lovers.

For me, the real hero was MacLeish. Nobody would touch the mortally wounded bat that lay on the ice - but Ricky had that flat-line pulse rate. He scooped the bat up in his glove and matter-of-factly skated over to the penalty boxes where the timekeeper sat and casually dropped the bat over the boards. Bat disposal problem solved.

Anyway, we wound up heading into overtime tied at 4-4. With the fog rolling in yet another time, Sabres winger Rene Robert took a shot from just inside the blue line on the right side that Bernie never saw. It zipped through the fog and squeezed between his pads. The Sabres had won Game Three, 5-4.

Having grabbed some momentum, Buffalo knocked us off in Game Four as well, 4-2, to even the series. With that, we headed home to Philly, where we were able to get back on track and win pretty convincingly, 5-1. Bernie was playing out of his mind at this point and we felt really good about our chances to clinch heading back to upstate New York for Game Six.

I remember noticing as the game began that the Sabres' grasped the gravity of the situation they faced. Their sense of urgency on the ice was obvious. They were two wins away from realizing the dream they had pondered since childhood - the very dream our team had realized the previous year — winning the Stanley Cup. At the same time, they were even closer to their nightmare - elimination.

Our situation was the mirror opposite of theirs and therefore less tenuous. We also had a psychological advantage. The Sabres had been in the National Hockey League for five years and had never won a game in Philadelphia. While our preference was to avoid exercising our home ice advantage in a Game Seven, we were confident that if it got to that point we would prevail. Thus far in the series, each teams' wins had come on their own home ice.

The game was tight early on and through two periods the scoreboard hadn't changed, still 0-0. As the third period unfolded, we seemed to raise our energy level and it wasn't long before Bob "The Hound" Kelly scored to give us the lead. From a scrum behind the net, he bulled his way to the front and jammed one home.

We held our lead through the next 14 minutes of the period but silently, as we took our turns on the bench after a shift, we each craved another dose of offensive aphrodisiac — a second goal. With less than four minutes to play I was sent out for what I knew would likely be my last shift. As we repelled another Sabres attack into our end, the puck suddenly squirted up the right wing boards through the neutral zone. With teammate, Orest Kindrachuk (The Little "O") in full pursuit, I dug in up the middle.

In an instant I realized the Sabres' defensemen had misread the play and were double-covering Orest - all racing for the puck. That left me wide open. All "O" had to do was get there first. Just as he tracked down the puck, both defensemen converged on him. The confluence of bodies crushed him into the boards as he dished the puck to me just inside the blue line. I was all alone on a breakaway.

It was as if time stood still as I skated in on the goalie, one-on-one. My first thought was, "Where am I going to shoot?" I had ruled out a deke or a juke even before the game. As I sat in my stall in the locker room, I had pondered a possible breakaway and felt that shooting was the way to go since Sabres' goalie Roger Crozier was one of the best in the game at stopping the deke. Now I had to take my pre-game decision to another level. Where would I shoot? I automatically computed that Crozier caught with his right hand and that he usually played in a crouched position, pretty low to the ice. There had to be room upstairs, over his catching glove, by his right shoulder.

While my brain steered me in that direction, my eyes were drawn to the five-hole (the pyramid shaped opening between a goalie's pads). Crozier's feet were set wide apart and there had to be two feet of air between his pads. In an instant, my game plan changed.

Good goalies never make the first move. They wait until the shooter commits, then they react to the shot. As Crozier waited for me to make the first move, I cruised in, untouched. By the time I got to within about five feet of him, he was still standing, holding the same posture, backing deeper into his net. I snapped off a quick, but controlled wrist shot and deposited the puck between his legs and into the back of the net. I was so close to him that my stick actually grazed his left pad on my follow-through.

The goal turned out to be the Stanley Cup clinching goal as we won Game Six, 2-0. What a thrill! Just like that, we were Stanley Cup champions for the second time in as many years. Bernie had posted his fourth shut-out of the play-offs and had simply dominated. Not only did he win the Vezina Trophy that year, as the league's top goalie, he also repeated as the playoff MVP, winning his second consecutive Conn Smythe Trophy. There were others who supplied unsung contributions as well. Orest was never the same after being hit on my breakaway play. He injured his back and suffered with it for the rest of his career. Little O was such an underrated player.

I will never forget how amazing it was to celebrate with my teammates out on the ice and then later in the dressing room after the game. What an incredible feeling of accomplishment, to go out and to achieve the goal you had set from day one. We were officially a dynasty and it felt pretty amazing — just as good as the year before.

The Stanley Cup-clinching goal unfolded so
perfectly that I thought it could be disallowed.
It seemed too easy at the time.

Days later, I mentally replayed the breakaway and had a revelation. The human brain can compute information and make decisions at light speed. I was amazed at all the thoughts that had traveled through my mind in a time span shorter than two seconds: the calling up of the information I had inputted before the game, the strategizing, the re-strategizing — all of it. What I had done ahead of time, I later realized, was created a mental video. I had visualized my options ahead of time and was able to recall and process the information in an instant. It's a preparation technique that is widely taught and used today but back then I had simply stumbled upon it on my own. Mental rehearsals are invaluable in sports, business and life.

Incidentally, many superstitious Buffalo fans would later considered the bat killing to be an "evil omen," pertaining to the result of the series. All these years later and they still haven't won a Cup. Who knows?

That night after the game, on our charter flight home to

Shaking with the incomparable Bernie Parent (far left) as our unequalled captain, Bobby Clarke, and NHL Commissioner Clarence Campbell look on.

Philadelphia, the euphoria was delicious. The raucous commotion in our locker room had been replaced with the wonderful, subdued glow of a group accomplishment. Some players sat and some roamed. I was a roamer, but for a few minutes I sat and chatted with my buddy Schultzie. Dave and I were close friends and still are. We had turned pro the same year and spent the same amount of time playing together in the Flyers' minor league system. As we reveled in our accomplishment, Schultzie quietly confided something that triggered two things inside of me — a feeling of sadness and an epiphany.

There had been an article written in a Buffalo newspaper that predicted a trade taking place as soon as the Cup finals were over. A list of names was mentioned and the writer speculated that at least one of the Flyers players on the list would be traded to Washington. Schultzie's name was on the list. So was mine.

I didn't think much of it because that's what newspaper reporters do, speculate. Stuff like that happens all the time and eventually you learn to just ignore it, otherwise it will eat you up inside. Well, this was eating Schultzie up inside. He told me that the article had truly sent him into an emotional upheaval. He said that he was so upset at the possibility of being traded that during the game, his head was miles from Buffalo and that he wasn't even close to being in the game. He was also thankful that he hadn't hurt our team's chances of winning on the ice, something that could have easily happened given his state of mind. Yes, on at least one of our players, the well-timed article had had it's desired affect.

I was saddened by the thought that someone I cared about had been unable to appreciate a magnificent experience as it unfolded. A lapse in emotional sovereignty had pushed Dave's thoughts to a place that had him, at least emotionally, miles from Buffalo. His preoccupation with something over which he had no control, had sabotaged the moment. His fear of a possible future event had prevented him from living in the present.

My epiphany came in two waves, the first of which helped me grasp that since my name had also been mentioned in the article, I had the ability to block out distractions. I had fortunately been able to react correctly under pressure and execute. I had maintained emotional sovereignty.

The second wave has become the most important universal truth in my life - that spending one second of time or one ounce of energy worrying about something over which we have no control is not only a waste of time, but it can also sabotage our chances for success — not to mention our appreciation of the present. No matter how much emotional energy any of us burnt up with anxiety and worry about possibly being traded - about being forcibly relocated - nothing would change the inevitable.

"Worry" can paralyze, that's a given - but only if we let it. It's a product of playing the "what if" game. "What if I'm traded? What if I lose my job? What if I'm criticized? What if I make the wrong decision? What if I fail? What if I fall off the tightrope? What if...".

When we try to fill in the blanks by writing the end of a bad story we instantly sacrifice what is going on in the present. Not only our enjoyment of it but also our ability to positively influence it. Pictures of negative scenarios collide like amusement park bumper-cars in our heads and without resolving anything, the present has vanished. Every successful person I have ever known has had the ability to stay in "the moment." The great ones, more than others.

In the end, Dave would spend one more year in Philly before bouncing to Los Angeles, Pittsburgh, and Buffalo, ultimately retiring in 1980. We remain great friends to this day and I absolutely love the guy. And there was indeed an irony to the end of the story that had been printed in the Buffalo News. It would unfold eight days after the conversation with Schultzie on the plane.

****

When we got back, the city of Philadelphia planned another Stanley Cup parade for us. Luckily they changed up the format for this one. Instead of having us in cars they put us all on two huge floats with platforms that stood really high so everyone could see us. We were also a whole lot safer.

More than two million people showed up - it was absolutely epic. They had the important people up on the first float - guys like Bobby Clarke, Bernie Parent, owner Ed Snider and the coaching staff. Then all of us grinders, we were in back. Well, we crept down Broad Street on these things, waving to the fans and having a great time. We had been drinking quite a bit of beer for a few hours though and eventually nature called - more like screamed to me - in the worst way.

I saw a gas station that was across the street and figured that was going to be my only chance to relieve myself. So I rappelled down the side of our elevated float as it was moving along and shoved my way to this gas station. I get there and the gas station attendant at first wasn't going to let me use the bathroom unless I bought some gas. No problem buddy, just fill up my back pocket. Luckily some fans reassured the guy that I was one of the players in the parade. He reluctantly tossed me the key and I was fortunately able to take care of business.

When I got out I realized, to my horror, that the floats didn't wait for me and were now a long way off. Then again, why would they? Nobody knew I was gone and even if they had, I was on my own. There was now a sea of thousands of screaming fans between me and my teammates and I didn't know what the hell I was going to do.

Just then, these two cops came over to me. They had seen me jump off the float and knew that I was in trouble - not just the bladder trouble but now trying to rejoin the parade. So they instructed me to grab onto each of their belts and hang on, as they then proceeded to take their billy clubs and make a "V" shape with them to wedge through all of the people. It was crazy. There I was, driving two plow horses, churning through all of these drunk fans. We were banging bodies out of our way as we went and I was hanging on to these two guys for dear life.

Finally, we got to the float, only I didn't know how I was

going to get back up on it. I didn't remember there being any stairs and there was no ladder. So they took a billy club and while each held onto one end of it, I was able to step on it and boost myself up high enough to where my teammates could grab me and pull me in. Nothing like a routine potty break. I then saluted the cops to thank them as we rode off. Unreal. I was never so happy to finally sit down in my entire life. What an ordeal.

Then, maybe two minutes later, both floats come to an abrupt halt. We all wondered what was happening. I figured something pretty important must be going on to stop this pro-cession. As it turned out, nature had also come calling on Bernie Parent. I am now watching with great interest as secu-rity guys magically pull out these secret stairs hidden in the side of the float, which I was of course oblivious to. Bernie then gets off like some sort of king with everybody cheering for him. Meanwhile, our traveling secretary had gone over to a row house along the parade route and arranged for Bernie to go inside to take a leak. So Bernie goes in, does his thing, and then comes out as we are all waiting for him. He kisses the homeowner, this little old lady who thought she had died and gone to heaven to have the world's greatest goalie pee in her toilet, then he casually walks back up onto the float so we can start again.

I am watching this and it was at that very moment that I realized my level of importance in the grand scheme of things within the Flyers organization. I had to pee and it was about a 30 minute odyssey requiring two police officers and billy clubs. Bernie, meanwhile, has to go and it's like the President getting off Air Force One. Unbelievable, but nevertheless ap-propriate in our hierarchy.

You know, I still have a recurring nightmare where I am begging the gas station attendant to let me use his filthy bath-room and him not believing me that I am actually a member of the Flyers. Then, in this hazy dream sequence, I see all these die-hard Flyer fans throwing coins into the row-house lady's toilet, which is now bronzed and converted into a shrine in Bernie's honor. How crazy is that? Fortunately, the parades left me with more pleasant dreams than nightmares.

****

I often get asked what it meant to me to win the Stanley Cup. To be honest, it didn't really have a deep, concrete meaning at the time, other than evoking a feeling of euphoria. Complete exhilaration. I was only 23 when we won our first Cup and it was almost like I was in a make-believe world because as a kid it was something I had always dreamed of. Always. I can say, however, that the strongest and most memorable emotion that I had when we won it was love. Immediately, it was love. The love I felt for my teammates at that moment was almost overpowering. I wanted to stay together with them for ever and ever. I never wanted that moment to end. It's very hard to explain. It was uncontrollable and quite overwhelming.

Both Cups were special, but the second one was more meaningful in that I could wrap my head around it and really appreciate it. The first time I was almost in disbelief that it was actually happening. The second one was neat because we won it on the road and as a result we were able to enjoy the moment as teammates. We were together without all the outside interference of fans and media and what-not, which made it really emotional to a lot of us. It was just us, nobody else, as opposed to when we won the first one at home and the partying started immediately, making it all pretty chaotic. We got to visit on the plane ride home and talk about what we had just done. Winning that second one validated us too and it proved that we weren't a fluke. That meant a lot as well.

I'm so proud of what we accomplished in Philadelphia. Even as we coped with our own fears, we used fear and intimidation to change the game. Hell, we took it to another level. We figured out pretty quickly that if our opponents were intimidated they had little chance for success. As soon as we won a pair of Stanley Cups playing the way we played, all the other teams took notice. Very soon size mattered in the NHL. All of a sudden toughness mattered in the NHL.

The wolf pack mentality that we were able to employ proved to be invaluable, it really did. Based on owner Ed Snider's philosophy and Keith Allen's execution, we took toughness to a whole new level in professional hockey. Being an expansion team, Mr. Snider had seen his Flyers take a lot of physical abuse in the first few seasons and finally said enough was enough. Seeking out players of character who were tough and exhibited a dedication to team, he built an organization that ensured nobody was ever going to push one of his teams around again. We had possibly the most colorful team of all time and I just felt very proud to be a part of it. To bring two championships to the City of Brotherly Love was an honor.

Looking back, I would have to say my big takeaway from winning those Stanley Cups was realizing that almost anything is achievable in life as long as everybody within the group is willing to subordinate their individual interests, goals and agendas for the good of the group. Whether it is in sports or business, unless everybody on the team is committed to this ideal, you will rarely - if ever - achieve success.

8) SHIPPED OFF TO WASHINGTON...

Eight days after winning a second Stanley Cup, after four wonderful seasons in Philadelphia, I was traded to the Washington Capitals. How ironic that Schultzie was so worried about getting dealt, in reality it was me that got sent packing. As I quickly learned, this was just another reality when you become a professional athlete.

I remember the moment like it was yesterday. My wife and daughter were already back up in Ottawa and I had packed up my car and was driving home for the summer. Our short term lease had ended and the rented furniture returned.

Along the way I had stopped to spend the night at my wife's aunt's house in Syracuse. I remember being awakened at about eight in the morning by Aunt Margaret. She knocked on my door and whispered "Bill, phone's for you, it's Keith Allen." I sat straight up in bed and said "Uh-oh!" It doesn't take a rocket scientist to figure out that any time your general manager tracks you down at your wife's aunt's house in upstate New York, that it's probably not going to be a good call. In fact, it was "the call" that all players dread.

Keith said very matter-of-factly, "Bill, as you know, it's my job to make difficult decisions and to do difficult things that we feel will help the organization. As such, we've traded you, along with our No. 1 pick in the draft, to the Capitals in exchange for their No. 1 — which is the No. 1 overall pick. I can't thank you enough for all the hard work you've given us and we'll never forget your contribution in winning those two Stanley Cups. Here's Milt Schmidt's phone number, Washington's GM. Good luck."

He was very respectful and businesslike - a picture of control. Me, on the other hand, not so much. Now, I was a bright kid academically, but maturity was certainly not my strong suit — especially at this particular stage of my life. I was not pleased and I let him know it. I'm sure he understood that I was emotional, but looking back it was probably not my finest hour.

I was upset that the Flyers were abandoning me and I felt thoroughly rejected. I was upset that I was going to be joining a second year expansion team, knowing full well that we were going to be losing a lot of games in the immediate future. I was upset that I was going to have to leave all of my friends and teammates, and make new friends all over again. I was upset that I was going to have to move and find a new place to live. I was upset and quite honestly, I was afraid. We had such a close team in Philadelphia, so close. You don't win two championships without being glued together and having the right chemistry, both on and off the ice. I was SO going to miss those guys.

As I finished my drive to Ottawa I was engulfed with a feeling of loneliness. I pictured myself as a sliver of a pie being taken out of the pan, and then watching that gap slowly close back up. I was sad.

On a day to day basis the team doesn't sit around thinking about the guy who's gone - they still have one another. But it's sure easy for the guy who's gone to have his thoughts dominated by the team he left behind. Sure, one of the soldiers was gone, but the platoon was still marching forward. Sometimes that's just a hard thing to accept.

I spent a few weeks of that off-season trying to pull myself together. My tightrope had been cut out from under me and I was on the floor of such a deep emotional gorge. Luckily I was surrounded by my immediate family, otherwise I would've been a complete mess. Finally, I reminded myself that the only thing in the world over which I had complete control was me. I started working out and running again and made a vow to embrace this new situation. After all, I was going someplace that truly wanted me. In fact, they gave up a lot in the trade, the No. 1 overall pick in the draft. That, if nothing else, felt kind of good. Out of the gorge, I climbed.

In early August the Capitals flew me in to DC and I spent a few days on the chicken, potatoes and peas circuit, driving around with the president of the team and shaking a lot of hands at various functions. It was quite by accident, driving around the beltway that I stumbled into a poignant insight on what it takes to win championships in pro sports.

As Peter O'Malley piloted our vehicle he stated that the Capitals were going to build a team with guys "...like you Flyer guys. Guys that just love to win." I reflected for a moment then it hit me and I turned and said, "You may want to consider getting players that hate to lose. Everybody loves to win but not everybody hates to lose." To this day I believe that championships are won with players who hate to lose.

****

In September I reported to training camp in London, Ontario. We were staying in a hotel up there and on the first day, Milt Schmidt, who was both the coach and the GM, called a meeting. His last item was about drinking and he said, "Men, no beer in the rooms." Well, not more than 60 seconds after Milt's speech, a bunch of guys jumped in a car and drove straight to the liquor store to load up on beer. They had completely defied him. I just watched that and thought to myself, if these guys are going to show that much disrespect to the coaching staff and to the management on the first day of camp, then what was I in for as the season went on? I was nervous.

To make matters even more interesting, I later found out that I had been named team captain. This was a real honor yet the responsibility quickly weighed on my mind. When a coaching staff makes you the captain, they're hoping that you can lead the way. Well, expansion teams lose a lot of games, that's just how it is. So trying to be a leader in a losing environment is extremely difficult. Don't get me wrong, I was humbled that I got to wear the "C," but at the same time it felt awfully heavy. I mean this was an entirely different makeup of guys. This was an expansion team about to enter just its second season of existence, so talent-wise, this was a long way from Philadelphia, where I had just won back to back Stanley Cups.

The roster was not loaded up with guys of the same character or the same drives or the same talents. Not even close. Expansion teams are mostly built with spare parts - leftovers from other organizations. That's just the reality of professional sports. They are the players that other teams "de-prioritized" and simply didn't want. In an expansion draft, teams can protect a certain number of players, always their top players and core guys, then they cast off everybody else by leaving them "exposed" in the draft. Such an appropriate term I've always thought.

So there was a disjointed blend of young guys and older veterans. Oh, we had guys that really cared, like Willy Brossart, Ron Low, and John Paddock, but most of us were cast-offs from other teams, each trying to find an identity. The bottom end of the food chain for sure, and I was the new leader. Yikes!

We lost our first nine games out of the gate and things were ugly. Real ugly. Management was leaning on me too, to rally the troops and to be their leader. You know, the more I've learned about leadership over the years, the more I've realized how much I still had to learn as a 24 year old. The organization asked me to be the team captain and I wasn't about to refuse. It would have helped to be in a winning environment with lieutenants and alternate captains to help navigate through rough waters, no question, but it was tough for me to assume that role and be effective at that particular stage of my career.

I found it difficult to have the tough conversations and to stand up for what I believed was right. To vocalize what might just be an unpopular position and to say it with conviction in front of the entire team, that was hard. It's such a common obstacle to leadership. When you stand up and say what has to be said, very often it will be followed by a period of alienation, by a period of distance, and ultimately by a period of loneliness — because you're not walking arm in arm with some of the people you had to speak to — at least until they get over it.

Today, I know now that if I say what has to be said and I am respectful, even if it is said in a firm tone, then I will be all right. Sure, there may be alienation but any loneliness that accompanies it will soon pass. Second, I learned that as long as I remain consistent with my values and with my demeanor, the people I deliver the message to will ultimately respect it and most likely respond to it.

Third, at the end of the day I can at least look in the mirror and say, "I stepped out on the tightrope...and I'm still here. I'm ok."

So, are leaders born or made? The answer is, both. I think of leadership as a craft, not unlike the craft of acting. Successful actors are born with an aptitude for the profession, but great actors never stop working at their craft or continuing to take chances with new roles or techniques. It's no different than what leaders do with their crafts.

As the team captain, up until this point I would have to

The uniform was different in Washington but my job of winning face-offs never changed.

give myself mixed reviews. Work ethic-wise, I felt like I was second to none. I would stay late and practice the fundamentals every day. I was not going to be outworked, no way. I was good at encouraging my teammates too, and truly felt like I was a team player. In these departments, I definitely led by example.

One thing that got in the way of being a consummate leader though was the fact that I was not a fighter or a physical player. Not only did I shy away from the rough stuff, there were a lot of games I played where I was scared to death. Then again, this just confirmed my sanity. Some players were crazy. Steve Durbano was crazy. I mean he'd try to pluck your eyeballs out with the tip of his stick blade. I remember playing against him in junior when I was 17. He was big and mean with so many screws loose even then.

My first time down the ice he speared me in the guts so I whacked him back. Next time down he speared me in the chest, so I whacked him back again. The next time he went for my throat with a full blown charge, like a bayonet. It was at that moment I said to myself, "OK, I have to make a decision

A ceremonial face-off against Bobby Clarke. The Flyers home opener just happened to be against the Capitals.

here. How far do I want to let this escalate?" I decided right then and there to back off, because it just wasn't worth it to me. I knew I wasn't that tough and realized that I didn't have the make-up, or the wherewithal, to play that kind of game. So I backed down and went about my business. Look, I knew I could fight...if I had to. But to go against a gorilla like that, who wanted to tear my head off and use it as a bowling ball, no way. My big fear was dropping the gloves to defend myself or one of my teammates, and getting completely thrashed. It's bad enough to get embarrassed in front of thousands of people, but to have no recourse on top of that — except to fight again and again and again until I eventually won one — no thanks. That was not my nature.

When I ponder the "complete leader" I always think of Bobby Clarke. He was very mature, very driven, and very courageous. He was just a year older than I was but he was wise beyond his age. One of his best qualities was his ability to have the tough conversation - to tell guys exactly what was on his mind. Yes, he could inspire with quiet endorsements of your play, but he could also take a teammate aside and say, "You're not giving us what we need." Or, "I expect you to work harder out there." That was one of his gifts - the courage to be able to talk to his teammates like that, with brutal honesty. You always knew where you stood with Clarkie. He was a tremendous leader, the quintessential captain.

For decades I have heard other players that played against Clarke say that he was gutless because he never fought his own battles. That bothers me. Bobby would have fought to the death but he simply never had to. Other players always dove in headfirst to take over the fight before it even started - not because they were told to but because they were so protective of our leader. Just as during the Civil War, Robert E. Lee's men surrounded his horse when he would try to lead his Confederate Army into battle and escort him to the back of the lines where he would be safer, Clarkie's teammates instinctively shielded him from harm.

Those Flyer teams were tough. We stuck together and won through fear and intimidation. Well, in Washington we lost through fear and intimidation - the great two-way street of hockey. We didn't have one player that scared anybody. Not one. We used to get the crap beat out of us on a nightly basis, both on the scoreboard as well as literally. It was brutal. I remember going in to Milt Schmidt's office adjacent to the locker room one night after a game. I hadn't even taken my gear off. I said, "Milt, I don't know if you're noticing what the guys on the bench are noticing, but we're getting the crap beat out of us out here. We need somebody who can calm the other teams' gorillas down because our guys are getting killed up and down the ice." It was open season on us. Milt said he was trying to trade for a tough guy but it never happened.

For me personally, it was even worse. I was skating around with a bulls-eye on my back and I didn't even really realize it at the time. Years later, when I was with Atlanta, we had made a big eight player trade with Chicago and wound up acquiring Phil Russell in the deal.

One day at practice Phil says to me, "You know, I gained got a lot of respect for you once you got to Washington."

I said, "What do you mean?"

He replied, "Well, we all tried to kill you."

Having no clue what he meant I said, "What?"

He said, "Yeah, everybody was gunning for your head. We were all going after you." He then proceeded to tell me about how every guy that had gotten cut out of the Flyer's wolf pack had been systematically targeted, one by one, and I was the first to go. He explained to me that because the "Broad Street Bullies" had tortured so many players during their reign of terror, that guys just couldn't wait to start exacting revenge. All those years of fear and intimidation had manifested into anger, and guys wanted payback. I had no freaking idea! He said that they would all sit around in the locker room and talk about how they were going to beat the crap out of me. I couldn't believe it!

Looking back, I was so glad that I didn't know because I was scared enough as it was. Had I known that everybody was gunning for me, I probably wouldn't have ever suited up.

As the season went on, things went from bad to worse. In addition to losing our first nine games, we went through a 25-game winless stretch right before Christmas that spanned 57 days — culminating with the firing of Milt. Tommy McVie came in as the new head coach, while Max McNab was named as the new general manager. I remember them sitting me down as the team captain and asking me if the team was really as bad as its record. I said, "We have some talent but we're not in very good shape." Boy, was that ever a mistake, because Tommy worked our asses off after that. Tommy was a task-master, a real physical fitness fanatic. He used to idolize the great American distance runner, Steve Prefontaine, and had patterned his philosophy on fitness around him. He was determined to work us to death.

I will never forget being in the sauna one day after practice with Tommy and him telling me about how he used to watch Prefontaine train in Portland, Oregon, and work himself to near death at practice - literally to the point of physical exhaustion, where he would collapse out on the track. He would then get up and start running again, only to collapse. And apparently he would do this over and over again. Well, Tommy figured it that could work for Steve Prefontaine, then it would work for us. He had to have had a clue that distance running was nothing like playing hockey, yet he still worked us well beyond the point of physical exhaustion.

No kidding, he would run us through full hour-long fitness practices on game days. On game days! I mean who does that? What bothered me about his methods was not the physical demand of the workouts. I loved that stuff - but not at the expense of putting up a win. One time we got into Minnesota late the day before the game so he had us practice at nine o'clock at night. That sonofabitch bag-skated us (no pucks, just stop-and-start wind sprints) for an hour and a half, and then had us back on the ice for another hour at ten in the morning - the day of the game - in full gear! It was insane. We died 20 minutes into the game and got crushed. We had nothing left in the tank, nothing. We were spent.

As a team we struggled through the midway point of the

season, but on a personal level I was playing some pretty good hockey. In fact, I was even named as Washington's lone representative in the All-Star game that year, which just so happened to be in Philadelphia. Normally it would be a huge honor to be named as an All-Star but given the fact that I was on the worst team in the league, and that I was named by the league to be my team's lone representative (starters were voted in by the media), it was sort of like, "Well, somebody has to go." The game was great though and I saw a lot of old friends too, which was really nice.

I remember the introductions by the PA announcer, Lou Nolan, at the start of the game. He would say the team name then the player's name and we would each skate up to the blue line for the National Anthem. So they are introducing the rival Wales Conference, which is my new conference, and we're the enemy since the Flyers were in the Campbell Conference. The guy just before me that gets introduced is hulking Buffalo defenseman, Jerry Korab who Flyers fans loathed. They let him know it too, booing him unmercifully. "Boooooo! Boooooo! It was just brutal. The guy introduced right after me was equally despised, Dan Maloney. He was Detroit's tough guy and the fans killed him too.

Sandwiched in between King Kong Korab and Dangerous Dan Maloney was, "From the Washington Capitals, Bill Clement!" The response from the crowd was the starkest contrasts you could imagine. They cheered and gave me a standing ovation. What a feeling.

Being back in Philly was great and seeing so many of my old teammates was really cool too. They were genuinely interested in how I was doing. We'd been to battle together and won, and that creates a bond that can never be broken. Ever. That's why it's so special. It's unlike anything you can ever imagine and one can't truly understand it unless you've lived it.

I was on a real high that night, but little did I know, my life was about to get turned upside down again. Now, the All-Star game was on a Monday night and I stayed late to catch up with some old friends over cocktails before driving in my

'77 yellow Lincoln Continental Mark VII about three hours back home to Washington. We went through a typical Tommy morning practice that following Tuesday and then suited up to play the New York Rangers that same night. Afterward I went out for a few beers with my closest teammates, who all wanted to hear about the All Star Game.

By the time Wednesday morning rolled around my body was just about out of diesel. Tommy worked us hard for two hours and I was never so happy to see a practice end. It was awful. Before I even left the ice, Tommy told me that Max wanted to see me in his office. So, I drove 30 miles back from our practice facility to the Cap Center to meet with him. I walk in and he's eating this huge hamburger. He says, "Sit down. Nice game last night." I nodded to agree and then proceeded to tell him that I felt like we were coming together as a team and that we were getting closer to turning the corner.

He's chewing and nodding and then he just blurts out, "Well, we've made a change and it's a good one for you...Atlanta." As he's sort of mumbling between bites he says "Here,

The 1976 All Star game meant another chance to suit up in the hallowed Spectrum.

Cliff Fletcher (the GM of the Flames) is on the line and he wants to talk to ya." He then takes another bite and hands me the phone. In shock, I take the phone and say, "Hello?" "Bill, Cliff Fletcher. We've been trying to acquire you for years but the Flyers would never trade you. So we're really excited that you're finally going to be a member of the Flames."

I thought, "Holy crap, what the hell just happened?! Have I really just been traded again?" It felt ok to be wanted like that, no kidding, but to be honest the only thing I was thinking about at that very moment was, "Please God, don't let their be a game that night, I can barely walk right now!"

He then says, "Bill, we're playing tonight in Philly and we really need you in the lineup. We traded two guys off of our starting roster along with a first round pick to get you, so how soon can you get to Philadelphia?" I remember just sitting there in shock. Another surreal moment. I was so pissed off at the way Max handled everything. I mean didn't the man know it's rude to talk with your mouth full?

Looking back, I think I was most disappointed by the fact that there was a job there that did not get done, and as the team captain I felt responsible for that. I felt like I was being measured in that regard and that hurt.

As I walked out the door Max said, "Bill, can you give Abe Pollin (the team owner) a minute of your time?"

I said "Yeah, I guess I can give him a minute of my time, that's about as much of his time as he's given to me since I've been here." I had never even met the guy, and now that he's traded me, now he wants to speak to me? Incredible. So I went to his office and met with him, not really knowing what to expect. I sat down and it turned out the man couldn't have been any nicer.

He had wanted to thank me personally me for my service and he wanted to wish me well in Atlanta. By him doing that he really earned my respect that day. It was not my finest hour, but that was a classy thing to do and I very much appreciated it. We stayed in touch over the years and he was a person I always held in high regard.

As I walked out of the Cap Center to the parking lot, I

just had to smile. Sometimes you've just got to roll with the punches, and at that moment — it felt like I had just gone 15 rounds with Muhammad Ali. I'd hardly had any sleep. I'd just been bag-skated for two hours. I played Monday night in the All Star Game in Philly, Tuesday night in Washington against the Rangers, and now I was going to be playing in a few hours back in Philly with the Flames against the Flyers. How in the hell was I going to pull this off?

So I got back in my car and drove three hours back to Philly. I get there, get my new uniform on, and hit the ice. Apparently we lost 7-2 but I am not really sure because it was all just a blur. I had never been more exhausted in my entire life. I slept the entire charter flight back to Atlanta, got checked into a hotel room, and slept for most of the next day. I then got up and played yet again in my first home game against Buffalo. We won and I played great, but man was I a mess.

On a side note, one of the silver linings of that entire debacle is that I am now the answer to a fascinating but useless bit of trivia that still stands today. QUESTION: "Who is the only player in NHL history to play in three games on three consecutive nights for three different teams?" ANSWER: "Bill Clement, — Wales Conference All-Stars, Washington Capitals, and Atlanta Flames." Dubious distinction, I know.

9) DEALT TO THE ATLANTA FLAMES...

Looking back, I knew that the Capitals were going to have to shake things up and make some drastic changes if they wanted to get better, and the fact that they chose to start by shipping out their team captain is just a reminder of how abrupt this business can be. To be honest, after the shock of being dealt twice in seven months had worn off, I realized this was a better situation for me. I was now on a team that not only wanted me, but one that had a much better chance of making the post-season. Once I got over the useless emotions of being hurt and angry and rejected, I accepted that I was in a much better place in Atlanta.

The move, however, from Washington to Atlanta exposed issues with my marriage. We were just barely hanging on by this point and I was really concerned. All the travel and stress had taken a toll. Our daughter, Christa was now two years old and I knew that Cathie and I needed help. We'd talked about getting counseling for some time but when push came to shove, Cathie didn't want to get any professional help. Sadly, when the trade went down I wound up moving into an apartment in Atlanta while she and Christa packed up and moved back to Canada to live with her folks in Ottawa for the rest of the season.

Meanwhile, I had hockey to concentrate on and that was going to be my focus 24/7. My new teammates in Atlanta welcomed me with open arms and that felt great. They were really good guys too, real quality people. The easiest part of the adjustment though, more so than anything else, was the simple fact that we won hockey games in Atlanta. We were winning.

Winning, it's a fascinating thing. There's only one

measurement of success in professional sports and that's winning and losing. We were raised to think that if we weren't winning, then we didn't deserve to feel good about ourselves. You got rewarded when you won and you got punished when you lost, right? You were supposed to feel bad about yourself if you lost. "What the hell are you smiling at?" God forbid you should ever look like you're having fun after a loss. That's how it is in high-stakes sports. The hatred of losing is supposed to temporarily strip you of any positive feeling about your worth and life is supposed to come to a stand-still - at least until your next game.

Have you ever been on a team bus after a loss? It's dead quiet in there. You're not supposed to talk, you're supposed to think about what you did wrong and about why you lost. The old-school coaches would basically reinforce the notion that if you lost you weren't supposed to enjoy yourself. If you went out with your wife you weren't supposed to laugh and smile over dinner; you were just supposed to go home and think about it. You were a loser. Only winners are allowed to feel good, not losers.

So it didn't take that long after I got to Atlanta for my self-esteem, part of which had always been tied to wins and losses, to fall back into place where it was supposed to be. Winning is everything to a highly competitive person, it really is. Being around winners, and being in a culture of winning, there's nothing better. Life is much, much easier when you are winning. No question.

What many people under-estimate is the ability each of us has to positively influence our immediate surroundings and thus contribute to that culture of winning. It doesn't have to come in the form of goals and assists. Contributions can come from encouragement - being the constant energy source teammates can plug into, especially if they are struggling. It can come in the form of sacrifice - like blocking a shot or performing an unsung chore such as killing a penalty. EveryDay Leaders don't need to be the statistical leaders or the designated captains. They just have to care about their teammates and the goals of the group.

There's little question that performance and self confidence are generally linked. At least they are for me. I had gone from Philadelphia, where we won 70% of our games, to Washington, where we won 2% of our games. So it was really hard to feel good about myself, especially caring as much as I did about team success. In Atlanta, I felt good again.

****

I had arrived in Atlanta mid-season and was introduced to my second "Freddie" head coach - this time Freddie Creighton, who I would immediately respect and bond with. He was tough but fair and I loved him as a coach. He was an ex-minor leaguer that never made it and if you saw him skate you would know why. He didn't really skate, he lumbered.

Freddie used to hit the ice for practice all juiced up with enthusiasm and head right to the closest loose puck which he would gather in. After stickhandling his way to center he demonstrated his awkward but full wind-up and took a huge slapshot at the empty net. Sometimes the puck actually made it all the way.

Every few weeks a couple of us would steal Freddie's stick, take it into the stick room and remove this little decal of stripes that went around the shaft of the stick, just above the blade. We would take a hacksaw and cut through most of the shaft and then delicately replaced the decal to conceal the incision. Once we snuck the stick back into his office (this sometimes required a decoy maneuver), we hustled into our equipment to get out on the ice before him. True to form every time, Freddie would bolt onto the ice, grab a puck and tee it up at center. Immediately on contact with the puck, his stick would snap like a used toothpick and he would fall flat on his face. Some days he laughed his ass off and others...not so much. Us players, meanwhile, we always laughed.

One day, in a quiet moment, I got talking to Freddie about motivating players and asked him if he had ever had a coach that had left an impression on him. With a smirk that told me there was going to be a twist to this story, he began telling me about an incident while playing junior hockey in Kamloops, British Columbia.

Freddie Creighton was a two-goal-a-year player, and that was in a good year. He rarely played in key situations or big games, but was a heart and soul type of player. When he was 19, Kamloops was facing playoff elimination and trailed by three goals in the third period. Looking for answers, Freddie's coach began a motivational rant. "Who's gonna get us a goal?! Who's gonna pick us up and be a hero?! Who wants to stand up and lead the way and get us right back into this thing?!"

Nobody stood up so the coach continued his plea for Superman to appear. Finally, completely fired up and feeling as if he could conquer the world Freddie sprung to his feet and shouted, "I'll get it coach!".

The coach peered down to the end of the bench where Freddie had been glued for half the game and sneered, "Ah sit down Creighton! You make me sick!" True story. Needless

The Atlanta Flames represented a new beginning... and a lot warmer weather.

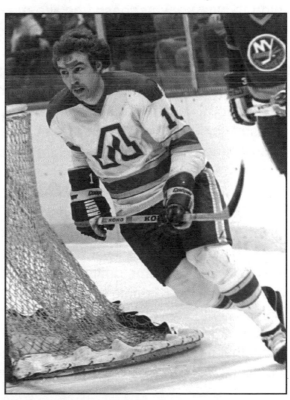

to say, this method of motivation didn't make my list of top 10 ways to be a quality EveryDay Leader.

****

By the time I became a Flame, the forward line combinations were pretty well set. I had to fit in somewhere and I wound up taking a bunch of ice time away from a player by the name of Claude St. Sauveur. He had been playing quite a bit until I showed up and this apparently wasn't sitting too well with him. I didn't know it at the time though, I just figured the guy was quiet — because he never said anything about it to me. In fact, after I was there for about a month and had gotten settled in, I remember saying to my teammate, Eric Vail, one day that I was surprised how quiet Claude was. Eric just started laughing and said, "He's not quiet, he just can't stand you. He complains about you all the time to the guys, he hates you."

I said, "Really? What do you mean? I didn't do anything to him, so why doesn't he like me?" Eric just looked at me and said very matter-of-factly, "You didn't do a thing to him, Billy C. You just took his ice time." Whoa. I had no idea.

By this time in my evolution as an EveryDay Leader, I had learned from watching others and by creeping out onto the tightrope now and again to have tough conversations, that I wasn't going to fall and hurt myself. The next day I discreetly approached Claude and asked him if I could buy him a beer after practice. He begrudgingly agreed.

We sat down and I said, "Look, Saint, I want you to understand something. I never asked to come here, I never asked for ice time once I got here, and I don't do anything other than what the coach tells me. I heard that you were upset with me about your ice time getting cut and you're pissed off at the wrong guy. If we're going to win, I need you and you need me just as much as we need our ice time. We need to pull together. If you have a problem go to Freddie and talk to him." I said that if he could earn some of his ice time back by pleading his case, then God bless him, go for it. I was fine with that

- and I really was.

We cleared the air and he was cool with me after that. We got along fine and that meant a lot to me. I was happy that I was able to address him man-to-man and put it behind us.

So the moral of the story for me with Claude was to confront the situation head on. Whenever you have any type of division between two athletes on a team, or people involved in a group effort, it can truly disrupt team harmony and chemistry to the point where under-achievements become more commonplace than successes.

Friction is never invisible - people instinctively take sides - and focus becomes cloudy. I recognized something counter-productive energy-wise and wanted to rectify it as quickly as possible. Energy vampires will create conflict when there doesn't need to be conflict, and unless you address that head-on, you're going to have problems that almost never go away on their own. He was upset and decided to take out his frustration by avoiding me and bad-mouthing me to my new teammates. I didn't care if he was bad-mouthing me, that didn't bother me. What bothered me was the fact that his negative energy would eventually hurt our team. That's what mattered most to me.

****

On the ice I felt liberated. I tore it up in Atlanta that first half season, clicking at almost a point per game rate. By my standards, I was on fire. It was so invigorating being in a winning environment again and flourishing as a player. We finished the regular season strong and wound up facing the L.A. Kings in the first round of the playoffs. We were favored to win, but we got swept, two games to none in the best-of-three series.

The best-of-three series for the first round of the playoffs was one of the worst things the NHL ever did and thank goodness it only lasted a few years. It was awful. You worked for 80 games to get into the playoffs and all you had to do was come up a bit flat in one game then run into a hot goalie in the next and you were toast. Season over.

****

That summer Cathie and I bought a home outside Atlanta, in Marietta, and I spent time getting it ready for our little family. I was really excited we were again together in our own place and I was committed to working things out. Things were good at first but eventually the same old problems came back. Our marriage was getting weaker instead of stronger. Communication was becoming less as opposed to more. Neither of us was a perfect spouse and I knew the issues weren't going to self-cure without some sort of intervention. Since that possibility was never accepted as an option, I knew it was over and by the end of the season it was. I felt as if I had failed as a husband and a father and it was the toughest decision I had ever made in my life.

****

On the ice that season, things went better than they did at home, but only slightly. After a career best 54 points the season before, I slipped back to 43 points. Turns out athletic performance is inversely proportionate to the size of your personal problems.

As a team we went 34-34-12 and were playing well enough at the end of the regular season that we thought we could make a run in the playoffs. Frustratingly, however, the L.A. Kings knocked us out of the first round yet again, two games to one. Losing the deciding Game Three in Atlanta was a huge disappointment. Again, we were favored to win that series but ran up against such a hot goalie in Rogie Vachon. I will never forget watching Bob Berry as he stood at the post jamming away at the puck until it went past our goalie, Phil Myre, for the 1-0 game-winner with just 58 seconds to go in regulation. The dream we dared dream - of skating the Stanley Cup - was over just like that. We were eliminated.

****

Sadly, I ended it with Cathie for good that summer. What a difficult conversation that was and I knew it would be devastating to her and her family. I don't think I slept for 10 days leading up to it. I remember going back up to Ottawa with her, like we had always done every off-season, to spend the summer with her folks. I will never forget the day I mustered the courage to ask her if we could talk. I began with, "It's over."

She was devastated and frankly, so was I. I walked out of the house with tears streaming down my cheeks and was greeted by Christa running up the driveway to get a hug, yelling, "Hi daddy! Hi daddy!" I realized at that moment that things were never going to be the same again. I picked her up and just hugged her, crying, and then set her down. I walked straight to my car and drove 30 miles to my parents home. I had to pull over to the side of the road three different times because I was crying so hard. It was such a horrible feeling.

Luckily we had an amicable split and I was always able to see Christa when my schedule permitted. It wasn't easy since I was playing in Georgia and Cathie stayed in Ottawa. My parents were my surrogates and got to spend a lot of time with her, taking her out to dinner at least once a week. They would bring her down to see me in Atlanta quite a bit too, which was so nice. I don't know what I would have done without my folks during that time. As usual, they were there for me through it all.

One of the hardest parts of the whole thing was having to say good bye to Cathie's family, because I was very close to them and thought the world of them. They were such a vibrant group of people - family and friends - and leaving them left a real hole in my life. The emotional distance that was now between us was also sad, but understandable. I had gone from being the guy who could do no wrong with them to being the ultimate villain dressed in black.

I spent the last part of the summer back in Atlanta, running and working out on these new, state of the art exercise machines at a local fitness center. I loved going golfing too, but I was never very good at it. People expected me to be a great golfer because I was a professional athlete, but the truth was I was just a hacker. I think I broke 90 once. Later in my life, when I was about 40, I got serious and took some lessons and played a few rounds in the 70's, but prior to that I didn't know what the hell I was doing out there. It was fun to get outside and hit it around though, especially with my buddies over some beers.

Meanwhile, I had this four bedroom house that was pretty empty so I wound up having three of my teammates move in with me — Harold Phillipoff, Pat Ribble and Greg Fox. It was like a giant frat house - what a blast we had living together. I didn't feel like being alone now that I was single, so it was great to have guys around and to have that camaraderie. We would hang out and talk hockey, talk life, talk women...whatever. Harold and I even showed our sensitive sides and wrote poetry now and again. They were great guys, dear friends.

To say there were a lot of players with great senses of humor on our team would be an understatement. The Flames roster was more like a busload of stand-up comics. Eric Vail, Guy Chouinard, Kenny Houston, my housemates - all could make people laugh. They were good people too and rallied when the opportunity to help someone presented itself.

One Christmas I read about a boy who was in Scottish Rite Children's Hospital because he had lost his leg. His parents were poor and couldn't afford a state-of-art prosthesis. When I approached the guys about chipping in to do something charitable, they all jumped at the chance, and a handful of us went to the hospital and presented a check to the boy and his parents. That's what Christmas is all about.

My relaxed, stress-free state of mind helped me to a 20 goal, 30 assist season. I even wound up sharing team MVP honors that year with Bobby MacMillan. It wasn't the most points I had scored in a season, but it was my best all around season as an NHLer.

I even made it back to the All Star game too. It was in Buffalo that year and I was able to get tickets for my mom and dad to come down, which made it even more special. I never really played well in those things though, they just didn't suit my style of play. I was a workaholic, and a checker, and a puck-hound. So to drop me into the middle of one of those star-studded, no-defense affairs was just useless. I don't think I ever felt as if I belonged and it probably showed.

That season I centered my roomie, Harold Phillipoff, to my left and John Gould on my right, and we had instant chemistry. We were the go-to line for much of that season and we were able to deliver. It was one of the only times in my career where I played on a line that had offensive magic. John was a good passer and shooter and a really smart defensive player.

Harold, meanwhile, he was really tough and he put up 53 points to boot. I totally trusted him out there. He and I be-

I was completely frustrated losing in the first-round of the playoffs in Atlanta so one year I kept growing my playoff beard all the way into the next season.

came such good friends and did just about everything together. He was bigger than me but was like my little brother on and off the ice. He always had my back too. I remember one time we were playing Chicago and Phil Russell hooked me from behind and raked me across the face with the blade of his stick. He deliberately went high with his stick, which is a huge violation of our code, and in the process damaged my right eye. I went down right away and was immediately concerned that I could lose the sight in that eye. It was bad.

I wound up having to leave the game and the team doctors put a patch on it but said I didn't have to go to the emergency room. Luckily, there wasn't any permanent damage to it, but it was pretty scary. Anyway, between periods Harold found me in the medical room. He had been out on the ice with me when it happened and was really upset. He said, "Don't worry Duke." One of my nicknames in those days was "Duke," because I did a killer John Wayne impression. "Don't worry Duke," he says, "I'll take care of that prick."

I got into my civies and went out to watch the third period. Sure enough, with the game out of hand and about three minutes to go, Harold grabbed Russell and just beat the snot out of him. Afterward he just smiled at me and said, "I told you I'd take care of him, Duke!" I wish I could've repaid the favor, only I couldn't beat anybody up.

****

Being single proved to be great for my career as it turned out. I had conflict resolution and I could just concentrate on playing hockey, nothing else. I was having fun and just loving life. It was work hard, play hard, every day. That was it. All in all, I had a great season because for the first time in a long time I felt really good about myself again. I could concentrate and focus on hockey without any distractions and my head was clear. I mean it wasn't like I worked extra hard on my conditioning or on my shot or anything like that with all the extra time I had, because I had always worked hard. The difference for me this season was my outlook on life. My confidence was back and it showed on the ice. When part of your heart and part of your mind are trying to deal with something really important to you that is atrophying - withering before your eyes, it's hard to maintain consistent focus. Unlike the Buffalo newspaper article which was simply a one-and-out distraction, my marital problems were constant. So when my marriage was finally over and I had that closure, once and for all, then I felt completely energized.

I also started to date again and felt good about myself in that regard too. Heck, I just liked who I was again and it felt great. In fact, towards the end of that season I wound up dating a beautiful young woman by the name of Jan. She was from Stone Mountain, just outside Atlanta, and she worked as an orthodontist's assistant. We were introduced by a mutual friend and hit it off right away. We dated a couple of times early on but then, for whatever reason, didn't see each other for probably close to a year. Once we finally reconnected again, it was as if it was meant to be.

The Flames finished the season strong once again and we were looking forward to finally making a run in the playoffs. Boy were we wrong. We wound up getting beat by the Detroit Red Wings, two games to none. We lost the first game in Atlanta and then were swept away in Game Two at the old Olympia Arena in Detroit. I remember Bill Lochead scoring both goals on Dan Bouchard to beat us, 2-1. If I disliked the best of three format before...I hated it by now!

****

Towards the end of the following season something happened that really tore me up. We were playing just OK hockey and management wanted to shake things up, so they made a blockbuster eight player deal. We sent five players to the Blackhawks and we got three back. Well, three of the five guys we traded away just happened to be my three roommates - Harold Phillipoff, Pat Ribble and Greg Fox. Talk about empty-nest syndrome! It was insane. I went from having my three buddies with me 24/7 to being abandoned overnight, literally. I didn't like that trade so much.

Luckily, it all worked out because Jan was able to move in with me and in the end I didn't have to evict any of my room-mates. It was wonderful to have someone to share that big house with too, just fantastic, to be able to come home to someone you cared deeply about. I was so happy.

After the 1977-78 season, the NHL got rid of the best-of-three preliminary round... but not before we were eliminated one last time. Toronto did us in that year and this one still stings. I will never forget, we lost the first game in Atlanta by one goal and it just so happened that it came as the result of a hooking penalty that I was called for while we were already a man short. My personal pain aside, we really didn't match up well against Toronto. They were so tough.

When we got up to Toronto for Game Two, they were like caged pit bulls that had been let loose. They just came after us and we were so in over our heads in a physical sense. They had some real bad-ass guys - Dan Maloney, Dave Hutchison, Jerry Butler and of course, Dave "Tiger" Williams. Man, those guys played like starving animals and their wisely crafted game plan was to beat on us all night, and they never let up. It was a helpless feeling. We couldn't do anything to stop them either because we knew we were over-matched. We were in a gunfight and only had knives.

In 1979 Fred Creighton was let go and Al MacNeil took over as the new head coach of the Flames. I didn't know a whole lot about the guy but I remembered a pretty negative quote about him from the legendary Henri Richard after his Montreal Canadiens had won the Stanley Cup in 1971. Mac-Neil had taken over midway through the season from Claude Ruel and he and Richard had not gotten along. He was the first Canadiens coach who didn't speak French, which some thought was an issue, but no one knew for sure. Anyway, after they won the title Richard was quoted as saying they had done so with a "midget (15 and 16 year olds) coach behind the bench." He even referred to him as "incompetent," which was quite a statement coming from a guy like Henri — with 11 Stanley Cup rings - more than any player in NHL history. I remembered thinking at the time what an awful thing that was to say about your coach, but it all made sense to me after I played for the guy.

Al MacNeil to me, on a scale of one to ten in motivation, communication, and organization — which at the time I felt were the three main tenets of leadership and coaching — ranked as a minus one. He wasn't even a zero in my book, he was beneath that.

It was easy for me to dislike Al because the moment he arrived in Atlanta he had a negative opinion of me. Despite the fact that I had made the All-Star team the year before, I was bench material in his eyes from the day he got there and nothing more. I could see it in his eyes and I could hear it in his voice anytime I asked a question. I was a leader on the team and maybe he felt threatened by that, I don't know. He didn't like the way I played or the style that I played. When I asked him what was up he just spoke in circles. He never talked to me about how I might be able to change and adapt to his liking or anything like that either. He just came in with a preconceived notion and moved me to the fourth line. The man was not a Clement fan, for reasons I did not know, and my ice time reflected that. I went from All-Star to role player and accompanying the demotion was an unhealthy drop in my confidence level. I scored a career-low seven goals and was totally confused, really down in the dumps.

We wound up finishing the year with a 35-32-13 record and then took on the New York Rangers in the first round of the playoffs. We had played so poorly in the post-season over the past four years and we really wanted to go deep into the playoffs.

We got off to a slow start in the series and then were told by management that if we lost the series, that the franchise was going to be relocated to Calgary. Wow, how's that for pressure? They weren't kidding either. From that moment on I was on a mission.

I will never forget jostling with the great Phil Esposito

out in front of the net that next game. He jabbed me in the ribs with his stick, so without dropping my glove I hauled off and punched him right in the face, knocking him on his ass. Dave Maloney, one of the Rangers young leaders, was right there and he screamed at me, "Dammit Clement, leave the old guys alone!" I just looked at Dave and said "F--- you! You have no idea… I'll do anything to win this f---ing series!" Well, whatever I did wasn't enough. We lost the series and as it turned out we were moving one way or the other. Management knew that all along.

Big changes lay ahead, that much I knew for sure.

10) HEADED BACK TO CANADA...

That summer Jan and I decided to get married. We exchanged vows at sunrise on the beach in Longport, NJ, near Atlantic City. Luckily she was on board with making the move north of the border, because in 1980 the Atlanta Flames franchise was relocated to Calgary. We had a strong fan base and drew well in Atlanta but our owner, Tom Cousins, had apparently lost a lot of money on some real estate development deals and wanted to recoup some of it. As such, he sold the team and off we went to Canada.

It was a bittersweet time for us as players. On one hand we were sorry for our fans, yet on the other hand we were excited to be heading to such a great hockey city as Calgary. I loved Atlanta though, the quality of life there was just unbelievable. The cost of living, the weather, the people, it was an easy place to live. To be honest I was really sad to go.

In August, Jan and I packed up our stuff into a moving van and then drove up to Calgary in my 1978 Corvette. I remember staying overnight in a hotel in Great Falls, Montana. We went to bed in shorts and t-shirts but when we woke up it was 40 degrees outside. Jan thought she was going to freeze to death it was so cold. I just had to bite my tongue because she had no idea what was in store for her in the ensuing months to come up in Alberta. She was a trooper though, all-in, and she just embraced the changes.

It turned out that I was the first player to arrive up in Calgary and that was a lot of fun. I did all sorts of TV and radio interviews to promote the upcoming season, and it was really neat because the fans were so excited to finally have an NHL franchise to call their own. Jan and I rented a house and once we got settled we started making plans to build a home of our own that next year. She was really excited about the project and it gave her something to focus on, which was good, since she was so far from home back in Georgia. We settled in, made some new friends up there, and were looking forward to a long and prosperous future together.

Next up for me was to get back out onto the ice and start out with a clean slate. I was hoping that I would be starting anew up there but those thoughts of optimism were quickly squashed once we had our first practice in our arena, the old Stampede Corral. The place was tiny, only seating around 7,000 fans, but it got pretty loud and crazy in there. The fans were so passionate but it took us a couple of months to win them over. I will never forget the first times we played Montreal and Toronto at home, the crowd would give them each standing ovations — out of respect. That was who they used to root for prior to us coming there and they were deeply loyal to them, so at times we sort of felt like the road team in our own building. It was crazy.

Optimism was running high with our change of scenery and I could tell early on that the competition for ice time was going to be tough. I knew how hard I was prepared to work each and every day though, determined to skate my way back into the lineup. As the season got underway I worked and worked, skating my butt off, yet my ice time didn't change from the year before. Even so, my numbers grew slightly and I was able to tally 32 points in 78 games.

"Ice time" is everything to a hockey player. Want to know how much ice time a player is getting without even looking at a stats sheet? Just ask him how things are going. If he says, "Great!", you immediately know he's playing a lot. If he matter-of-factly says, "Ok", then you know he's not playing as much as he would like. If he won't even respond to the question, he is communicating disgust through his silence. It's ALL about ice time.

We only lost five games at home that year out of 40 contests and finally wound up making a deep playoff run. In fact, we made it all the way to the conference finals.

We swept the Chicago Blackhawks in the first round

and the highlight was winning Game Three in triple-overtime. I remember how tired I was climbing those 14 stairs as we went from our basement dressing room in the old Chicago Stadium up to the ice for the start of that third extra session. I will never forget how it ended either.

Willi Plett was one of our tough guys, but he could also play. Tony Esposito (Phil's brother) was Chicago's goalie and he had a reputation of being a party guy. For years, before every period of every game against Tony, Willi would scream out in the locker room, "Shoot from everywhere on that fu---ing wino, he can't see the puck!". "Wino," that was Willi's nickname for him. We knew that whether he was hung over or not, Tony didn't see too well from long range.

So, the third overtime starts and Willi skates the puck up to center ice and rips one from the red line. All I see is the red light go on. Score! Sure enough, he let it fly and it found the back of net. We all just about died, it was as if he had finally called his own shot. We all jumped over the boards and started celebrating on the ice and what I remember most about

Our first season in Calgary was magical because winning was commonplace. I also finally started to protect my head with a helmet.

it was how we were all laughing so hard. For six years, every time we played against Tony O, we knew what Willi would yell at the beginning of the period. Finally, in the biggest NHL game of his life, he scored on him from long range. It was hilarious.

Personally, the win against Chicago meant a lot to me because it was the first playoff series I had won since being traded away from Philly. It felt really good. After sweeping the Blackhawks we then went on to upset Philadelphia in the second round, four games to three. It was a tough seven game series - just a brutal, bloody series. In my opinion, this was the toughest team the Flyers ever had.

We went up three games to one only to see them rally back. We had a chance to end it in Game Six at home but they came after us and tied it up. So we actually wound up winning the series on the road in Philly. That Game Seven in the Spectrum was epic. Nobody wins Game Seven in Philly. Nobody. The Spectrum was still the most intimidating building in the league at the time because the Flyers were still the most intimidating team. Our Flames team was so quiet and businesslike before the game, it was an eerie calm. We just sort of decided, collectively, that we were going to go out and play as well as we could play — and then let the chips fall where they may. There was no rah-rah, nothing. In the end our approach worked, and we won 4-1. It could just as easily have been 8-1 too, because we dominated them that night on their home ice.

The Flyers had no business being on the same ice as us that game and it was obvious to me that they weren't prepared to play. They thought that they had won the series by winning Game Six in Calgary and some of them got cocky. I remember looking into Kenny Linseman's eyes on face-offs and seeing this bizarre look of disorientation. It was like his hands were tied behind his back and he wasn't quite sure what to do about it. They were struggling to find the switch to turn their A-Game on, and to ratchet it up, and they just weren't emotionally prepared to play that night. Years later I talked to a few of the veteran guys on that team and they said they knew on the plane ride home from Calgary they were going to have a problem in Game Seven when they saw younger players acting so excited and saying things that were overconfident. In the end that was the main reason we wound up dominating them. They were looking past us and they got burned.

Part of my limited role under Al was being the team's go-to faceoff specialist. For non-hockey fans, a face-off occurs whenever there is a stoppage in play. Two players line up across from each other and the linesman comes over and drops the puck between them. The objective is to gain control of the puck by getting it back to your defensemen — at which point they either take a shot on goal or move the puck up out of the defensive zone — depending on whether or not you are in the offensive or defensive zone at the time. Well, I was our top face-off guy and it was my job to win those battles and protect our lead. Bobby Clarke, the Flyers' captain I revered so much, taught me about how to win face-offs back when I played with him in Philly. I was a good faceoff guy anyway but I learned so much more just by watching him - so many effective techniques, he was just amazing at it. It's an art, it truly is, winning a face-off.

As it were, I had a complete book on Bobby in the face-off circle from all the time I had spent studying him, and I could usually neutralize him because I was bigger and stronger. So to win face-offs in the offensive zone when they fell behind in Game Seven, the Flyers put a hulking rookie by the name of Tim Kerr out there against me instead of Bobby. Kerr would go on to be a prolific scorer but at this stage he was just a bull. After watching him and facing off against him a couple of times I realized he only had one move. He would just come in under your stick and pull back with his incredible power. That was it - but he was REALLY good at it. I struggled against him early on in that series because he was so big and strong. I would try to block his stick blade with my blade but he would blow right through me.

Halfway through Game Seven I realized I had to find a way to stop this kid, and fast, or we were going to be in serious trouble trying to hold the lead. I had to devise a way to beat him. I knew he wasn't that creative, he was just overpowering so I hatched a plan. The next time I lined up against him, I leaned my weight forward on my stick in the face-off circle and pulled my skates back, back, back — so that my bottom hand was bearing all my weight on my stick. I had basically become a human tripod and it must've looked crazy. Then, as soon as the linesman dropped the puck, I quickly move my tripod forward so my stick blade, bearing all of my 200 pounds, was beside the puck. As expected, Kerr came around behind my blade to pull the puck back towards him but now his stick got stuck. He was forced to release pressure and try to go around the other way, and as soon as he did, I would just flick the puck back to one of my defensemen.

As soon as I figured that out, I beat him almost every time. It was a little thing, something 99.9% of the fans had no clue about, but my teammates knew and that was all that mattered. That was my role and I took great, great pride in it. One of the personal mottos I live by is, "There is Always a Way". The degree of difficulty in this instance was the element of time, or lack thereof. I had to make adjustments quickly on the fly without panicking. I think I was prone to panic when I was young, but as I got older and somewhat wiser, I was able to focus and complete the task at hand...usually. Panicking in sports, in the wild, in business, as I found out years later - can get you killed - if not literally then at least figuratively. Luckily I was able to find a way to beat Tim Kerr on those face-offs and it played a part in us advancing to the conference finals.

We then met up with the Minnesota North Stars in hockey's version of the final four. We were coming off of such a high in beating Philadelphia, and unfortunately we peaked too soon. We were exhausted coming into the series and it showed. Minnesota came in riding a lot of momentum and we came up short, losing four games to two.

The playoffs are such a grind, both mentally as well as physically, and you just never know how you are going to match up with your opponent each round. The North Stars were a good young team, led by their star rookie Dino Ciccarelli, and I will never forget seeing all of those inflatable green "Dino the Dinosaurs" everywhere at the Met Center. God, I hated those damn things! The North Stars beat us in six games then went on to get devoured by the New York Islanders in the Finals. New York was in the midst of winning four straight Stanley Cups in those days, they were truly one of the NHL's great dynasty teams.

Personally it was really tough. I only scored three points during our entire playoff run and that was difficult to accept. I wanted to contribute more but the table wasn't being set for me the way it once was and I just wasn't given as many opportunities. I was getting older at this point in my career and wondered how many more opportunities I would have to get back to the Stanley Cup Finals.

11) MY SWAN SONG...

That off-season I was able to really enjoy some of the fruits of my labor. Jan and I had moved into our new house and we were able to relax and live life to its fullest. Summer in Alberta, man, nothing better. What a beautiful place, just gorgeous. So stunning to see the Rocky Mountains so close by, it was as if you could reach out and touch them. Truly awe inspiring.

Our house was built on a golf course about 12 miles outside of Calgary in an area called Bragg Creek. Building that house was significant to me. It meant I had been with one organization long enough to put down roots. It also meant that I was at a place financially where I had never been before. It felt really good.

I trained like an animal that summer, totally motivated, working on everything I could possibly imagine in hopes of gaining more ice time. Training camp opened and it was great to see all the guys again. I came in refreshed, re-energized and ready to go. Just before the season started we had to choose a new team captain because ours had been traded. This, as I knew, is a sacred honor in hockey - to choose your captain to wear the "C." Management would sometimes appoint a Captain but a lot of teams allowed the players to elect who they thought should wear it. That was how we had done it in the past and we just assumed that was how it was going to go this year as well. Guys were talking about who they were going to vote for, but then just before we voted, management stepped in and appointed someone. A few days later one of my teammates, Jim Peplinski, who was a good friend of mine, came up to me and said, "Duke, I just want you to know that I've asked enough players on the team who they would have voted for to get a majority answer, and it would've been you."

That meant a great deal to me, that my teammates thought that much of me and had that much respect for me. I had worn the "C" in Washington when I was just 24 and would have relished the opportunity to represent my teammates one more time now that I was older and wiser at age 31. I imagine once management got wind of the fact that there was a chance I was going to be elected captain, they decided to appoint someone else, and I can understand that. What coach would want a captain that he had an almost adversarial relationship with?

The season started and in no time my hopes for gaining more ice time were dashed. My shifts would continue to dwindle. After training hard all summer I had led the team in strength tests and stamina tests and broke records for this and for that at training camp, but it didn't matter. I was determined to show Al that I was worthy of more ice time but his mind was made up and had been since the day he arrived. There was simply nothing I could do about it.

Whether I wore the "C" or not, I knew I could continue to influence my teammates in positive ways - to put the team first and to work as hard as I could at being a high level Every-

I had hopes that my second year in Calgary would put me back on the map as a key contributor.

Day Leader. One thing was a certainty. I would not allow myself to become an energy vampire by letting my attitude slip.

I tallied a paltry 16 points that season, a career low. I was even a healthy scratch for some games. My confidence had grown fragile as it was and this just helped it atrophy further. It was also very humbling. Like most athletes I needed my coach's approval and in hockey your ice time is what tells you just how much value you offer to the team. Obviously, my value wasn't very much.

We finished the season with a 29-34-17 record and snuck into the playoffs, only to get swept by Vancouver in the first round. Despite those hideous Duraflame Log jerseys (big V-shaped black, yellow and orange chevrons on their sweaters), the Canucks got hot and rode a wave of momentum all the way to the Finals that year. Anyway, personally, it was just an awful ending to a very painful season.

****

Al MacNeil was fired after the season by our GM, Cliff Fletcher. Finally, after three miserable seasons with the man, I was going to be vindicated. In his place Cliff hired "Badger" Bob Johnson out of the University of Wisconsin. I was so excited to have the opportunity to play for Bob because he had such a terrific reputation as a player's-coach, a progressive thinking-man's coach. I was going to have a clean slate with Badger, a chance to start over. Well, Cliff Fletcher made it pretty clear that he was going to be making all kinds of changes that off-season. He followed through, trading guys, cutting guys, and basically letting everybody in the organization know that it didn't matter who you were, he was going to shake things up from the top down. So I called Cliff every couple of weeks to ask him where I stood in his grand plan. Every time I called he would reassure me and tell me not to worry - that I was fine.

Feeling a bit overconfident, I suppose, I made a tactical error in judgment that would really cost me. One day, after consuming a few margaritas with a bunch of the guys at a local Mexican restaurant, I decided to go meet with Cliff. I sat down across from him and initially proceeded to tell him how much I was looking forward to playing for Bob Johnson. Then - and this is where I screwed up - I said to him, "Cliff, you knew 60 days after you hired Al that it was a mistake, didn't you?"

Cliff had signed Al to a five year contract for $125,000 per year, which was huge money for a coach in those days. Cliff looked at me and said, "Yeah, I did." He then proceeded to tell me that it would have been pretty hard to fire him after his second year with the organization, when he led the team all the way to the conference finals. He knew that when he crashed and burned that past season, however, that he would be able to "re-assign Al" within the organization. I could tell Cliff was a bit upset with me for bringing this up but I didn't make too much of it.

With just a couple of weeks to go before training camp, Cliff scheduled individual meetings with all the players. Sitting down in that same seat, sober this time, I jokingly said to him, "Well Cliff, am I still part of the organization?" I just smiled and looked over at him waiting for him to pick up on my humor. But with a straight face he said, "No, you're not. We're phasing you out." He then went on to say that it was Bob Johnson's decision, not his.

I went into shock - I really did. My head started to spin. I knew that my life was going to be impacted in a big way, I just wasn't quite sure at that moment how bad it was going to be. I had let my agent go at that point and Cliff told me that he would see if any other teams wanted to bring me in. Two days later I went back to see Cliff and he told me that the Hartford Whalers and New Jersey Devils had showed some interest in my services.

I had one year left on my contract and figured I could go to either place and collect a paycheck for one more season, but my heart wasn't in it at that point. I just wasn't interested. After scoring just four goals that past season my confidence was shot and I didn't feel like starting all over again. Twelve years into my pro career I had a firm grasp of the theory of taking one step backward in order to take two steps forward. I just wasn't sure about my ability to take those two forward steps. I figured I would just be prolonging the agony for one more year, rather than biting the bullet and entering the real world right then and there.

I started thinking about what I was going to do with my life after hockey. With that, I knew I could get one third of that last year's $137,000 salary, as a buyout — and that was what I chose to do. So, I took the $46,000 spread out over two years (one-third of the contract over twice the length of it) and retired. I was hangin' em' up for good.

I thought back to the advice I had given to Claude St. Sauveur all those years prior, and about how there's only one thing in this world over which you have complete control, and that's you. Ironically, I never took my own advice. I resented Al MacNeil and really blamed him for a lot of negative things that had happened in the past three years, including losing all of my confidence and ultimately being forced into retirement.

I realized a number of years later that it was me who was responsible. He may have been responsible for making team decisions concerning his line-up but I wasn't being held

I sure hadn't planned on this.

prisoner. There's only one thing in this world over which you have complete control, and that's you. Not the economy, not your spouse or your kids, not the weather, and certainly not the coach. It was me, I was responsible for my actions, for my career. In retrospect, I could have and should have asked to be traded when I was still in Atlanta. I should have done my homework and sought out a team where I would have had the opportunity to not only be best utilized, but also appreciated.

By avoiding doing that, because of my fear of change, I had essentially killed my career. Staying with the Flames was safe to me. I liked my teammates and they liked me. I didn't want to start over somewhere else. I didn't want to uproot and move again. I feared the prospect of having to recreate that immediate environment that I was so comfortable in. That fear kept me from exercising control over the one thing that I had complete control over, which was me. I had no problem giving that same advice to Claude, yet when it came to my own career and I was the subject of the issue, I seemed paralyzed. I had really turned my back to the gorge and pretended that I didn't see the tightrope.

There are a couple of certainties about what lives down in the gorge. First, whatever's down there has the potential to limit our performance and therefore our levels of achievement and success. Second, these RESISTORS are pushing against us based on part of the 90-10 principle. This is a principle (the percentages may vary slightly) I speak about today that was authored by philosophers hundreds of years ago that states that 10 percent of the things working against our success are External - coming from outside forces - and 90 percent of what is pushing against us is Internal, coming from inside us. It's a pretty exciting ratio when we consider we are in control of the 90 percent.

I had control of my situation and instead of stepping out onto the tightrope I practiced what I call "rationalized inertia" - pretending I was still moving forward while refusing to step out. When procrastination leads to rationalized inertia, success becomes a distant if not unachievable target.

Looking back, my opinion of Al MacNeil as a coach has

never changed. However, my opinion of what Al MacNeil was responsible for in my life has completely changed. The guy may have been a horrible coach, but he wasn't responsible for anything negative that happened in my life. Nothing.

As I was being "phased out" that off-season, the oil and gas industry throughout Canada completely crashed. As a result, home prices plummeted. When we moved to Calgary there was close to a zero percent vacancy rate. Homes sold in hours for more than they were listed at. It was a boom town at that point, with tons of new money coming into the area every week. It was a totally different vibe in those days. Then it came crashing down and it all bottomed out.

Sadly, our new house that we had built turned out to be a bust for us financially. In fact, a lot of guys who had gotten traded or released at that time simply walked away from their homes. It was crazy. They owed more on their mortgages than their homes were worth and they just decided to let the banks have them. I eventually wound up selling our house to a friend of ours and it took me two years to collect a lot of the money that he owed me. You know the old cliché, "When you lend money to your friends, in the end you usually lose both?" That wasn't completely true in this scenario. I knew that he was upset because the house was continuing to drop in value, and I was sympathetic to that, I really was. But when your signature and your handshake are your bonds, then there's an obligation to do the right thing and keep your word. That was just an awful experience, it really was. In the end I wanted to maintain my friendship with him, so I just took less than the agreed amount and moved on.

I learned some valuable life lessons though, about the perils of doing business with your friends and also about trying to take the high road. Both have served me well all these years later.

So there I was, 31 years old, re-married, with a new house that I was inevitably going to take a loss on. Oh, and I was suddenly unemployed. I knew that I was going to be packing up and heading somewhere, I just wasn't sure where. I was sad to be leaving my teammates too, because I had made some really good friendships with those guys. Guys like Jim Peplinski, Paul Reinhardt, Lanny McDonald and Jamie Hislop. They are such good people and it was easy to get close to them. I knew that I was going to miss them. A week before training camp the guys threw me a surprise retirement party which meant a great deal to me. The whole team was there - I will never forget that.

Because of my reluctance to walk the tightrope, that's exactly where I found myself. I could only wonder at that point, what could have been? Years later I spoke to our team trainer, Bearcat Murray, and he said that Bob Johnson had asked two questions about me when he took over as the head coach. He asked "How hard does he work?" and "Will he play hurt?" Bearcat told him that I played with pain a lot and that I was one of the hardest workers he had ever been associated with. I also learned from one of the assistant coaches that the staff was looking forward to having me on the team. It turned out that it had not been Bob Johnson's decision after all. Too bad. I would have loved to play for Badger. I always loved his classic line, "It's a great day for hockey." And it would have been.

Bob would go on to win a Stanley Cup with Pittsburgh in 1990, only to die of cancer a year later. What a great man.

12) FROM CENTERMAN TO RESTAURATEUR...

In a blink, my 12 year professional career was over. My hockey epitaph was complete: I had tallied 148 goals and 206 assists in 719 regular season games, plus a handful more in the playoffs. There it was. Had I possessed the confidence at the time I probably could have played professional hockey for another four or five years — possibly into my late thirties. No question, I was still in great shape and had value as a veteran presence.

I left some money on the table too, no doubt about it. But I had lost so much self-assurance that I decided to leave the game on my own terms. Ironically, as my ability to deliver the product as a player decreased, my courage on the ice and enjoyment for playing the sport increased. That was the thing that made me the saddest about saying good-bye to this magnificent game. Looking back, I wish I had found that confidence, but I doubted my abilities at the time and decided to move on.

The big question was, "on to where and what?" To be honest, I had no idea what I wanted to do with myself at this point in my life. I knew that I wanted to start my own business though - entrepreneurship had always intrigued me. That last year in Calgary I had gotten involved in raising a large amount of investor capital for a couple of friends of mine who were acquiring the rights to a Canadian bakery/deli restaurant franchise called "Grandma Lee's." They had territorial rights to open restaurants in Arizona, Colorado, Utah and Nevada. I figured if I was going to find investors for them, then I had better understand how the business model was put together and if the food was any good. So I dove in and tried to learn as much about the business as I could. I even went in and worked in one of the stores for a few days, learning about their products and about how they ran their operation. I gave the food great reviews and really liked what I saw, so when life after hockey presented itself, I felt it might be a good fit - maybe this would be a huge opportunity. As it turned out, the parent company was in the middle of a cash crisis and needed to raise some capital, so they offered me the opportunity to buy the territorial rights to Georgia, Tennessee and Alabama for $10,000.

I knew that Jan wanted to move back to Atlanta when my career was over and I was fine with that. I had really enjoyed my time in the south and was anxious to put down roots there again. My master plan was to open a pilot store in Atlanta and then, after the incredible success of that one store, sell hundreds of other franchises throughout the Southeast. That was the "plan." With that, we packed up and made the move back to the Peach State. I would have loved to just move back into my house in Atlanta, but we had renters in it at the time and couldn't get in. So, we moved into my in-laws basement. It wasn't ideal, but I figured it would be a good move considering the fact that I was going to be working so much. We would wind up staying with her folks for about a year, until the lease ran up on my renters.

As soon as we got back to Atlanta I hit the ground running. One of the first things I had to do was spend a week in Toronto at the Grandma Lee's training school, where I learned the ins and outs of running a restaurant and bakery. I really enjoyed it.

It was also immediately apparent in checking my own net worth that I needed to raise some money. A lot of money. I needed about $400 grand to get the restaurant up and running and for someone whose top single-year salary had been $137,000, this seemed like a bunch. So, I formed a Limited Partnership and started beating the bushes for investors. I called a few of my old teammates and friends and asked them if they wanted in on my "soon-to-be-money-making" business. It took a few months but luckily I found enough takers. So with most of my life savings in there too, I was now ready to build store No. 1.

Now the pressure was on to get my friends a return on their investment. While raising money I scoured Atlanta in pursuit of the perfect location. It was repeatedly pounded into my head during training that the key to a successful franchise was location, location, location. So off I went, on a quest to find "THE" right place. There was just one problem that I hadn't counted on: Atlanta had more food and beverage establishments per capita than any city in North America. Ah, what's a little competition?

Undeterred, I set off on a quest to find some prime real estate and even brought on four real estate agents to scour the city. I didn't have the money to build a free-standing building so rented space was going to have to do — at least in the beginning — for store No. 1. I wanted to be in a mall or strip center, with solid anchor stores to drive traffic. Having a free-standing building was not important, I just wanted to be in a high density, high traffic area with a lot of people nearby. That was key.

A pattern started to repeat itself. Invariably one of my agents would find prime space that had a lease expiring. I would go in and make my presentation to the building owners but they never chose me as their tenant. Many of them didn't want to convert their space into a restaurant but most were simply unimpressed with an ex-jock turned restaurateur who wanted to launch a Canadian bakery-deli in the south. It turned into a real grind. I spent a whole year just trying to find the right location, an "A" site. It was THAT important.

Because it was taking some time to land the location a financial noose started to tighten around my neck. I had some substantial investors who were anxious to start receiving a return on their money. After all, this was the 80's, the halcyon days of Limited Partnerships when everyone made money. A return on investment was kind of hard to produce, however, without as much as a lease. It was a new kind of stress that I had never felt before. This was a kind of pressure I wasn't sure I liked.

Finally, fearing that my investors were going to back out, I settled for what I knew was a "B," or second-rate location.

I was convinced I could overcome the disadvantages of the location though, no question. I had a marketing strategy all planned out and I was completely confident in the product. I was going to have the nicest décor, the cleanest bathrooms, the service was going to be second to none, and the food was going to be amazing. It was all set. Basically I felt that if I could create a better mouse trap, then it would all work out.

With that, I dove in and started phase two of my life after hockey. I was officially a restaurateur. My franchise opened in a strip center just north of Atlanta in an area called Sandy Spring. It was a retail space that we converted to a restaurant and the construction build-out proved to be very costly. I had always been a do-it-yourselfer and was very hands-on during the entire process. I spent days jack-hammering concrete up to lay pipe and conduit. It was tough but I wasn't about to spend even more money on hiring contractors to come in and do the work. I knew I could do a lot of it. Dad had shown me the way years ago as a kid. Eventually, we got all the equipment in, along with the tables and chairs, then hired a staff. Everything was finally coming together.

****

The day we opened the doors I was undercapitalized. I quickly realized that it was going to be a struggle. Nevertheless, I really enjoyed being there and being a part of building something from scratch. That was very satisfying. I went into the venture with the same work ethic and positive attitude that I did as a professional hockey player and I was determined to succeed, regardless of the obstacles that lay in front of me.

In the beginning it was all so new and exciting. Every morning as I arrived at Grandma Lee's I was greeted by the aroma wafting out of our baking ovens in the kitchen. The cinnamon from the Chelsea loaves and sticky buns always dominated, and the butter we brushed on our biscuits always seemed to find its way into the mix. We had a great lunch menu with our signature homemade pot-pies. It was wonderful food, it really was. With a hint of chocolate in the air from our cookies and the smell of our bread baking, the experience was more than satisfying. For me, the smells represented hope and prosperity, and that today had a chance of being a better day. Same idea as the smell from the paper mill growing up...except WAY better.

Each day as I greeted customers and kept an eye on our overall operation, I would silently keep a tally on how many people came through the door for breakfast and lunch. We weren't really a dinner destination so I knew we had to do significant numbers before six o'clock when we closed. Each day I counted. Some days were better than others, but we never seemed to get over the hump. By the time our first anniversary arrived, I knew we were in trouble. I spent pretty much every waking moment working at the restaurant. I would get in around 5:30 in the morning to check on our bakers and then stay well into the evening before I left for home. Jan even got a job at a clothing store right next door, just so we could see each other every now and then. Like my breakaway in Buffalo, it was all such a blur.

Running a restaurant, as I learned, is a numbers game. You need a certain number of people to get into your establishment to try the product and you need to have them spend a certain amount of money. Then you need a certain number of them to become repeat customers. While this is building you have to control your food costs and your payroll. It's obviously easier said than done, that's for sure.

I tried all sorts of different marketing ideas to drive traffic. One thing I used to do that our waitresses hated, was to have them go out and stand along the side of our busy street wearing a sandwich board on the front and back of them, offering free coffee in the morning. I just wanted to get people in the door and I was convinced that if they just came in, they would see how great it was and come back for breakfast or lunch. I was kind of like a drug dealer, giving them their first hit in hopes that they would get hooked and keep coming back for more.

Our problem, as I eventually learned, was that it was all

drive-by traffic in our location with far too little pedestrian activity. And it was difficult for cars to turn off and come into our parking lot, because of our location in this strip mall. Before I even signed the lease I would go over there at 5:30 in the morning and just sit there doing traffic counts. I could see that there was plenty of traffic going by, but what I couldn't see was that by the time lunch rolled around many of the cars were miles away at their places of work. I also hadn't observed that the cars that WERE there at lunch had trouble pulling in and out of our parking lot. It was just too congested. I needed a plan to fix this.

So, I went to the other 20 or so neighboring business tenants and convinced most of them to chip in on paying for an off-duty cop to help direct traffic over the lunch hour. I told them that if more people were able to get into our strip center over the lunch hour, especially to eat a meal, then we would all mutually benefit from it. Some said yes and some said no, but the majority of them agreed — so we started doing that. I wanted to be a lunch destination, not just a breakfast stop, and

Even pictures like this accompanying newspaper publicity didn't seem to help business.

for a while at least — the traffic cop helped us to achieve that.

That was just one of the obstacles we had to overcome. Sadly there would be many more. One especially hurt my chances of building the business and I discovered it too late to salvage. When we first opened, we had a guy come in from the corporate office to serve as our store opener. He was the one who originally priced all of our sandwiches for us, only it turned out that he priced them way too high based on our food cost calculations. We were charging too much. I remember customers would complain that our product was too expensive, but I knew the quality of our product and figured this was just what a premium sandwich must cost. Fantastic ingredients, large portions and homemade bread, all made from scratch. And, each sandwich was made from to start to finish with everything on it that they wanted in 30 seconds, so it was very convenient too. There was a whole methodology to how we did everything. So when I found out after the fact that our sandwiches, which were really our life blood, were priced too high — that was extremely disappointing.

Should I have checked? Known better? Absolutely. Especially after customer objections. What a mistake. I went with what the corporate office told us to do, after all, these guys had restaurants up and running. Who was I to tell them how to price the sandwiches? Someone who wasn't curious enough - that's who.

Making decisions every day really appealed to me and I also found it extremely gratifying managing my employees. I had never hired anybody prior to this, so being a boss was completely new to me. It was challenging at times dealing with all of the different personalities and with all the drama, but I enjoyed it.

Looking back, my hiring practices were at times flawed. I hired a guy when we launched named Larry. He was a young fellow that didn't own a car and he said that he had walked three miles to the interview. I remember being so impressed with that. He had also been an avid Flames fan before the team moved and he recognized me, which probably helped his chances of getting hired. He said that he really wanted the job and that he was a great worker. I wanted to give the guy a break so I hired him. He worked hard at first but then started taking short-cuts.

One day I had asked Larry to make sure to sweep up under the sandwich tables. It was his turn to stay and clean after we closed and I reminded him about how important cleanliness was and that my expectations were that it look spotless. He assured me that it would get done right. So the next morning I came in and swept under the sandwich tables and pulled out all sorts of nasty stuff. Clearly he hadn't executed as he had said he would. I swept it all up onto a tray and put it in my office. When Larry arrived I called him in and he sat down. I asked him if he had swept under the sandwich tables and with a convincing tone he said he sure had. I then told him that I was going to have to let him go.

He had already been on probation for other incidents, and this was the last straw for me. He then asked me why he was being let go. I told him it was because he wasn't able to execute at a level that represented the quality I wanted to maintain and that he not only lacked honesty with others but also himself. I mentioned the debris under the sandwich tables and he protested, "But I did sweep under there, I got everything." That's when I then pulled out the tray, with all the crumbs and dust and sandwich papers and crap on it and showed it to him. I put it right in front of his face and said, "Larry, you're dishonest! Not only with me but with yourself and this is why you're getting fired this morning."

What I learned from Larry was to not confuse the investment somebody will make in themselves, with the investment they will make in you. It turned out that all Larry wanted was material things for him. Once he started getting paid and was able to take care of himself, then the level of excellence at work suddenly wasn't that important anymore.

There was also an 18 year old girl who worked for me by the name of Rita. She was living in a real bad situation at home. Her dad was emotionally abusive to her. I remember she called me one night just sobbing and said, "I can't live here anymore." So, my wife and I went to her home. Jan stayed in the car and I walked up to the door. Rita's mother answered the door and let me in. I told her who I was and said that Rita had asked me to come pick her up. Just then I looked up and I saw her husband, Rita's father, standing at the top of the staircase. He weighed 400 pounds conservatively and as he starts talking to me in a friendly tone, he comes walking down the stairs towards me. As he gets to the bottom of the stairs, he lunges at me and grabs me by my throat with both hands. Here I am, in the front foyer, with this giant guy pinning me up against the wall trying to strangle me. It was yet another, "Is this really happening?" moment. I thought I had left hockey behind.

Thinking quickly, I dropped down to get some leverage with my strongest asset, my legs, and with a mighty heave, shoved him backwards. His weight literally crushed in the wall behind him. I remember the sheetrock just imploding into a cloud of dust when he hit it. I then took his hands off of my throat and twisted them under him. Luckily I had incredible hand strength. So I am now standing there, holding his hands with him pinned up against the wall and I say to him very calmly, "Rita has asked for my help - she has the right to leave and I'm taking her out of here." I then said, "I'm going to let you go now, but if you try to take a shot at me I'm going to really hurt you." He backed off and as I moved away I looked up at his wife, who was now standing at the top of the stairs. I calmly said to her, "You need to get this man some help, he's not well."

Rita came running down with a bag packed and we got into our car. I wasn't sure what to do but I knew I couldn't let her go back there, so she moved in with us. Jan and I both agreed it was the right thing to do. The next day I took Rita into work with me. Later that morning one of my employees, Larry (yes, *another* Larry...), an African American baker who had previously done some time in prison — but who I was willing to give a second chance, came over to me and I could tell something was up. He says "Boss-Man" (the nickname was an "inside" thing, since I was the only one at the store that knew he had done time), "Boss-Man, we got a problem." I said

"What's up, Larry?" He then proceeded to tell me that Rita's uncle, who was about the same size as her father, was out front along with his son — and they wanted to talk to me. The son (Rita's cousin) was about 20 and built like an NFL linebacker. Oh boy.

So I go out front and see these two gigantic guys, who are wearing their hunting camouflage fatigues, and they want to "talk" to me. I walk over and introduce myself and the uncle says very directly, "We're here to get Rita." I said, "OK, come on back and let's chat a little bit." I wanted to get them out of the restaurant area, just in case the proverbial sh-- hit the fan. Not good for business, I figured. So we sat down and by the time our conversation was over I had them nodding in agreement that Rita's father needed help. I convinced them that he just wasn't right emotionally and that for Rita's safety she needed to be someplace else. As they walked out they each shook my hand and said thanks, which was a sense of relief. Another tightrope crossed.

After they left I sat back and took a deep breath. Just then I looked over and saw Larry, smiling at me from across the room. He says to me "Good work Boss-Man. I had 'Black Joe' ready to go just in case." I looked at him very inquisitively because I had no clue and said "Who's Black Joe?" He then holds up this old canvas bag that he had gotten out of his trunk and pulls out a pistol. My eyes just about popped out of my head. "Larry! What the hell are you doing? You're an ex-con, if you get caught with that thing they're gonna to throw you back in the joint!"

He wanted me to know how much he appreciated me hiring him and this was his way of letting me know. Incredible. To be honest, I was completely flattered. To think that he would risk his own freedom and safety to have my back, that meant a lot. I had always wanted to create a close-knit team environment with my employees and based on that, I think I had succeeded. I have always wondered what has happened to Larry. He had his demons, but he was a good man.

Rita wound up living with us for a couple of months until she was able to get a place on her own. We were happy to help her out at a time when she needed someone to give her a hand. Having her live with us was tough though because at this point all the troubles at the restaurant had started to take a toll on our marriage. Things were beginning to crumble on the home front due to money problems and the fact that we were both completely stressed out.

I could see that the restaurant was failing and I had no way of fixing it. My motto of "There's always a way!" seemed to be failing me. Jan was fighting against the restaurant, thinking that's what was taking me away from her. She figured it was either going to be the restaurant or her, but in essence what she was doing was pushing me away in competing for my time and for my affection. I WAS the restaurant.

Not only did I not have as much time to devote to her as I once had, but my head was spinning about a thousand miles per hour most days. I would wake up and chase my own tail all day, and then come home and crash. I was a mess. Eventually she wanted me to spend less time there and more time at home with her. I got that. I completely understood where she was coming from, and for the most part I agreed with her. But I just couldn't take a step back and do that. I was so concerned about making the restaurant into a success and so concerned about getting my investors a return on their investment and so paralyzed by the thought of failure, that everything else got shoved to the back-burner — including my marriage. What a confused human I had become.

13) FAILING, IN A VERY BIG WAY...

Ultimately, Jan and I split up. Our relationship was over. I had hung in there for about 18 months until I finally had to stop the bleeding. I needed to establish myself in a new post-hockey career and be successful and I realized that I couldn't do that with her in my life. I was now in my mid-thirties and she was in her late-twenties, and I knew that if we weren't going to work out, it would be unfair of me to take up any more of her time with regards to having children.

So, we parted ways, got a divorce, and said good bye. Could I really have failed twice at marriage this early in my life? It was tough, it really was, but I felt like it was the right thing to do at the time. Everything was crashing and burning around me and I just didn't want to drag her down with me. In the end I had to sell my house too. I had borrowed against it in order to keep the restaurant afloat and eventually I was financially upside down in it. When Jan found out about that she went ballistic. I told her that I needed to do everything I could do to keep the business alive but in retrospect she had every reason to be upset with me. I made so many mistakes during that phase of my life, so many.

The weeks leading up the closing of my restaurant were the loneliest and scariest of my life. Cash register receipts delivered a daily confirmation of the impending demise. On many days, I found myself trying to will my adding machine to lie to me. Sadly, it wouldn't. I was about to fail and I realized that it would not be a little failure, but a great big one. Closing the doors and having to tell all my people they were out of work was up there in that category of tough conversations. This was going to be one of the toughest things I ever had to do.

Looking back, the experience of running a restaurant

was both rewarding as well as nerve wracking. As a friend of mine once said about the restaurant business, "It'll eat the flesh from your bones." It did. I remember the day the bank called me and told me that they were going to foreclose on our home unless I brought my mortgage payments up to date. This wasn't their first warning. I owed them just under $5,000 which represented being six months behind on the payments...and this time they were serious. They wanted it all.

My daughter Christa, who was only nine at the time, had flown by herself to Atlanta to visit me. So I took her with me when I went down to the mortgage company to try to negotiate with them to let me keep the house. I told them that I had begged and borrowed $900 in cash from friends. It was in my pocket and I would hand it over if they would be willing to give me another 30 days to try to sell my house. Reluctantly, they agreed. Luckily Christa didn't know what her daddy was up to at that moment.

I then met up with this realtor. Chuck was his name, a real good ol' southern boy. Eventually we got it sold. And thank God he did because I was broke. I had to file corporate as well as personal bankruptcy, which about killed me. I was a mess.

I knew closing the doors to Grandma Lee's would lead to an emotional wasteland, so I searched for ways to survive. I thought that if I could just stay in business for another six months then maybe I could turn the corner. I met with my accountant and spent an entire day attempting to come up with a way to stay afloat. For every viable option we thought we had uncovered, there were three counter-balancing factors that dragged us under. I was behind on payments and installments to so many suppliers and vendors, as well as to the IRS, that I had trouble keeping them straight. Creditors were coming at me from every direction, trying to put leans on anything they could. There was only one option.

I hired a bankruptcy attorney and began my education on yet another phase of my post-hockey journey. My attorney's name was Jim Macie, a man who had left the priesthood to become a lawyer. For every lawyer who contributed to the profession of law's less-than-stellar reputation and image, Jim Macie restored the faith. He was a gentle and considerate man who cared about his clients.

One of my creditors was Dewey Thomas, who sold and leased restaurant equipment. An ex-teammate of mine, Tim Ecclestone, who was also in the restaurant business in Atlanta, introduced me to him. Dewey was in his 40's and had a classic southern drawl. His height, weight and build might have been average, but his eyes weren't. Perhaps they were simply "set up" by his dark beard, but I found they communicated different aspects of Dewey's personality and style. The first was strength and decisiveness, almost as if to say, "Don't screw with Dewey." Another was a sense of how he played the game, almost as if his eyes were warmly communicating, "I'm a fair guy and my business is built on integrity."

When Grandma Lee's opened, I decided to purchase the equipment rather than lease it. The plan was to be in business long enough to pay it off and own it outright. Plus, the payments on a purchase were roughly the same as the payments on a lease and my philosophy has always been that life is simply a game of cash-flow. Dewey had agreed to finance the equipment and the selling price was right at $100,000. Slicers, giant mixers, toasters, baking ovens, regular ovens, a stove, a ventilation hood, and a walk-in refrigerator...all of my equipment came from Dewey. I had only put 10 percent down, so the value of the paper Dewey was holding was $90,000.

As Jim and I analyzed the loan documents I had with Dewey, I assumed Dewey would just repossess the equipment once I filed bankruptcy. He had enough faith in me to finance 90 percent of the equipment and I wanted him to recoup what he could. For that matter, I wanted all of my creditors and investors to walk away unscathed but was sadly aware that the creditors would receive roughly five cents on the dollar, the investors nothing. Still, it was my goal to minimize the loss for as many people as I could.

I was so conflicted. My dad had always taught me to think things through, then to do what was right. "Doing what was right" trumped everything else. It had become both fundamental and foundational in my life but there seemed to be no "right" in any of this. There would be carnage almost everywhere, one way or the other. Some days I felt as if I were in a giant gyroscope, spinning out of control — desperately trying to get my balance and regain my equilibrium, only to be rocked by another negative. I was floundering.

I was shocked when Jim explained that the equipment would not go back to Dewey, but would be absorbed by the bankruptcy court, sold, and the proceeds applied to my long list of debts. Dewey was my largest creditor and stood to lose the most. As I drove away from Jim's office that day, I was determined to find a way to make Dewey whole. There had to be a way. If we converted the loan with Dewey to a lease, I thought, then Dewey would own the equipment, not me, and it would go back to him instead of being taken over by the bankruptcy court.

The following day I visited Dewey in his office and confided my financial situation and my plans to close. He had been in business a long time and I knew this was not a new story to him. His eyes seemed to convey more resignation than surprise. I also sensed a relief on his part that I was sitting across from him explaining my situation and that he had not simply received a letter in the mail notifying him that Grandma Lee's was closing and that in my bankruptcy filing I had listed him as "just another creditor." Nowhere in his eyes did I see, "You'd better not screw with Dewey." I offered him the lease alternative and we executed the paperwork to convert the loan to a lease. Despite the fact that Dewey would lose some money as a result of my bankruptcy, I felt good about the fact that he would lose far less in this scenario.

About a month after the doors to my restaurant closed, with the bankruptcy hearings behind me, I received a phone call. It was Dewey Thomas and I'll forever be grateful and humbled by what he said to me that afternoon. He had called to tell me that if I chose to go back into the restaurant business, he would be more than willing to lease or sell equipment to me again, down the road. He explained that he had been around the restaurant business for over 20 years, and that when he had visited my place he had really liked what he had seen. He said that I had what took to own and operate a successful establishment and that it was simply my location that had done me in — something that I had realized from the outset, but stubbornly thought I could overcome.

And he didn't stop there. He then explained to me that he had been financially burnt by Chapter 7 bankruptcies and failed restaurant ventures more times than he could remember. The fact that I had come forward to try and protect him even as my ship was sinking, had meant an awful lot to him. His final words were, "I respect what you did and I'm here if you need me." I sincerely thanked him for the call and hung up. I then sat by the phone reflecting on what I had just heard. I was touched. Here was a man that had lost money with my venture who was offering to join business hands with me again. Yes, he had said that he felt I had the ability to make it in the industry, but the fact that I had earned his respect meant even more to me. EveryDay Leadership is built on two things that are never handed to us - they must be earned: trust and respect.

I was reminded that the only thing I truly owned was my credibility and as I sat there my father's words softly echoed somewhere deep in my mind. "Always do what's right…always do what's right…always do what's right."

When it was all said and done I was in for quite a lifestyle change. I had gone from making $137 grand a year playing hockey and owning two homes, one in Calgary and one in Atlanta, just over a year and a half ago — to now eating dinner at TGI-Fridays, where for $3.95 I could enjoy all-you-can-eat appetizers and two-for-one glasses of wine during happy hour. I had cashed out of everything. Everything I had ever saved or property I had ever owned, everything was gone. My bank accounts had been seized by the IRS. So all I had was what I was walking around with in my pocket, trying to get from day to day.

I was able to rent a small apartment and keep myself going until I could figure out what I was going to do with the rest of my life. I felt like a complete failure and really didn't know what I was going to do. It was certainly the low point for me, no question. It was humiliating.

I had to be on a complete cash basis at this point because I wasn't allowed to put myself in a debtors position while in the bankruptcy program. I couldn't even have a credit card. Luckily, I was somehow able to lease a small car.

I had stopped making payments to the IRS for employee tax withholdings, which was not a smart decision. It had become a choice between sending the IRS what I owed them, or buying raw ingredients for the restaurant to try and keep it open. The IRS was an invisible entity that didn't seem threatening at the time so I chose the latter and, boy, did that ever turn out to be the wrong decision. If I had thought the restaurant industry would "eat the flesh from my bones," I hadn't seen the IRS in action.

I will never forget having to make those phone calls to my friends who had invested in me. In the tightrope category I always refer to as "the tough conversations," these were gut-wrenching. There were about 20 investors in all, each at different amounts ranging from $5,000 to $25,000 apiece. I remember calling two of my closest teammates in Calgary, Jim Peplinski and Paul Reinhart, and having to tell them that their money was gone. Their one question that they each had for me really hit me: "Why didn't you tell us sooner that you were in trouble, before you let it get to this point?" My answer was probably not what they wanted to hear. I told them that I didn't think it would help the cause to let the investors know that things weren't going well. It might've softened the shock for them, but I don't think it would have helped the bottom line. I didn't think that they could help at the time, other than throwing more money at the problem, so I chose to just try to work it out on my own through grit and hard work. I had so much respect for those guys and was so humbled that they had the confidence to invest in me. They didn't lose their life savings with me by any stretch, but it was enough to leave them frustrated and disappointed. Luckily it didn't affect our relationships long-term and I am proud to still be able to call them my friends today.

Each conversation was different and each person took it differently too. My great friend John Quattrocchi lost $25,000, which was a significant sum of money to him at the time. Within a few days, after the shock had worn off, he became more concerned about me and about my well being though, more so than his money. He is the man who really opened my heart and my eyes to human development.

John was more concerned with where I was emotionally than he was with the money that he lost, and that was so profound to me. I will never forget what he did for me - he brought me a copy of the iconic Napoleon Hill book "Think and Grow Rich." The book is a study of what made the most successful people in the world so unique and was way ahead of its time. It was first published in 1937 during the Great Depression and it's not about monetary wealth as much as it is growing rich in other deeper, more meaningful ways. Anyway, the gesture touched me deeply and I have never forgotten it. John and I remain very close to this day.

****

So, it's 1984, I'm 34 years old and I'm a mess. I had jumped into the restaurant business with the same intensity I had exhibited as a player, yet little did I know the intensity would not be enough. Within two years of my retirement, I had plunged into corporate and personal bankruptcy and had lost everything — including my second wife.

My morning showers were often marked with tears brought on by bouts of depression. I had failed in a career for the first time in my life. To make matters worse, I had no job, no training, no college education, no career, and no money. Well, very little money.

It was now springtime and the spring had always been my favorite season. In Georgia, it meant beautiful foliage — magnolias, dogwoods and azaleas in bloom. In hockey, it meant the NHL playoffs. Every player lived through the long, grueling regular season in hopes of his team making it into the playoffs. I had been lucky in this regard. In 11 NHL seasons, I only missed once — my first year in the league. Springtime, for so many years was the symbol of so much to look forward to. This spring, sadly, would be very different.

When I look back, I'm still proud of my mouse trap. I know that I created a better mouse trap. No question. In the end, however, it still wasn't enough to overcome the disadvantages of the location. To this day, whenever I see a Grandma Lee's I still can't bring myself to stop and go in. It's just too painful. I miss those sticky buns though. Man, were they good. Interestingly, there's a franchise today that's not too far from where mine was in Atlanta. Obviously it's far enough to be considered a prime location, so I have to tip my hat to them.

A happy interlude in an otherwise tumultuous time was my brother Pete's wedding day.

14) REINVENTING MYSELF...

In addition to the $4 grand "survival fund" I had stashed in my attic, I was also making a few bucks in royalties for some TV commercials I had shot the first year I moved back to Atlanta. You see, while I was searching for a site for my restaurant, I wound up doing a little acting work, shooting some local TV commercials. Acting was always something that I had thought about in the back of my mind but was never able to pursue until my hockey career had ended. I had always been good on TV doing post-game interviews and what-not, so I thought it would be fun to try it out. You could make some easy cash doing something that took very little time, so I figured it would be perfect for me.

I was a bit camera shy at first but it turned out that I was actually pretty good at it so I hooked up with a local talent agency. They had me take some head-shots and before I knew it I had auditioned and landed a couple of commercials. One of the first gigs I got was for Hardee's Restaurants, a fast-food burger chain. I played a plant worker and had one line, I will never forget it: "We took a vote at the plant! Hardee's biscuits? Number one!" And with that, the seeds of future income were planted.

Now that I was unemployed, I figured this "acting thing" could be something that I could pursue in the next chapter of my life. I was decent at it, I was highly motivated, and let's be honest — I had no other employment options at that point. So I dove in and started pounding the pavement, going to casting calls and doing as many auditions as I could. I'm sure that my friends and family thought I was crazy when I told them I was planning on earning a living as an actor, but I was determined to do this with the same level of intensity and hard work that I had employed as a professional hockey player.

Whenever I would get lines to memorize I would dive in and practice-practice-practice. I read everything I could read about acting and enrolled in every type of acting class I could get into. I became a student of the game all over again: cold reading, unscripted text, movement — all the techniques — I wanted to succeed so badly and was willing to do whatever it took. Quite frankly, I was desperate to reinvent myself.

Sure enough, before long the work started coming in. With it, my confidence started to come back as well. I was embarrassed to even call myself an actor for the first year because I didn't feel I had earned the right to. Acting is a craft and landing a few commercials didn't make me a craftsman. In my eyes it was like some guy who played senior hockey with his buddies calling himself a professional hockey player. So I used to cringe when I would hear someone call themselves an "actor" after one audition.

The stereotypical "struggling actor" always waits tables but I swore I never would. I didn't think my ego could handle

BILL CLEMENT

Every actor needs a headshot. This was one of my first.

it, I wanted all my energy focused on the goals I had set after reading "Think And Grow Rich." Believe it or not, I exceeded my financial goal and made $68,000 my first full year as an actor. It was amazing. By now I was registered with every talent agency in town and was landing so much work that I was considered to be at the top of my acting category, which was "Caucasian Male: Age 31-38." If a client called a talent agency looking to audition a caucasian male aged 31-38, I would get the call. Then my competitive nature would kick in and I would head off to the audition, determined to kick every other 31-38 year old male caucasion's ass who showed up to take MY job!

Things were going well and I was feeling really good about where I was and where I was going. Life was good. In fact, it was about to get great.

One day I headed off to an audition for a national Blue Cross – Blue Shield commercial. It involved two parts - one was for a husband and one was for a wife. For such auditions the casting director would pair up an actor and actress and run them through their lines in order to see them simultaneously. Well, I wound up getting paired for the reading with this gal I had seen before at some other auditions. She had seriously caught my eye. I thought she was so beautiful, just gorgeous, like a Vogue model. Her name was Cissie and without a doubt as soon as we introduced ourselves I was in trouble - completely intatuated. It was love at first sight… at least for me. Truth be told, Cissie took one look at me and thought I was gay. Today, she jokes about it and says it was because I was handsome and funny.

I assured her that I was very much a heterosexual. She was from Columbus, Georgia, and didn't know the difference between a Dixie Cup and the Stanley Cup. We began dating and really hit it off. She too had a daughter, Regan, who was 10 years old at the time. Regan was born with Down Syndrome and I immediately fell in love with her. What an amazing child.

Cissie was apprehensive at first about me, so I had to make sure she understood that I wasn't going to just disappear on her. She had gone through a couple of negative experiences with men in her past and she was reluctant to commit. So I had to let her know that I wasn't going anywhere. Finally, after six months of dating, she came up to Canada for Christmas with me to meet my folks. It was at that point that she realized our relationship was real. I wanted us to plan a life together but I was ready to start over with her somewhere new, away from Atlanta. If I was going to get into a new relationship, I wanted it to be somewhere that was fresh — without any memories of Grandma Lee's lurking around.

So, I asked Cissie what she thought about moving to New York. I felt I had conquered all I could conquer in Atlanta at that point, so I threw out the idea. I guess it was my competitive nature but I always wanted to compete in the major leagues — and New York was the place to be if you were an actor. I wasn't completely sure if I had what it took to make it there, however, so I went to a handful of the talent agents that I was working with at the time and asked them what they thought. They all thought I was good enough and that I should go for it, which was a huge confidence builder. I asked them about Cissie too, and they wholeheartedly agreed that she could thrive there as well. Now, at the time Regan lived with Cissie. She knew though that New York might be a tough place to raise a child with special needs though, so she made the decision to have her live with her father until we got settled into a home at some point down the road. She felt that it would be a great opportunity for Regan to spend some time with her biological father and also felt that it could be great for her career to try something outside of her comfort zone. With that, we packed up everything and headed to the Big Apple, in search of an apartment.

Finding a place to live in New York City is next to impossible. I felt like a carpenter trying to split an atom. Luckily we wound up being able to stay with some actor friends of ours until we got our bearings. No sooner had we unpacked than I got a call from an agent back in Atlanta telling me I had gotten a gig in Miami. Ahh, a gig. Of course I had to take it so I jumped on a flight, People Express, and headed down to Florida. Poor Cissie now had to try to find an apartment for us by herself.

The first place she looked at was in a terrible neighborhood, so she continued on her quest. Eventually she was able to find a semi-decent place out in Queens that fit within our budget. We wound up getting this tiny little second story row house apartment for $1,100 bucks a month that didn't even have its own thermostat. There was no tenant in the apartment below us for the first few months we lived there and that's where the thermostat was. So the landlord left the heat real low. Eventually we went to the guy and asked him if he could let us in to turn the heat up. It was October by now and starting to get pretty chilly. Incredibly, the guy said no! We just laughed it off. I mean what were we going to do? Heck, we were just happy to be settled. Fortunately a couple moved in before it got too cold and as it turned out she was from Panama. Needless to say she turned the heat WAY up.

Once we got settled, we set out to find work. Neither of us had an agent in New York, so we were basically starting from scratch. It was daunting and the competition was insane.

Cissie and I often competed head to head when a client wasn't sure if they wanted a man or a woman as their spokesperson. She beat me out every time.

Cissie Clement

We were determined to make it though. One of the things that both drove us and scared us was the fact that almost all the actors we knew from Atlanta who had gone to New York to try to make it, wound up coming back to Atlanta. Looking back, I think one of the reasons for that was they always left avenues of retreat and never severed their ties. For instance, they would keep their apartments in Atlanta as opposed to ending the lease. They also made short-term commitments to try it in NYC for six weeks or a few months. They didn't really make a commitment to go all-in, whereas I "burned the bridges of retreat." I didn't give myself a chance to go back because there was nothing for me to go back to. Cissie and I, we HAD to make it, there was no Plan B — no other option.

We were the Greeks burning our ships as we went ashore. In essence we had set ourselves up to start our NY existences a half inch past the midway point on the tightrope. In doing so it was now closer to safety moving forward rather than retreating.

With no agents, we had no work. Luckily, however, while in Atlanta, I wound up doing some side work in video ed-

A composite card I used for modeling and acting. The more "range" you had, the more work you would get.

iting. I had met these guys who had all of this editing equipment and they let me sub-let it late at night, when they were closed. So I basically taught myself how to edit video. I would then create and edit other actor's demo-reels for a few bucks, which turned out to be a nice little side business for me. I knew we had done quality work so I made sure Cissie and I had really good demo-reels that we could deliver to agents' offices...if they would let us in. A good demo-reel was everything in this business, especially in those days, before the internet. I knew if we could get people to watch our reels they would take us on and start sending us out on auditions. We would drop them off, make follow-up visits and then hope for the best.

I put a desk in our kitchen, which became my office, and I set up a big map of Manhattan on the wall. We did our homework, finding out which agents were good and which ones were sleeze-balls, and we would prioritize our plan with different colored pins on the map. Every day we would get up, pack up, and take the E or the F train into the City to try to find work. We had a 30 block rule for our first six months there too, which meant if the distance we had to travel was under 30 blocks — we would walk it — and if it was over 30 blocks, we would break down and take the subway, which at the time was 80¢. Cabs were a luxury we didn't even consider, we were way too poor.

We had some residual money coming in from work we had done in Atlanta but it was tight that first year, real tight. It was the silly little financial victories that meant the world to us. In fact, I remember coming home from the local supermarket in Queens one day and scaring Cissie half to death.

"Hey, hey! Guess what!", I screamed as I bounded up the stairs, grocery bag clutched tightly. From the sense of urgency in my voice she jumped up and blurted, "What?! What?!"

"I just found a 10 pound bag of rice for $1.89!", I panted.

It was crazy, it really was, but I was so excited about this amazing deal I had found. We pretty much ate rice every day and every way known to man. It was those little victories that kept us going though because we were just so poor.

We tracked our finances every day and kept a little ledger booklet for our budget. Everything that cost us over 50¢ we would write down. Honest truth. As an NHLer I rarely ever looked at the balance in my bank book. If it had a positive balance, I knew I was ok since more money from my salary was always coming in. That was my version of budgeting. Now I needed to be completely organized in order to create a budget for us. More importantly, to see if we were making enough to stay in the black. I would make simple spreadsheets with pencil and paper, just to see where we could cut here and there in order to stretch every dollar. In addition to rent I was still paying off my Chapter 13 Bankruptcy debt, plus I had a child support payment.

When I met Cissie, believe it or not, she was almost in worse financial shape than I was. In a twisted irony, at times I felt like a bankrupt financial advisor. Such an oxymoron. But we were both determined to succeed — no matter what. It was so far away from the days when I was a professional hockey player, just spending like crazy on stuff I didn't even

Acting out a scene was predictable. At this stage of my real life, however, I didn't know what was around the next corner.

need. When you're a player and you're living that lifestyle you naively think that the money is never going to go away, and that it will always be there. In today's world of major league sports that's pretty well true, unless you completely lose your mind. When I played, there was always a new "something" I had to have, and invariably I would just buy it. Living that lifestyle then going though those tough times like we were experiencing in Queens, it really grounded me and made me appreciate things a lot more. It was humbling yet infinitely valuable.

It didn't take long for me to see that we were making some headway in our careers, slowly but surely gaining traction. I was knocking on a lot of doors and finally a big one opened up. I was out delivering demo-reels to agents one day and I stopped into Abrams Artists, one of the biggest and best agencies in New York, to follow up and see if they had gotten a chance to look at our tapes. The receptionist sort of blew me off as she did to most of the starving, desperate, out of work actors that came in every day.

I thanked her and stepped out of their expansive office to grab the elevator. As the doors split open and I took a step forward, a bit dejected, I heard someone yelling, "Wait, wait!" So I stuck my hand in the door to open it up and looked back out. As it turned out, one of the agents, Tracy Goldblum, had looked at our tapes after all. She loved them and just like that, agreed to represent us. What a relief, that somebody believed in us. They tried to sign us exclusively but I was ready for that and said no. It was a gamble to play that card but luckily it worked out because before long we were able to develop relationships with a half a dozen other agents in New York as well. Before long we were being sent out on tons of auditions and eventually we were even able to stop eating rice for breakfast, lunch and dinner!

15) A COLOR ANALYST IS BORN...

As luck would have it, I was asked to do some hockey color analysis on TV for the New Jersey Devils. The color analyst sits next to the play-by-play guy in the broadcast booth and provides in depth analysis and insight from the player's perspective. I would fill in occasionally for their regular guy, Sal Messina, on their MSG (Madison Square Garden Network) broadcasts. It didn't pay a lot but it was fun to be back in the game. And it turned out I was pretty good at it. One day in early '86 I got a call from ESPN, asking me if I was interested in working as a color analyst for their hockey broadcasts.

They had just gotten the broadcast rights to the NHL and were putting together broadcast teams. They wanted to see if I would be a good replacement for Brad Park, who had been doing it for them but left when he was offered the head coaching job with the Detroit Red Wings. So they called me to see if I wanted to come in for an audition. I was ecstatic. ESPN was televised coast to coast and I knew this was the opportunity I had been waiting for. For the audition they told me that they were bringing in four former players and letting them each do a live game, on the air. Whoever did the best, got the job. That was it. So I flew up to Chicago and did the Blackhawks vs. Minnesota North Stars game and did my thing, which involved extensive preparation, including decisions on the information I would try to get in and the knowledge I would attempt to showcase. Always a plan. I apparently did all right because they called me shortly after and offered me the job.

I had no idea where this new broadcasting gig was going to go, or how long it was going to last, but I was thrilled to have a quasi-steady job doing something I really enjoyed. The games were sporadic, so it worked out in the sense that it didn't infringe on my acting career too much. And, as I did more and more of it, it started generating some really good income.

I had a hard time adjusting to it at first though. You see, ESPN was auditioning play-by-play announcers at this time as well, so I actually wound up working with five different play-by-play partners in my first five games. Trying to find any chemistry and rhythm under those circumstances was a challenge, but my partners were all pros and I did all right.

Something else interesting happened when I went to work for ESPN. I had been working really hard at making a name for myself as a serious actor to that point and I didn't want to be recognized at any auditions as a sports announcer. I thought it might hurt me if casting directors figured I was a broadcaster just dabbling in acting. So when I started my new job at ESPN I asked the producers if they would mind if I changed the pronunciation of my name on-air to Cle-ment', with the emphasis on the second syllable, instead of the way I (and my family) had always pronounced it - Clem'-ent, em-

ESPN wasn't a global force in television in the early years, but I could tell by the quality of the people I met every day that it wouldn't be long.

phasizing the first syllable. I just wanted to remain incognito and fly under the radar at auditions.

They said sure, no problem. To be honest, I figured the acting thing would take off and the broadcasting would subside, but the opposite happened. The broadcasting just grew and grew to the point where I have now ended up stuck with a mispronunciation of my name. My whole family still goes by Clem'-ent, and they routinely scoff at my "mispronunciation" that I created for myself. I'm still allowed to come to family reunions though. That's a good thing.

Between broadcasting and acting, I was starting to generate some momentum on two career fronts at this point. One day I went in to audition for a Deep Woods Off commercial. It was a pretty big deal and wasn't sure if I would get it or not. Days went by and then out of the blue I got the phone call telling me I got it. It was a national campaign and I was really excited about it. The agency called and as it turned out, they needed me in Florida the following Wednesday for the shoot. Now, I was broadcasting with ESPN at the time and as it

I felt comfortable playing a cowboy or farmer because of my experiences growing up.

turned out, I had a Tuesday playoff game in Philadelphia and then a Thursday playoff game in New York. I had a tight window to get it done, but I was determined to do so. I didn't want to let the agency down and I knew the payday would be significant.

I discussed the tight schedule with my producer and close friend, Bruce Connal, and he said, "Go for it!" So I flew down to Miami on Wednesday morning between games and when I arrived there were about 10 people waiting for me at the hotel — the director, the producer, the ad agency people, the client — everybody who had anything to do with the commercial. They all came right up to my room with me and nervously sat around on the beds while I ran through my lines for the director. The first thing he asks me is, "Are you off book?" — meaning, "Do you have your lines memorized?" I said, "Yup, I'm ready to go."

With everybody looking at me I took a deep breath, smiled and said "We filled this tent with 10,000 hungry mosquitoes and biting flies. But they're not biting me. I'm using

Getting dressed in a tuxedo was a bigger pain than putting on my hockey gear. It took some getting used to.

Deep Woods Off, it repels extra tough mosquitoes and biting flies...", and finished the 30 second script without a stumble The director then says, "OK, now how about really punching it. Get nasty with it, let me hear you do it meaner, with some more authority." So I did it again, with a totally different voice inflection. I would call it, severe.

"All right", he said, "now lighten it up. Show me your range."

"No problem," I replied, and I did it again for him with a much softer, warmer voice. Just then, everybody in the room gasps this huge collective sigh of relief. I looked over at them wondering what in the world they were doing. It turned out they were all scared to death to hire me because they weren't sure I could take direction or that I had any range. Because of my ESPN playoff schedule I hadn't been able to make either of the "call backs," where the field of auditioning actors is narrowed down to just a few and the director runs the audition to really put the actors through their paces. As it turned out, the lady from the ad agency, as well as the one representing the client, Johnson & Johnson, really wanted me — but the director and producer needed to know if I could act — so they wanted nothing to do with me. Luckily the ladies prevailed and in my Florida hotel room I was able to win everyone over.

We wound up shooting in the Everglades that night and it was an adventure, let me tell you. When I got there I saw that they had a tent set up with cameras inside. I was escorted to the wardrobe and make-up trailer and met Jack, my wardrobe guy. This had to be the easiest money he ever made because all I wore in the commercial was a pair of shorts. If nothing else, Jack was thorough. He handed me the shorts to try on and also presented a pair of Speedo type undies. He said he wanted to make sure I was protected from the skeeters. And he didn't stop there.

He reached into his pocket and said, "Don't laugh, but I brought some of these too because those bugs might get real aggressive", and with that he produced a handful of condoms. Condoms! I almost peed myself laughing.

I'm a pretty practical guy so I said to him, "Jack, the last time I checked, a man has to be in a certain state of arousal to apply one of those things. Am I just supposed to wander off to a private place in the everglades in the pitch dark and take care of this?" Needless to say, he didn't have an answer.

I knew my fear of snakes and alligators would have prevented me from "performing" anyway, so I thanked him for his concern and told him I would be ok flying without protection.

Then a group of people from the University of Florida's entomology department showed up with 15,000 mosquitoes and biting flies. Turned out they didn't want to get busted for truth-in-advertising laws, so they brought 5,000 extra critters to crawl all over me. Box after box after box of bugs were unloaded and dumped into this tent. Once it was full, I lathered up with Off and headed in. It was insane in there, totally freaky. The stuff really works though, no kidding, I only got bit twice during the entire shoot and that just happened to be when I was standing outside the tent. Those damn flies were the ones that got me too, once on my cheek and once on the back of my leg where the spray kept rubbing off due to how I was sitting in the tent.

It was well worth it though, because I would wind up

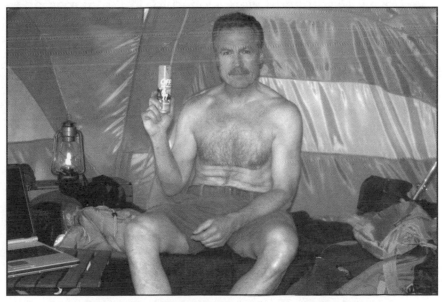

At age 53 I went back into the tent to reprise the Deepwoods Off campaign.

raking in a total of $96,000 for doing that one 30 second spot. Incidentally, in 2004 I did a remake of it due to the fact that West Nile Virus had become an issue. The crazy thing with shooting it this time though, was that instead of having 15,000 hungry mosquitoes and biting flies, they had 40,000! I still get the heebie-jeebies when I think about being in that damn tent.

****

In 1987 the NHL decided that instead of having an All-Star Game they would have a two game series in Quebec City featuring the best players from the NHL versus the best players from the Soviet Union. It was the first year that they let the fans vote on who got in, which was pretty neat, and they really hyped the thing up. "Rendezvous '87" it was called, and it was for global bragging rights. It would be held in conjunction with the Quebec Winter Carnival, which is such a fabulous extravaganza - a winter Mardi Gras. It was billed as a sports spectacle - a hockey summit - and it turned out to be even better than advertised in my opinion.

Ken Wilson and I were slotted to do the games and I was really looking forward to it. Now, when you work as a broadcast team you really get to know your partner. You're with that person on the road and you spend long hours together. Ken was an interesting guy. I nicknamed him "the island," because he did everything by himself. He would walk through the airport separated from the crew, he ate by himself, and just chose to do everything alone. He was the farthest thing from a team player I had ever been exposed to.

We had our first production meeting the day before Game One of the series and I could tell right away that this was being taken very seriously. It was an all-hands-on-deck command performance meeting, complete with operations producers and technical staff. There must've been 40 people at this meeting and most were wiped out after having ridden up on a bus during a snow storm for 12 hours to Quebec City from ESPN's headquarters in Bristol, Connecticut. As soon as they got there the technical men and women had to get to work, pulling cable in 40-below weather. It was unbelievably cold during this weekend - almost unbearable.

Our producer was Bruce Connal, a real pro, and a friend of mine to this day. In fact Bruce's dad, Scotty, was the man who originally hired me. He was a real legend in the business who had come from NBC and was one of the original patriarchs of ESPN. He was loved by everyone, just a great man. Anyway, Bruce is orchestrating this entire operation and I could see that his crew was exhausted and that tensions were running high.

At one point in the meeting Bruce says to Ken and me, "I would like you guys in the building at 4 o'clock tomorrow." Ken immediately says to him in his deep voice, "Well, I'm not coming at 4 o'clock. I've never come to a game in my life at 4 o'clock and I won't be there tomorrow at 4 o'clock."

I'm hearing this and I'm saying in my mind, "Holy crap! I can't believe my ears!" There are people in the room probably suffering from frost bite after being out in sub-zero weather pulling cables all night for us, and Ken can't make it to the warm broadcast booth a little bit early?

The next night Ken arrived about 4:30. We did the game and everything went pretty smoothly. Afterward, we went down to the production truck to talk to the crew. Out of the corner of my eye I noticed a commotion near the back of the truck. I look over and there is Scotty Connal, with Ken up against the wall and he's about to drive his index finger through his chest. "You arrogant son-of-a-bitch who the hell do you think you are!?"

I was in shock and couldn't believe my eyes. Later that night I ended up at a big reception talking to Ken and his wife. I was there with Cissie and I eventually pulled Ken aside to talk to him. I said to him "Ken, what was the deal in that meeting yesterday? Why did you tell Bruce in front of all those people that you wouldn't come in to work early?"

Do you know what I found out? Ken had a routine of preparation that he religiously went through. He was an old pro as a broadcaster and he had his own way of doing things.

He had always showed up to games at about 5:30 in the afternoon, so for him to come in at 4 o'clock really threw him out of his comfort zone. His routine was really important to him and he didn't want to mess it up. Contrary to what most people think, there's a lot of prep that goes into calling a game — especially one in which you had to learn a bunch of new, very difficult name pronunciations for all the Soviet players. As the play-by-play guy, you have to know that stuff cold. Anyway, that fear of not being as prepared as he could have been or would have been ultimately caused him to overreact.

He found himself at a gorge with something pushing against his success and he panicked. Into the gorge he dove, without even attempting to step out on the tightrope by coming in at 4:00 pm...outside of his comfort zone.

I've seen it more times than I can count and have often been that "over-reactor" myself. It has cost me credibility, respect and even jobs. The singular lesson I continue to attempt to master and learn is, it's never 'what' you say but 'how' and 'when' you say it. If we can be nimble enough to intercept that emotional impulse before it travels from our brain to our mouth, we have a fighting chance.

If Ken had taken Bruce aside after the meeting and quietly explained his discomfort with the call time, he most likely would have come to a compromise both he and Bruce could have lived with and avoided damaging his reputation in front of 39 co-workers. As it were, the 'how' and 'when' he chose, were counter-productive for a group effort.

So there we are after the game at this huge cocktail reception and I'm listening to Ken explain this to me and I'm starting to feel bad for him, thinking, "Aha...now I get it." I'm thinking to myself, "Maybe he's got a point. This is Ken Wilson, if he wants to come in at 5:30 in order to stay on his routine, then so be it."

Just then, Ken spots some TV executives from another network across the room and it was as if a switch flipped inside of him. His eyes get real big and while I was in mid-sentence, he grabs his wife by the hand and takes off. He nearly ran Cissie over, dragging his wife across the room to talk to these people. It was hilarious. Here we are in the middle of a pretty deep conversation and he just bolts. He "big-timed" us.

As I stood there with Cissie, dumbfounded, I looked at her and said, "Well, that sort of says it all right there about Ken."

****

One of my most memorable moments as a broadcaster came at the end of that '87 season when I got to do the Game Seven, four-overtime Stanley Cup playoff thriller between the New York Islanders and Washington Capitals. I was working alongside Doc Emrick, who is one of the all-time great play-by-play men in history. It was the Patrick Division Finals and I was so excited that I wound up taking my shirt off and tying my tie around my head.

In my mind I was channeling the great Apache leader Cochise. It was one o'clock in the morning and we were just punchy. Hell, we were loopy. We were trying to fill up intermissions on camera between the overtime sessions so I de-

One of the goofiest nights of my life.
Doc Emrick would probably agree.

cided to do some impressions: from John Wayne to an East Indian Soothsayer to Boom Boom Geoffrion (an iconic French Canadian hockey legend with a thick accent), all sorts of stuff. I can do some pretty good accents and Doc just kept feeding the monster.

I was just being spontaneous, it wasn't like I had planned any of it. Well, as it turned out most of the viewers loved it. Some of the ESPN execs hated it but most liked it. Most TV critics liked it but some cut us into tiny pieces. Believe it or not, I still have people come up to me all these years later and ask me about that night. How crazy is that? What it taught me though is that if you're not willing to get out on the ledge - step out onto the tightrope - you'll remain that same old slice of white bread on the sandwich of life. Just OK, ho-hum - no whole wheat, rye or seven grain - nothing memorable or note-worthy. It was a great lesson for me in that without taking some risk, there is seldom a healthy reward.

I often use the "slice of white bread" expression to describe something "vanilla." The first time I heard it was taking an acting class in New York, shortly after Cissie and I moved there. I did a scene where I was supposed to be on the phone talking to an old friend I hadn't spoken to in a while. After the scene the teacher, a lady named Joan See, said, "Well, you're a real slice of white bread."

"What do you mean?" I asked.

"I saw nothing there. No texture, no emotion, no whole wheat. Just white bread," she answered.

I didn't like hearing it but took it to heart and never forgot the expression. I vowed then and there to always try to deliver something more than white bread.

****

By now Cissie and I were more in love than ever (if that was possible), so that summer we decided to get married. We chose to exchange our vows in the Atlantic City area, with my great friends, John and Marie Glassey agreeing to host the weekend as they had when I married Jan. Ahh, A.C., what a place! Cissie's sense of humor is just one of her beautiful qualities and she often quips "Atlantic City? Oh yeah, that's where Bill always gets married."

By this time Cissie was getting a decent amount of commercial work and then caught a break of her own when she landed a pretty regular role as a day-player on the soap opera "All My Children." Ironically, her character's name was "Nurse Callahan," which just so happened to be her ex-husband's name. She was Susan Lucci's, or "Erica Kane's," lead nurse when she was in the hospital. Luckily for us, "Erica" was a confirmed hypochondriac, which gave Cissie plenty of air time and more importantly, a steady paycheck.

In all we spent a year and a half in Queens before saving up enough money between the acting and broadcasting work to escape from New York. Once my three-year Chapter 13 bankruptcy repayment plan concluded, we were finally in position to get a mortgage and buy a house. I will never forget calling my bankruptcy trustee to finalize all the details. To my surprise he informed me that I had not quite satisfied all of my debts. There was one more thing that had been overlooked, somehow, to the IRS. I asked him what he was talking about and he then proceeded to tell me that at some point a document had fallen out of my file, which he later found. As a result, I now owed the IRS another $7,000.

My heart started to beat extremely fast. I had just busted my butt to navigate my way through a three year personal bankruptcy reorganization and had established two new careers — all in an effort to save enough money for a downpayment on a home. And now I had the IRS after me again? The frustrating part was that if the document hadn't been misplaced, the debt would have been satisfied at pennies on the dollar - in with all the other creditors. For two weeks I tried to plead my case, but to no avail. Knowing that it could be an expensive proposition to take legal action against the trustee's office that might eat up $7,000 in no time, I just gritted my teeth and paid it. That was a hard check to write.

Committed to moving forward with our lives, not backward, we bought a little home just across the river from Trenton, NJ, in Morrisville, PA. We looked at New Jersey, but it was cost prohibitive. We had ruled out Long Island because we didn't want to fight traffic to the city all day long. So, we went out a bit further to Pennsylvania and figured we could just take the commuter train 60 minutes into New York for auditions and work there. We had wanted to get out of Queens and live in our own house and start a family, so this was a really big step for us on a lot of levels. For me, personally, to be able to get a mortgage and own a home again, this was a pretty significant step in my comeback.

Cissie and I were really happy together. I knew that our marriage was going to work too and I knew it for a couple of reasons. When Cissie met me I had nothing. I wasn't a famous hockey player, I was a broke restaurateur. And, when I met Cissie, she had nothing. So we kind of built our lives back up together, and went through a great deal of adversity together.

I also vowed to learn from the mistakes of my first two failed marriages this go-around as well. I made a very, very strong commitment to making sure that I would do whatever had to be done to be the best husband and the best father and to make our marriage work. I recognized at this point in my life that every marriage has three entities: you, your spouse, and your relationship. Well for me, I committed to working as hard as necessary to nurture the relationship, to making sure that it was as healthy as either one of us as individuals. I was determined not to let this marriage fail.

Hey, it wasn't all roses either, we've had some rocky times. But we've communicated and we've gotten through them. We actually went to a marriage counselor to see a psychologist real early in our relationship. When we hit a pothole, my feeling was that if we had some objective input — we would both be able to see the light and find common ground. I wanted us to be able to step out of the pothole before it became a gorge. It turned out to be really valuable that we did that. Whenever we would come to an impasse over something, one of us would ask the other, "Do you want to go see our lady?" "Yeah, I do." And off we would go to get some professional guidance to help us navigate our way through whatever obstacle was in front of us.

I set up the ground rules and they were pretty simple. First, we both had to like the person we were seeing. If one of us disapproved or wasn't happy with that person, then we would change — no questions asked. I wanted us to both be very confident and very happy with this person who we were sharing all of this intimate information about our lives with. Second, we would always dedicate ourselves to the process. We agreed that we would stick with it, no matter what, and work on whatever they suggested we do — for the sake of our relationship. Cissie was right there with me and I'm really glad that we did it because that commitment has proven to be incredibly valuable to us over the years.

I really think that my true understanding and dedication to leadership started with my third marriage. It's been wonderful being with Cissie for all these years and I can honestly say that I love her more and more each and every day. I'm proud to say that we're now at 25 anniversaries and counting.

For a lot of acting jobs, Cissie and I were a great fit as a couple. Life has imitated art.

16) NEW BEGINNINGS...

Life was good in our new home and in our new situation. We kept plugging along, doing our things, and eventually once we felt that the time was right we decided to have a family of our own. Our daughter Savannah was born in 1989 and she was beautiful. What a blessing. We stayed in our little house in Morrisville for a little over a year before realizing we were going to need more space. We were doing well financially and decided to buy a new house while continuing to rent out the old one. So, we moved to Newtown, about 15 minutes away in nearby Buck's County. We now had a much bigger house and a yard. It was wonderful.

Once we got settled, Cissie's daughter Regan moved in with us. It was an adjustment, but without a doubt one of the best decisions that we have ever made. She brought so much light into our lives, it was unbelievable. Knowing that the clock was ticking, our son Chase was born just 15 months later in 1990. Cissie was 40 by now and decided it was time to try her hand as a full-time mom. It would turn out to be her dream job, truly. She's an incredible mother.

Just as we settled into our new home and our new life with three kids, I got a call one day from my first wife Cathie. She was in tears. She said that they couldn't handle our daughter Christa any more. She was 13 years old and like most teenagers, had a mind of her own. Independence was something she craved and boundaries were often just challenges to circumvent. So, Cathie asked me if Christa could move down from Ottawa and come live with us.

It wasn't that difficult a decision even though we were just getting our own family going. I knew that it was the right thing to do. Cissie and I talked it over and felt that we could provide the structure for her that we felt she needed. In so many ways my little angel was moving through the "teenage rebel" stage and we felt she would benefit from discipline and structure in a loving environment.

We swallowed hard and said, "We'll take her, absolutely." Life was hectic, and it was about to become even more crazy. Looking back, I can honestly say the next two years presented some of the greatest leadership challenges of our lives. Christa would prove to be a handful as advertised, but our whole family unit - our circumstance - was changing so drastically. In less than two years we went from no kids, to four. Kind of like zero to ninety in three seconds. Different ages, different challenges, different needs.

It made perfect sense to me that Christa was searching for an identity and pushing the outer boundaries as a kid. She was a product of a broken home and failed marriage before she was three. She was also never able to meet her biological mother - something that became important to her at a young age. We adopted Christa when she was just six days old and when she was 11, prior to a summer visit with us, she asked me to help find her birth mother. Since it was a private adoption through one of the Flyers' team doctors, it wasn't that tough.

I was able to get the contact info and tragically learned when I called that just 30 days before, Christa's mother had died of a brain tumor. We did, however, get to meet Christa's biological grandparents who lived not far from us in a nearby Pennsylvania town. They gave Christa a lot of photos of her mother and were able to comfort her, but I know that was always tough on her.

With Christa moved in, our family was growing. One day I was playing in a golf tournament and a course employee came out on a cart to tell me that I had an emergency call waiting for me in the clubhouse. I hurried in only to find out that Christa and her friend Melissa had gone out for a walk in our neighborhood and Cissie couldn't find them. Our neighborhood had been carved out of farmers' fields and wooded landscape and wasn't necessarily isolated, but it also wasn't connected to other developments. I raced home to meet with the police, who requested pictures of Christa in preparation of filing a missing-person report.

When you find yourself waiting for news about a loved one and you're not sure which way it will go, it feels as if you have stopped breathing. We must have washed the dinner dishes three times trying to stay busy. Finally, about an hour after sundown Christa and Melissa quietly came through the front door and made a bee-line upstairs to her bedroom. Regan came running into the kitchen to tell me, "Dad, Dad, Christa's home!"

Cissie, ever the compassionate mom, said, "Honey, what are you going to do?" I said, "I'm going to take a deep breath and try to under-react. These are two very vulnerable 13 year olds, I'm just happy that they're home and that they're safe."

So, I went upstairs and I could see that they were under the influence of something. Raising my level of concern was the fact that they were both scratched up and scraped pretty good. Christa was hurting while Melissa was in better shape, so she was able to tell me that the only thing they had in their systems was beer, which was actually a relief. It turned out they had left our development and gone off exploring, eventually wandering into a condominium project that was under construction.

A framing crew from Mississippi had knocked off early having completed their commitment in the area, and was about to shove off for points further north and another job. They had cracked open a few cases of beer. Sure enough, they invited the girls to join them and proceeded to get them drunk. Thank God they weren't raped and luckily they were able to get out of there and try to weave their way home. To do so they had to navigate a stretch of woods in the dark.

Once into the thicket they lost their bearings and fell into an empty, rocky creek bed. Bruised, but determined to get home, they were then sliced up trying to negotiate their way through a large patch of blackberry bushes. By the time they made it to the safety of Christa's bedroom they looked like they had gone through a blender.

Melissa lived 15 minutes away so I drove her home and when I got back I took a big piece of cardboard and wrote on it in huge letters "We love you so much." I put it on the floor by Christa's bed so she would see it when she woke up. I knew she was dealing with some emotional demons and knew what some of them were. Disciplinary measures and consequences for her actions would all come very soon. For now, my goal was to make sure she knew how much she was loved.

We went through different chaotic episodes for close to two years and maturity finally began to outpace rebellion. Cissie and I never waivered from our commitment to be the best parents we could for Christa so we decided to enroll her in a private school called Villa Victoria, in Trenton. I pulled all sorts of strings to get her in because she wasn't a model student. It was also expensive, but like most parents I wanted to give her all the help she needed to continue her growth.

I remember her first day of school. It would also be her last. I was at a function and called Cissie that afternoon to see how it went and she told me that Christa had arrived home from school and announced that she was moving back to Canada. I hurried home to find out what was up and Christa was adamant about leaving.

As it turned out I learned that her mom and Grandma had convinced her over a period of time to move back to Ottawa. They undoubtedly missed her - the only child, the only grandchild - so they painted a picture of life back home, in public school, without so many rules and so much discipline and structure. It was a devastating pronouncement but I was not going to stop her or talk her out of it at that point.

Initially Cissie and I were really hurt by her decision to leave us after we had opened up our home and our lives, to say nothing of the emotional roller-coasters we had had to endure. Within a few days though, we began talking about unconditional love and what it truly means - giving and asking for nothing in return. Once we stopped feeling sorry for ourselves we were able to go right back to loving Christa the way every child should be loved - unconditionally.

Back in Ottawa, Cathie soon realized that the feisty rebel still lived inside Christa. Now 16, she was going to call her own shots and an amazing transformation took place. She moved out and lived with a girlfriend's family. Incredibly, as soon as she got away from everybody telling her what to do, the rebel began to disappear. She started to do it all on her own, including going to school at night to get her high school diploma. She worked her butt off for a number of years and ultimately graduated with a degree in accounting from Algonquin College in Ottawa with a perfect 4.0 GPA. She never got anything lower than an A. I think she was the only student in their history to accomplish that. How incredible is that? Amazing.

Today, Christa is one of the most remarkable model citizens I have ever known. She worked so hard to turn herself around and I couldn't be prouder of her. Through sheer determination, she put herself through college and became a very successful CPA (CGA in Canada) in Ottawa. Shortly after graduating she was diagnosed with Multiple Sclerosis, which was difficult for her at first, but she has done just a fantastic job dealing with it. She and her husband Blaine have two adorable children, Todd and Amy, my grandkids, and I love them all dearly.

We went through some incredibly difficult times together, absolutely, but Christa is truly an amazing story. Despite all the chaos, I learned so much from her over those rebellious years. Looking back, I really grew as a person from having to deal with all the different parenting adversities. Christa helped me become a better leader. She pulled me out of my comfort zone and forced me onto that tight rope. I know too that at the end of the day, Christa is a better person for having come to live with our family.

Unknowingly, I think we helped each other become better people.

17) SPREADING MY WINGS AS A BROADCASTER AND SPEAKER

Despite the chaos at home, my career as a broadcaster was really going well. By now I had become one of ESPN's top color analysts. The only downside was that I was on the road an awful lot. Being away from my two new babies was rough, no question. I was able to fly in and out of the Philadelphia airport though, which made things a little easier due to the fact that it was only about a half hour drive from our new house.

The regular season wasn't too bad, maybe a night or two a week I was gone. But come playoff time, Cissie knew that I was going to be gone for the better part of two months. I would come home for "conjugal visits," but otherwise I was on the road working. As a former player, I was used to that lifestyle. I knew that it was a price that I had to pay in order to provide for my family - just part of what I did.

In 1990 I was presented with another right angle turn in the road, when I got a call from the Philadelphia Flyers. They were going in a different direction with their broadcast team and asked if I was interested in becoming their new color guy, alongside Doc Emrick. My instant reservation was that a former teammate of mine, Bobby Taylor, was the analyst I would be replacing. I was assured that a change was going to take place one way or the other though, whether it was me or somebody else coming in — which made me feel better about it. ESPN had only ever given me single year contracts up until that point, so I was free to go where I wished. The stability of a five year contract sounded pretty darn good to me at that point, so I happily signed my second pro contract with the Flyers organization. Plus, I would now be sleeping in my own bed a whole bunch more considering half of my games would be in Philly.

The timing of it all, as it turned out, was pretty remarkable too. As it turned out, just a few weeks after I signed my new contract, ESPN lost the rights to broadcast NHL games to Sports Channel America. Had I not taken the job I would've been out of work at ESPN anyway. Luckily, Sports Channel

Bill Clement
PROFESSIONAL SPEAKING,
BROADCASTING, APPEARANCES

WEBSITE: www.billclement.com

A playing career montage I sign for genuine autograph seekers, not dealers.

America needed broadcasters at that point too, so Doc and I wound up broadcasting for them as well when our Flyers schedule permitted. So I was really kicking butt career-wise at this point. Life was good.

Something else profound happened to me that year - I delivered my first motivational speech and it was life-changing. It turned out to be one of the most powerful experiences of my life. A friend of mine had invited me to speak at a local Chamber of Commerce breakfast at a hotel in nearby Langhorne, PA. He said that there were going to be about 250 people there and I told him I really didn't want to do it. Believe it or not, I was still scared to death of getting up on stage in front of people. I had never forgotten that speech (more like a non-speech) I had given as a 21-year old rookie with the Flyers at the private school — where I bombed on stage and almost passed out from hyperventilation. Right after that, I had promised myself to always get back out on the tightrope and not let it end that way, but the fear of public speaking was down in the gorge pushing like hell against me moving forward.

Well, he begged me to reconsider. Not wanting to let him down, I asked him what in the world I could possibly talk about. He looked at me sort of confused, as if to say, "Are you serious?" and said, "Just tell your story." I thought about that and started to wonder, what was my story?

"Look how fast you established new careers and got back on your feet after your failed business venture," he said. "You were able to buy a home exactly three years after being broke - as soon as your bankruptcy obligation ended — that's a helluva story."

He suggested I speak about the steps I took to get back to my feet. Take us on your journey of two Stanley Cups, your train wreck in business, then your recovery. The life lessons will present themselves as you speak. Then he told me to just be myself and speak from the heart. I had always felt an obligation as a pro athlete to entertain audiences while on stage and truth be told, I didn't believe I was very funny or entertaining. He made it sound so easy, so I reluctantly agreed.

When I got up on that stage and told my story, spoken

straight from my heart, you could have heard a pin drop. People were genuinely interested in what I was saying. As I relaxed more I saw openings to inject some light-hearted comments and people laughed. And I didn't even try to be funny, that's what was so amazing to me. For 30 minutes I just told meaningful, personal stories from the heart. That was it.

All these years later as a professional speaker, that was the single best advice I have ever gotten from anybody in this business — to just speak from the heart. From the second I finished that speech I knew that I wanted to be a professional speaker. What a high. I had mined an ability I didn't know I had, all because I, albeit reluctantly, stepped back onto the tightrope. It was almost as if I was dancing on it.

I believed that if I could just speak honestly and openly about some of my travails, both in sports and business, then I was destined to succeed and on my way to helping others. Sharing the lessons I had learned, as well as their values, became very important to me. It all began with that first speech, which I had titled, "From Hero to Zero and Back." And it was, straight from the heart.

****

In February of 1992 I got to cover the Olympics in Albertville, France. It would be my first opportunity to broadcast Olympic hockey and I had been looking forward to this for what seemed like an eternity. Little did I know, however, that it would also prove to be one of the most interesting and emotional months of my life.

While the Olympics were staged in Albertville, the hockey venue was in Meribel, a small town about a half hour away up in the French Alps. Cissie and I got there five days before I had to do any work and we had the time of our lives spending a romantic week in a cozy chalet drinking wine and seeing the sights. It was so beautiful, just breathtaking. I wanted to enjoy that time because once the hockey started I knew the schedule would be insane.

I had signed on to do both TV analysis for TNT as well as color analysis for CBS Radio. My partner on TV was to be broadcast hall of famer, Jiggs McDonald. Jiggs and I had worked together before at Sports Channel America and had also known one another from our days during the late 70's working for the NHL's Atlanta Flames — me as a player and Jiggs as the TV play-by-play man. Our work schedule was grueling. In one stretch during our first week on the air, we broadcast ten games in five days.

Three games were played each day during the preliminary round alone. We would broadcast the first game which began at noon, have the middle game off, then broadcast the third game which began at 7:00 PM. Most days I would simply stay in my seat while the middle game was being played and ready myself for the 7:00 PM start. Be careful what you ask for, right? Trying to learn all the name pronunciations alone of all the foreign players was a major challenge in itself.

In the month leading up to the Olympics I had spent literally days on the phone gathering information on the 12 teams I would be covering. I wanted to develop an overview of each country's philosophical approach to the sport as well as the different types of game plans they would throw at prospective opponents. I was also in search of insights, information and profiles on the performers I would be watching. I have always felt that a good portion of the entertainment value of the information I deliver lies in its originality as well as its power to take the viewer to the under layer of the competitor's existences. In other words, if I can humanize the faces on the screen, I can create a level of interest which hopefully transcends the sport. My philosophical foundation props me up to this day and is the basis for my preparation on all NHL telecasts. Driven by this personal tenet, I networked my way to the home phone numbers of coaches, managers and scouts. If I wasn't interrupting a supper table in Czechoslovakia, I was acting as an alarm clock in Italy.

The first week of competition whizzed by. Many long days, but Jiggs and I were on top of our games. TNT was thrilled with our work, the ratings were good, and the reviews from the mainland were all positive. We were on a roll. Then came week two. The euphoria came to a screeching halt when I found out I had inadvertently been double-booked. You see, the understanding going in by all parties was that at no point would TNT TV and CBS Radio have to televise or broadcast the same game. Well, as it turned out, the big surprise of the tournament was Team France. They were clearly on a roll playing in their home country and despite being heavy underdogs in almost every game, they had advanced far enough to find themselves scheduled to play a crucial game against the Team USA. The winner would advance to the medal round, so it was a very big deal.

All of France was amped up on patriotism. For that matter, so was the U.S. America still cherished vivid memories of that improbable gold medal in 1980, the "Miracle on Ice." Hope was that perhaps it hadn't been a miracle at all and could therefore be repeated. Hockey interest was so high that both TNT and CBS decided that they were going to broadcast the game. For me, this was a major problem.

I remember my heart stopping because I knew that I couldn't possibly be in two places at the same time, working for both entities. Unfortunately, there was no wording in either of my contracts as to whom would take precedence - after all, this was "never" going to happen. It was a mess and I had only a little time to get the situation resolved.

The phone calls came just five minutes apart. The first was from Glen Diamond, our TNT producer letting me know what our schedule for the next few days looked like. Naturally we would cover the Team USA vs. France game the next day. The second call was from Frank Murphy, the Executive Producer of CBS Sports Radio. CBS would be broadcasting the USA vs. France game as well. So much for Shangri la.

I was contractually obligated to be in two seats at the same time. Since the laws of nature strictly prohibited this, I had a serious problem on my hands. So for the next 24 hours I searched for solutions, attempting to sort out this unexpected crisis. If I had David Copperfield's phone number, I would have called him. "Hello, David? I need you to teach me how to be

Harry Houdini and we've got less than a day." I made repeated calls to the U.S. to my agent, to radio and TV execs, as well as to my empathetic Cissie. The predominant emotion I felt was one of anxiety. I knew that I had no choice but to breach a contract which I had signed in good faith. I just didn't know which one. I kept calling and calling, so you can imagine my phone bill.

My agent informed me that while this confluence of commitments was never supposed to happen, he was told in no uncertain terms by both parties that I would be expected to be in THEIR seats come the start of the first period. It was now decision time. I mulled it over and finally made the decision based on which partner I would strand the most by NOT being there. In the end I figured it would hurt Jiggs more than it would my radio partner, Gary Cohen. Both are tremendous announcers and good people, so it was just brutal to have to make that call.

In the end I went with TNT. In my rationale, I concluded that radio is far easier to carry off as a solo broadcaster. Because there are no pictures for the viewers, when the play stops your subject matter is driven solely by you. Because of the "visual" on television, you are more obligated to accompany the pictures with appropriate dialogue. At the Olympics, all TV entities from each country take what is call a "World Feed." In other words, it's the same pictures for everyone. So you have to talk about what's on the screen as determined by a producer and director you've never heard of, sitting in a control room somewhere. What you get is whatever they give you. So unlike your own show where you coordinate story lines with your producer and director, in order to make the pictures the viewers see match up with the predetermined stories being told, you are forced to play "follow the surprise pictures." It's not easy and I was not going to put Jiggs in that kind of predicament. He had worked too hard for too long to be dealt that kind of hand. Plus, I knew Gary could handle radio flying solo, he was a true professional.

I went over to talk to the guys at CBS Radio and they fired me on the spot. I will never forget walking to the back of the broadcast trailer to talk to the producer. He just looked at me and said, "You're done." Then everybody in the trailer turned their backs to me. I felt like I was walking around with a flashing neon sign on my forehead that announced I had leprosy. It was like "dead man walking."

It had gone from being one of the greatest experiences of my life to one of the worst, just like that. What a contrast of emotions - from euphoria to white water without a life preserver, then disappointment. As it turned out, CBS had a roving reporter covering hockey and he simply slid into my spot. CBS radio execs, however, were extremely irritated and they let me know it.

Later that year ESPN re-acquired the NHL broadcast rights and they wanted me to work for them again as their lead color analyst. It was a privilege doing nationally televised games and I was really excited about the possibility. It was also an honor calling games in Philly. I had so much respect for the organization and the way owner Ed Snider ran the franchise. I didn't want to have to choose between my regular gig with the Flyers or ESPN though, so I tried to see if I could make it work to do both. I looked at the schedule of my Flyers games compared to the ESPN games and saw that there were about a dozen or so that overlapped. While I was at the Olympics, my former Flyer teammate Gary Dornhoefer filled in for me and did a great job. Figuring he might be able to fill in for me for those dozen games that upcoming season, I pitched the Flyers on letting me do ESPN's national games, with Gary covering for me when I was gone.

We had a pow-wow that included Ed Snider's son, Jay, who was handling the day-to-day operations of the organization. I liked and respected Jay as much as I did his father and it didn't take long for Jay to put his cards on the table. First, he was not keen on me working for ESPN on top of the job I had with him. He wanted me to work exclusively where I was. Second, he let me know I would be taking a sizeable pay cut once my contract was up. I was in year three of my five year deal so I could see the writing on the wall. Jay was willing to let me out of my contract and in the end I decided to leave the

Flyers and go back to work with ESPN. It turned out that ESPN's deal was going to represent a pay cut as well, but with them, I would only be doing one third as many games. My feeling was that I would take a step backwards income-wise in order to use the extra time to focus on developing my speaking career.

I knew that being a professional speaker would require the same amount of preparation and hard work that I had given in becoming a professional hockey player, actor, and broadcaster. So I decided to get real serious about it. I knew that the world of television was very subjective and that if the wrong executive didn't like my work I could be replaced at any time. I looked at speaking as a way to not only subsidize my income, but also as a possible exit strategy if I was ever out of broadcasting altogether down the road.

With that, I was offered some backroom office space from a friend of mine. I then went out and bought a desk and a chair and a book case. There were still no personal computers at this point, so I bought Brother's top of the line word processor-typewriter. From there, I started researching everything I could get my hands on about this new business. I was a sponge, soaking it all in. It was fascinating. I started watching tapes and listening to cassettes of other speakers. From Dale Carnegie to Zig Ziglar, you name it. I read their books and took notes. I learned about speakers bureaus. I went out to speak wherever I could and to whomever would have me. Pretty soon I had files of articles and ideas, I became obsessed. I would get up at five in the morning and start writing. I needed to develop stories about human development from all of my experiences both in and out of hockey, and then figure out the appropriate life lessons that I could share with people. I would define and then redefine my message. My desire to help people and to motivate them could now be facilitated and that really excited me. To this day it remains my main takeaway from presenting - the knowledge that I gave something of value to an audience. The fact that it could now be monetized was a welcome bonus.

Meanwhile, working for ESPN again was great. The

NHL was determined to expand into some non-traditional hockey markets, especially down south, and the game's popularity in the U.S. was growing. To capitalize on that, ESPN launched a sister station, ESPN2, and with the extra reach the network expanded its hockey coverage big-time. My work load suddenly tripled and the good news was so did my income. Life was all good. I was also experiencing a newly found sense of celebrity on a national scale that I had never really known as a player. TV is such a powerful medium and having that much exposure as an analyst really pushed me out into the national spotlight. I was now being recognized in airports and in the street and since most people are polite when they approach to say hello or get an autograph, it was seldom a burden.

Celebrity status is powerful. When celebrities speak, others listen, so there is a constant podium from which to influence. When the podium is used for the greater good amazing things can be accomplished. Even the simplest act of signing an autograph can make someone smile, which is why I have always considered it a privilege to be in the position to do so. You just never know the amount of sunlight you may be infusing into an otherwise dreary day, or even disadvantaged life.

I was working with Gary Thorne and with our expanded workload we were spending a lot of time together in the booth. He was and is such a pro that there was always something to learn from him. One night, however, I learned a life lesson the hard way about the power of communication when I teased him and wound up embarrassing him on-air. It was our second year of working together and during a broadcast one night in Pittsburgh he mistakenly called Vancouver's Sergio Momesso, Sergio "Mimosa." I chuckled and decided to have some fun with it. I said, "It sounds like you're ready for a tall drink and a vacation, Gare!"

We then went to commercial and were off-air, so I quipped, "Maybe you were thinking of Minnie Minoso, the baseball guy?" It was sort of a shot at him because he was also working like a dog in those days, traveling coast to coast almost daily doing Major League Baseball games. It was insane and I honestly don't know how he was able to do it. Anyway, I thought I was just having fun with him like any partner would, but he got really upset. He stood up, snatched off his head-set and said, "Maybe you shouldn't correct your partner's mistakes on the air, a--hole!" and then threw it down on the desk. He then walked out of the booth. I was like, "Oh my God, what just happened?!" Being the consummate pro, Gary wasn't going to jeopardize our broadcast so he came back in just before the commercial break ended and sat back down. I said to him, "Why don't you cool down and just relax." He looked over at me, his eyes got real big, and as he leans into me he says, "No! You relax, a--hole!"

When you hear "5-4-3-2-1-go" in your ear, you know it's time to perform, so we both calmed down and were able to finish the game. Afterwards, I went for a glass of wine with our producer, Tom McNeeley and director, Doug Holmes. They were good friends and stars at what they did. I was still upside down emotionally and they both said, "We're done. We're screwed. Our show will never be the same again."

I looked at them and said, "No, you're wrong. We'll get past this and things will actually be better than before." I wasn't sure what I was going to do, but I knew that I had to do something to make it right.

Within a few days the playoffs started and we were back in Pittsburgh for a game. I approached Gary before the game and asked if I could talk to him. I apologized and we sort of cleared the air, with both of us getting some things off of our chests. It turned out he was fed up with me correcting him, period. You have to understand too, that with the influx of Europeans and Russians into the league at this time, some of these names were nearly impossible to pronounce, so it was tough for everybody — especially if the player was a new guy who just got called up and we weren't familiar with him. If Gary mispronounced a name, I would hit the "talk-back" button to tell our producer the correct pronunciation so he could relay it to Gary. Even while calling the game with his headset on, Gary told me he could hear me.

I explained I wanted to be a safety net for him and was trying to help. To my surprise, he said that the correct pronunciations were seldom relayed to him so he figured I was having a laugh at his expense with everyone in the truck. No wonder he was irritated. We talked it out and in the end I told him that I wanted to be the best partner he ever had. We agreed that individually we would never be perceived to be the best at what we did unless we're perceived to be the best team.

We had a wall that was being built up and I didn't even realize it. I recognized that we needed to tear it down though, and in a hurry. I told him that if he ever had a problem with me or with something I did or said, that I hoped he would tell me about it so I could fix it and make it right. I encouraged open dialogue.

It was crazy, here we were talking together for hours on end, night after night, yet we weren't communicating. I also later reflected on something that added even more insight into the situation. Gary's mother had just passed away that Mother's Day and I knew that had to be incredibly difficult for him. Here we were, in the playoffs, still working — and I'm sure his heart was still very heavy.

Personal things, like what happened in the booth are always best left that way. We were handling it internally and I thought we could keep it in the family because nobody outside of the booth and our truck knew what had transpired. What we didn't know, however, was that some dweeb back at ESPN's studios pirated the recording of what was exchanged off-air and wound up distributing it. It would get written up in various publications and turned into quite a distraction for not only Gary and me, but for ESPN as well.

From that moment on, I vowed to make sure that I thought about everything I said on-air, especially if it was a joke at somebody else's expense. I also vowed never to assume that people had thicker skin than I expected them to have. In the locker-room, nothing is sacred and everyone is fair game, but I wasn't there any longer. At the end of the day I was committed to being the best partner I could be with Gary and to be honest I felt very fortunate that we were able to put all of that stuff behind us and move forward. I have the utmost respect for Gary, the guy is brilliant and the best in the business.

It's an honor for me to say that we are still friends to this day and while we're not a TV pair any longer, we still work together. We are the voices for EA Sports hockey video games and have done commentary for the next-generation versions of the games NHL-07 thru NHL-13. We have a blast doing the recording work but it's a tough process. We don't just go in and read off a script. Hundreds of scenarios are written out for us then we have to ad lib the descriptions. It's demanding and the producers want us to paint the same scenario multiple times. Over and over and over again we go, with subtle changes each time. You have to reinvent the language and reinvent how you see and say things. It's some of the most rewarding, grueling, and fun work I have ever done. Then, to see actual NHL players enjoying EA Sports in the locker rooms before games, it's a real trip. What fun.

Audiences used to scare me. Not any more.

18) FINDING MY GROOVE...

By 1994, Chase and Savannah were four and five, respectively, and we really couldn't have been any happier with where we were in our lives. We lived in a nice neighborhood full of great friends we really enjoyed being around. The kids were in activities and school was about to start. Knowing that she was about to acquire some newfound discretionary time, Cissie got the itch to do something more.

So, we converted the kid's playroom into an office for her - more like a writing cave. She loved to write and was a wonderful story-teller, so she spent the next year pounding out a novel. It's titled "Moonlight, Magnolias and Sex at Earls," and it's really good. She met some resistance trying to have it published and set it aside after it was completed. I know that she would love to see it in print some day. Anyway, I told her I would be Mr. Mom as much as I could during that time so that she could focus on writing. She really appreciated it and it worked out great for both of us. I cooked and cleaned and hauled the kids off to their various activities, while she wrote and did her thing. Honestly, it was one of the most therapeutic and fulfilling times for both of us, for totally opposite reasons.

One of the highlights of the '94 NHL season was witnessing the New York Rangers finally win the Stanley Cup. It had been 54 years between Cups for the blue shirts and it was quite the spectacle when they finally won it at Madison Square Garden. New York was a team of destiny that season. They won a heart-stopping seven game series against New Jersey in the conference finals, even clinching it in double-overtime - the second double-OT game of the series, and then went on to beat Vancouver in another seven-game thriller in the finals to end the curse. It was just unbelievable. In fact, I would have to say that it was the most memorable stretch of broadcasts of my career. Unbelievable hockey.

Vancouver was down three games to one, only to rally back to tie it up and force a Game Seven. New York wound up winning Game Seven by a goal, but Vancouver's Nathan Lafayette almost tied it up with just over two minutes to go when he hit the post. Remarkable theater. The tension and the angst that fans at Madison Square Garden were feeling was palpable. The whole city of New York was on edge. When Mark Messier, the captain, hoisted the Cup over his head at center ice afterward with that huge grin — it was magical. Generations of Rangers fans were weeping. It was so emotional, I will never forget it.

In my mind I was evolving from a former jock-turned-TV-guy, to a respected journalist, and that felt good. I had honed my craft and become a student of the game. I was committed to being a championship caliber broadcaster and it showed, which meant a lot to me. I wanted each broadcast to be top notch, from the announcers to the producers to the technical guys, and I took it personally if it wasn't.

Preparation was the key for me. I had a template down by now and that was the secret to my success. The first few years I was working as a broadcaster I tried to prepare for the entire season before it even began.   I would get all the publications, make notes on every page about every player, and organize them into binders. It took me a few years to figure out that 90% of the stuff I had organized and prepared before each season became obsolete within a couple of weeks. Guys got traded, or hurt, or benched, or whatever — making everything beyond the original opening day lineups mostly useless.

So, I eventually came to the conclusion that it was a whole lot more efficient to prepare for one game at a time. I mean, during a game there is a finite amount of time that you have to get in all the information that you want to get in, and to also be able to follow the storylines that are developing in each game you cover. It's about creating that right balance of support information, historical information, and current events information — along with being able to follow the storylines of the game as it unfolds. Those are the keys and it's a balancing act, truly. From there, it's all about staying current in order to keep your finger on the pulse of what's going on not only in the news, but also behind the scenes.

Being a former player, I was welcomed in the locker rooms and could talk to the players. They trusted me - I was one of them. I had walked in their shoes. This was big for me as I did my homework and compiled information for my broadcasts. And I learned early on that in a perfect world, all of the support information that you prepared, you would never need. If the game is thrilling, so exciting, it will generate so many storylines that all the other stuff that you had drops way down the list in terms of priority.

If you're delivering excitement, something that is happening before people's eyes — whether it's a brawl or a tight game or an unbelievable performance by a goalie or a player who scored a hat-trick, that is what becomes the story. All that other stuff is what you use in case you have a boring 6-0 blowout with no storylines. That's when you have to be prepared and have things to talk about. As an announcer you pray for interesting, compelling storylines to develop, otherwise you are going to have your work cut out for you. It can get real boring in a heartbeat for the fans tuning in and you have to somehow make it interesting. That's the key.

You know, I've explained this many times over the years to young guys who have wanted to get into broadcasting: you earn your money when the game sucks. Period. That's why you have all that other interesting information and all those stories that you can tell. It's easy to do the job that I do when the game is a thriller. Heck, a 4-3 end to end game is easy. It's not so easy to be great, however, when the games aren't any good. That's what separates the true professionals from the rest of the pack. So that became my standard: I've got to be really good even when the game's really bad.

I was fortunate in that I was on ESPN's top crew with two different play-by-play guys, first with Doc Emrick and then with Gary Thorne. I always looked forward to going to work with such talented professionals. Everything that is any good comes with a price tag and the demanding part of the job on the top broadcast team was our crazy schedule in the playoffs. I remember doing a deciding game-seven in the early rounds of the playoffs one season and feeling rather drained afterward. Then, because we were the No. 1 team, we would fly off to another city to do another game seven for a different series the next night. In three nights we might go from New York to St. Louis and back to Washington. The tough part was trying to be "on" all the time, to be at your best when sometimes you felt like you just didn't have your "A" game. You would fly off, reading whatever you could get your hands on for the plane ride — trying to prepare. Then, when you got there, you would try to interview some guys at the morning skate to see what sort of storylines were developing.

I try to have an agenda of what questions I want to ask, to be prepared and to come in with a game plan. Truth be told, I am still driven by the embarrassment from my ill-fated "hyperventilation speech" as a 21-year old. Nevertheless, it was hard to just jump into the seventh game of a series without knowing all of the back stories and drama that had built up to this big crescendo. You had to go like crazy to try to bring yourself up to speed. Who was hot, who was nursing an injury, who was in the coach's dog house — as an analyst it's my job to find out all of that stuff.

It was grueling, yet incredibly rewarding. I took it as a huge honor to call a game seven. That was an historic game for whichever team won and for their fans and to think that you were going to be a part of that was very significant, so I always looked at it as a privilege. I figured I could sleep during the off-season. It was no different than when I was playing. You just sucked it up and went on adrenaline. My first pro coach Eddie Bush used to say, "Boys, the body follows the mind!" and he was absolutely right. We all have complete control over how we perceive and react to the things that at times are very demanding.

One of my favorite TV shows is "Dual Survival" on the Discovery Channel and one of the stars is Cody Lundin, a minimalist and primitive skills expert who has been teaching survival skills for over 20 years. This man wears shorts and no shoes - even in the winter! He will sometimes pull on a pair of woolen socks to trudge through the snow but that's it. He said something during one episode that really caught my ear. He said, "Survival is 95% psychological. If you fold mentally you will fold physically. The same is true in business and in sports.

Preparation is the key, and it's one of the foundations of success in my opinion. Just as I had learned to prepare to play the game, I learned long ago how to prepare to broadcast games, from the type of information to what I read, to how I organize it and process it, to how I actually input it onto a form that I look at before each and every game. All that stuff, that's my security blanket. I know that it's at my fingertips whenever I need to call it up. It's seamless at that point, nobody knows I'm looking at my cheat-sheet. Then, I just let the game unfold before my eyes. When I need some information, I will look down at my prepared notes - my plan "B." But at the end of the day, there is simply no substitute for being not just prepared, but over-prepared. When you are that prepared, your confidence level is higher and that allows you to relax, which in turn allows you to be yourself. That's when you can be insightful and engaging and even let your sense of humor show through, all of which leads to a connection with the viewers.

****

No sooner had the Rangers ended their curse than the NHL shut down for part of the season due to a lockout. The owners and players were in a standoff and as a result I wound up broadcasting minor league games with Gary Thorne in both the American and International Leagues, on ESPN2. They needed programming content and we needed a paycheck, so it all worked out. It was actually a whole lot of fun doing the minor league circuit and visiting some towns we never got a chance to otherwise see - places like Syracuse, Albany, Binghamton, Indianapolis, Milwaukee, and Houston — even Las Vegas. I thought it was marvelous and had the time of my life.

One time we had a game in Portland, Maine, on a Saturday night and I got in on that Friday. I wound up eating dinner at this fantastic little restaurant near my hotel called Street & Company. I thought the food was so incredible that I called Cissie when I got back to my room and told her to get a sitter because I had booked a flight for her to fly up and meet me for dinner there the next night. She flew in on Saturday afternoon and we had a wonderful little romantic dinner together after my game. Weekends like that are some of the most memorable for me.

I remember another time doing a game in Las Vegas and I got to do my part of our "open" (broadcast lead-in) sitting in the little special locker room that had been set up for Manon Rhéaume, the first women's professional goalie. I will never forget broadcasting that game, not so much because of Manon, but because of the arena. It was old and had some seats that jutted out and completely blocked our view of one entire corner of the ice. We couldn't see any of it whatsoever - we were completely blind. So whenever the play went into our blind spot, Gary would say, "And, they're in the corner…". Then after a few seconds, "And, now they're out of the corner…". It was completely crazy.

That's how it was in some of those older rinks though, they had unique and quirky idiosyncrasies to them. They were not all built for hockey and therefore not at all conducive televising the sport. It was demanding at times but the same principal applied as on those congested days without adequate preparation time - do the best you possibly can with what you have. As professionals, our only choice was to roll up our sleeves and go to work. That's what audiences expected and that's what we were paid to do.

We earned our money during those minor league months. We had to peel back some layers on a nightly basis in order to dig up compelling storylines. We had no star players to talk about and very few fans in the crowd for some games, so it was a challenge at times just to keep the conversation going in the booth. It was the first time I had been back in the minor leagues since my days in Quebec City and Richmond, and it definitely reinforced my appreciation for being in the major leagues.

One night we were doing a game in Binghamton, NY, and afterward I went down to the hotel bar to have a beer. There was a bartender there by the name of Matt Larson. He was a really interesting young guy. He had the most unbeliev-able look, and an incredible voice. We got to talking and I was telling him about my acting background. I asked him if he had ever done any acting himself, because he looked like he would be a natural. He said he had always thought about it and he tried to dabble in it previously, but that he had never been able to pursue it. We talked some more and I told him we would continue our conversation the next time I was in town for a game. Sure enough, I got back there a couple more times and each time we would chat. I was truly impressed with Matt's potential so I told him that if he was really interested in pursu-ing it as a career, I would help him. I even went so far as to in-vite him to come stay at our house for a few months, so I could introduce him to some agents in New York, help him with a head-shot (the actor's business card), and get him onto some auditions. It was a big leap of faith to take this kid in, but it just felt right. I really thought he had what it took to make it and I wanted to help him.

Sure enough, he left his job and came to live with us a short while later. I was still traveling quite a bit but Cissie met him and signed off on the plan - ever the supportive partner. We gave him our spare bedroom, fed him, and even helped him with some of his bills. I really believed in him and wanted him to pursue the dream. I started setting him up with some things in New York and it looked like he was gaining some trac-tion.

As I spent more and more time with Matt, however, I started to notice a pattern of behavior that was troublesome. For starters, it looked like he drank way too much at times. I didn't care if he helped himself to our liquor cabinet now and again, but occasionally he went overboard. He also wound up getting his girlfriend pregnant during this time and with that came heavy doses of drama. He was trying to do the acting thing in New York but it was getting tougher and tougher. We were sticking with him though and really encouraging him to keep his eye on the ball.

One night I was chatting with him in my downstairs office. He asked me if he could make some phone calls in there and I told him sure, no problem. I just said to please be careful not to mess anything up. I had tons of articles cut out of newspapers with notes on them spread out and organized all over the floor because I was going to be putting them into binders to be used as research for some upcoming games. "Absolutely," he said.

Now, he had an audition the next day that was big — a significant opportunity for him. If he nailed it there was no telling where it would go, maybe even a regular gig on a network show. I was genuinely excited for him. So I left him in the office and went to bed. The next morning I came downstairs and saw him laying on the floor. At first I thought he was dead, but then I could see that he was just passed out drunk. He had been rolling around down there too, and had destroyed all of my prep work. Incredibly, it was also past his departure time to catch the train to be on time for his audition. Man, I was pissed. I remember taking my foot and sort of rolling him over, like you would roll over a corpse, and yelling at him "Matt! Get up! Get up Matt!" He finally woke up and I just looked at him, completely disgusted, and said, "Go to bed." For whatever reason, Matt had sabotaged himself and missed his big audition. A few hours later he woke up and I told him to come with me for a walk around the block.

We started walking and before he could say anything I said to him very matter-of-factly, "Matt, within 24 hours you WILL be gone from our home. The reason that you will be gone from our home is because of your behavior. I don't feel that my family is safe when you're here and I'm not home." I then went on to tell him that the reason I was sending him packing was for his own good. I told him that I was disappointed in him but that I still believed in him. I told him that I wanted him to do some soul searching. I told him that he abused alcohol and that he needed to address this if he wanted to lead a productive life. I told him that I wanted him to start asking himself some honest questions about the obstacles that he had in his way that were stopping him from succeeding. I wanted him to identify what was in the gorge and what his tightropes were.

I had watched his pattern of behavior and every time it looked like he was ready to take a big step forward, he found a way to self-destruct and take a step backward. We talked about fear of success and fear or failure. I reassured him that I thought he was immensely talented, that he was a really nice guy, a good human being, and I wished him all the luck in the world. Matt felt bad, but all he could do was nod and agree. He thanked me and later that day he packed his stuff and away he went. That was it.

It's interesting, but when I tell people the "Matt" story they usually say to me, "Boy, what a mistake. I bet you really regret that experience." And my answer is and always has been no, not a bit. In fact, I learned a great deal from it. First of all, my motive was to try to help somebody mine their talent and reach their potential, that otherwise might not have even discovered. I will never regret the gesture - but I learned that when people aren't willing to help themselves, then it's usually a lost cause. I also learned that others can't do it for them. It taught me a lot about my own nature and about my desire to help others.

From then on I started creating standards and benchmarks for people to achieve on their own before I invested any time and effort in helping them with their careers. What I realized more than anything from this though, was that I tended to be an enabler. I often tried to do too much for people because I genuinely wanted to see them succeed. I wanted to do everything I could to help them, not realizing at times that I was doing it FOR them, depriving them of ownership of their success.

I go back to my dad and his ladder and all of his tools. He would help anybody who asked. I realized that this was me, all these years later, only my desire to help others had manifested too strongly. Looking back, I would still do it all over again with Matt, only next time I would have different ground rules for myself - a different style. I would guide from well behind him, as he blazes the trail himself.

Fifteen years later, out of the blue, Matt left me a voice mail on my cell phone. I don't even know how he got my number. He said "Bill, it's Matt Larson. It's been a long time and I'm just calling to see how you're doing." He went on to say that he was living with his girlfriend (now his wife) and their child down in the Carolinas somewhere and that things were going good. Then, at the end of the message his voice cracked just a little bit and he paused. He then said, "I'm just calling to thank you, because you had a profound influence on my life. You helped me and I'll never forget what you did for me." The message ended. I just sat there, reflecting on what I had just heard. For me it was complete validation. It just reinforced that it had not been a mistake helping Matt. It happened for a reason. I learned and therefore grew from that experience, and in the end I believe he did too. I still get chills when I think about that call.

*Warming up
for a Flyers
Alumni game.*

19) REDISCOVERING MYSELF...

By 1996 our two youngest kids, Savannah and Chase, were finally at ages where they were involved with sports and other activities, and I wanted to be able to spend more time with them. As a result of the New York Rangers winning the Stanley Cup in '94, followed by the New Jersey Devils winning it in '95, I had gotten spoiled. For two straight years I was able to just drive to work for all of those playoff games and avoid airports altogether. They were geographically speaking, desirable series and it was incredible.

Well, in '96 that all changed when the Colorado Avalanche beat the Florida Panthers in the Finals. I don't think I slept in my own bed for two months during that post-season. I didn't want to miss my kids growing up so after the playoffs, to free up more time with them, I decided to quit playing golf. Cold turkey. I loved to golf, and really enjoyed all of the charity/celebrity tournaments with the guys, but I had to make some tough choices with regards to how I was going to spend my time. So golf had to go. Golf is almost an all-day commitment by the time you factor in driving there and back, hitting balls at the range, having lunch, and then spending four or five hours out on the course. It turned out to be one of the best things I ever did. I knew those years were going to fly by and I wanted to be there as much as I possibly could.

I had gotten really excited about my son's interest in hockey at that point too. Chase had been playing mites (youth hockey) for three years and I was hoping that he would fall in love with the sport, but then unexpectedly at the age of seven he decided to give it up. I was torn. One part of me wanted him to experience the thrill of one day hoisting the Stanley Cup, like I had done. But then another part of me was just relieved that he would never have to worry about living up to other people's expectations as to how good a hockey player he had to be. For anybody whose dad was a professional athlete, there's always an evaluation platform that's unfair. And for him it would have been even worse considering the fact that not only was I a former NHLer-turned TV announcer, but that we were living outside Philadelphia — where everybody would compare him to me at every stage of the game. It would have put so much pressure on the kid and to be honest I was relieved he wouldn't have to go through all of that. He wound up playing soccer instead, so I became his soccer coach. It was great. I really got into it too. In fact, I learned as much about rearing kids and leadership doing that throughout the late '90s as I had doing a lot of other things in my life, which was very rewarding for me.

****

In 1999 I branched out of my comfort zone a bit and wound up broadcasting the "Great Outdoor Games" on ESPN. What was neat for me in doing this was that it was the first time I was going to be able to do play-by-play, versus color analysis. The play-by-play guy to me is the "what," as in what's happening right now, whereas the analyst is the "why and the how it happens." They are completely different disciplines and I was excited about trying something new.

My first broadcasts were with the target sports, which included archery, rifle, and shot gun. I wound up working with a former Olympian and world champion by the name of Shari Legate, who was fantastic. Later on I branched off into doing timber sports - the lumberjack and lumber "Jill" stuff - which included log rolling, boom running, tree topping, speed climbing, and hot-saw competitions. Those were such a blast. Just to watch those athletes, it was awe inspiring. They were so tough. Since I had grown up in the woods with a chainsaw in my hands I could directly relate to a lot of it. I was teamed up with a pair of lumberjack analysts, John "Mad Kiwi" Hughes and Sean Duffy, who got his start on MTV's "Real World" and is today a U.S. Congressman in the state of Wisconsin. Wonderful men and we had some great high-quality times together.

Working with those people gave me a chance to be a teacher and a mentor, which was really neat too. They were all bright-eyed coming in as analysts and I could relate to everything they were experiencing. Doing the broadcasts was rewarding but also very difficult in that all of the voice-over work we did was done in post-production, believe it or not. So we would hang out all day and watch the events, doing very little work other than occasional interviews.

Then, afterward we traveled to Indianapolis and got locked into these sound proof booths with producers and sound technicians. They had already edited everything down into segment increments for TV purposes, and now it was our job to narrate all of it following the storylines and the pictures. We had to pretend that it was all live, which is really quite demanding unless you've had acting training. My resume came in handy.

It was totally different than being there in person, calling it as you saw it happen before your own eyes. In fact, we already knew all of the outcomes but had to sound objective and not give anything away. I loved being live, it made you focus harder. You only had one shot to get it right. Once something is out of your mouth, it's gone, and you can't get it back. Here, meanwhile, we could say something and if we screwed it up we would simply do it again. The challenge then became making it sound fresh - like it was the first time you said it. Anyway, because I knew we had multiple opportunities to get stuff just right, I demanded excellence from my analysts. I pushed them pretty hard towards perfection. I know there were times when they resented the hell out of me, yet at the end of the day when they looked at the finished product I know they were thankful that I continually asked them to raise the bar.

One of my most vivid memories from those days was the time this speed climber named Dustin Beckwith came flying down this gigantic 60 foot pole during a climbing race and cut his leg wide open with one of his metal gaffs. They wear these razor sharp gaffs, or climbing spikes, and once they've climbed to the top, they basically free-fall down to these big pads at the bottom. It's controlled chaos at best, no kidding. Anyway, Beckwith rips his thigh open on the crash landing, basically impaling himself and immediately winds up laying in a pool of his own blood. The medical guys came running over and I was worried he might have severed an artery or something because blood was just pouring out of this poor guy. He sees my eyes amongst the faces crowded around him and as he's getting patched up, very calmly with a smile he says, "Hey Bill, I bet that's gonna make Sports Center!" I just about fell over. Sports Center was ESPN's daily highlight show and that seemed to be what he was concerned about. You know you're "somebody" if you make it to Sports Center. Lumberjacks are brave - and crazy! I love them.

I loved everything about the Great Outdoor Games and worked every one of them for their entire run, until ESPN discontinued them after 2005. The Games were held in some fun places too, like Lake Placid, Reno, Madison and Orlando. I was so disappointed when they got cancelled because I always looked forward to doing them. They were a great escape for me. They let something else besides hockey find its way into my large head, which at times was a welcome distraction.

****

Later that same year, 1999, I had something interesting happen regarding the issue of trust while I was covering a game in Denver. The Mile High City is always a favorite stop on the broadcast tour. Any time the Colorado Avalanche appear on my schedule I have something to look forward to. Terrific city with wonderfully friendly people and excellent restaurants. Throw in the Denver climate and the Cherry Creek jogging trails and I know I'm at peace with the world. For a number of years, ESPN programming had us frequently in Denver. We could always count on the Avs to ice a competitive team with extremely colorful players — Patrick Roy, Ray Bourque, Joe

Sakic, Peter Forsberg — the list was long and dynamic and our ratings reflected the country's affinity for the boys from Colorado.

On one trip to Denver I was approached by our director who asked me to do him a favor. Brad and I had worked together 20 times or so over the years, so I was happy to oblige. He wanted an autographed Joe Sakic hockey stick for his mom. I have a good relationship with most NHL players and my nature is to help people. Depending on the timing of such a request, this is usually something I enjoy doing. This particular day Brad's timing sucked. On game-days, teams skate in the morning and players are accessible. They almost always honor polite requests from people they know for things such as an autographed stick. Brad had waited until I arrived at 5:00 PM for a 7:00 PM game. The players at this hour do not want to be disturbed, nor is it appropriate to be autograph seeking while they are in their "game prep" mode.

My comment to Brad was, "Wow. I was here all morning and could have approached Joe then. Now my only window is after the game and I'm going out for a bite to eat with some old friends. How bad do you need this?" He said he was sorry and that he had only talked to his mom that afternoon and discovered she was a huge Sakic fan. I said I would see what I could do after the game. After all, it was for his mom, and I knew how hard I always tried to make my mom's wishes come true.

The game ended and I hooked up with the couple I would be dining with. We all went down and waited outside the Avalanche locker room. Finally, after 30 minutes it opened to the media and I dove in to find Joe. I was told he was showering. While my friends waited patiently outside, another 10 minutes slipped by. When Joe emerged he graciously signed the stick for me. I didn't expect less. Joe Sakic is not only a great player but a generous man who is discreetly philanthropic. He is a giver.

I gathered my company and headed for our ESPN TV truck parked outside the arena. I climbed the stairs to the main control area but didn't see Brad. I asked our crew if anyone had seen him because I had the stick for his mom. Without hesitation, a girl who worked part time on the crew stepped toward me and said, "Oh that's for me. I asked Brad for a Sakic-signed stick and he said he would ask you."

"I thought it was for his mom," I replied.

She smiled and said, "He didn't think you would do it if you thought it was for me so he told you that it was for his Mother." The first emotion I felt was anger. I felt as if I had been used. My quality time with my Denver friends had also been compromised. I immediately headed out for our late dinner without even seeing Brad, but with the indelible knowledge that he had been untruthful. If he had come to me at any point before I arrived at the truck with the stick after the game and said, "Listen, I need to tell you something - the stick isn't really for my mom, it's for Lisa, the girl in the truck. I wasn't sure you'd help me if I told you the truth so I stretched it a bit and before you go to any more trouble I just needed to square that with you," it wouldn't have been too late for him to salvage at least some of his credibility. I understand we all have egos and feelings and emotions and that sometimes they get the better of us. I would have understood. As it was, Brad had played the façade to the end.

The next time we worked together I wanted to get Denver off my chest so I took Brad aside and told him that what he did wasn't appreciated. He apologized and we went about our business. I've worked with Brad a number of times since that original Denver day and we have continued to have a cordial relationship. While we have moved well past the incident, I don't fully trust him. Because I don't trust him, it is difficult for me to respect him. Trust... It's something that takes years to create, and just seconds to destroy. And once it's broken, it's SO hard to earn it back.

****

In September of 2001 my world, along with everybody else's, was completely rocked by the tragic events of 9-11. Being on the East Coast, an hour from New York, I was a little bit closer to it than many people, yet far enough away to be completely safe. What an unforgettable day it was and it really effected me as it did most people. I still think about it often.

I was in our basement exercise room working out with Cissie that morning and I got a call from my landscaper. He said a plane just hit the World Trade Center. I quickly turned on the TV and saw the smoke coming out of the building. Like many others I had just assumed that it was a small plane that had lost its way. But when I saw the second plane hit I started to cry. Unable to watch what was unfolding, we walked upstairs and went out onto our deck. We both stood there crying in each others arms. I remember saying to her, "Our world will never be the same." The way I see things and the way I see people, it all changed in the blink of an eye. It was an incredibly emotional time. Even thinking about it now, more than a decade later, tears come to my eyes.

One of my teammates when I was a Washington Capital was Garnet "Ace" Bailey. Sadly, Ace was one of the unfortunate souls onboard United Flight 175, the second plane to hit. How lucky I was not to be traveling somewhere that day. I practically lived in airports, so I can only thank my lucky stars that for whatever reason I was home with my loved ones during that time — exactly where I needed to be.

September 11th is one of the reasons I became a U.S. citizen and the entire experience not only made me appreciate the people I loved and respected even more, it opened my eyes to our vulnerabilities. I count my blessings every day.

****

That next year I got the opportunity to work as a studio analyst for NBC at the 2002 Winter Olympics in Salt Lake City. I would have the honor of sitting next to Jim Lampley, one of the best broadcast journalists in the business. We covered both men's and women's hockey and it was so rewarding. With the Winter Games on U.S. soil, I was thrilled about being able to take part in such a huge spectacle. This was only the second incarnation of the "Dream Teams," where Team USA, led by coach Herb Brooks, went with the top American NHLers — versus the amateurs as they had done in years past. Team Canada was stacked with all of their top players as well and most everybody was praying that they would end up meeting in the gold medal game for the first time in 42 years.

Sure enough, they both advanced on to set up this epic battle that everybody had been anticipating. Canada was the favorite, but the U.S. team beat the Russians in the semis and were in really good position to pull off the upset. I remember it was close through the first two periods but Canada came on strong in the third and won the game, 4-1. It was marvelous hockey, just awesome. If you were a hockey fan, this was as good as it gets and I had a front row seat to it all. I was like a kid in a candy store.

I returned to work at ESPN completely invigorated. The hockey was so good, so pure, and it was almost as if I had a new lease on life. I remember the regular season winding down and then the playoffs starting. I felt so confident in my abilities as a journalist at this point, after having established a lot of credibility for myself as a broadcaster at the Olympics. It carried quite a bit of prestige to be selected for sports' grandest stage and I was very honored by that.

****

Near the end of the regular season, I wound up doing a game in St. Louis with Gary (Thorne) and an incident happened that really threw me for a loop. Gary got to St. Louis late because he had a baseball game he was calling the night before and as a result, he missed the morning skates - hockey's version of basketball's "shoot around."

I was there and wound up sharing info with him, including a tidbit gathered following some chats with a few of the older veteran Blues players after practice. At the time, Brent Johnson was their No. 1 goalie and he was just a kid. So I asked a couple of these guys if they thought they could win it all with him in goal? I sort of whispered it, implying that it was off the record — just between friends. And it was supposed to be.

They each looked at me with a concerned look and said, "No, we don't think we can." Now, I had complete under- standing of the rules of engagement with stuff like this. I knew that I could never mention that on the air as a quote. No way. What I could do, however, was maybe bring it up as a rhetor- ical question during the game if Johnson started to struggle in goal. I could ask, "I wonder if he has the confidence of his teammates right now?" Something like that.

That night up in the booth with Gary before the game I told him the story, about how the veteran guys I spoke to didn't have much confidence in Brent Johnson. As we got well into broadcasting the game there was a stoppage of play. We weren't going to commercial, so we needed to keep the con- versation going about the game. My jaw began to drop as Gary says on-air, "And Bill, some of the veteran players at this morning's skate admitted to you they just don't think they can win big and win it all with Brent Johnson in goal…". I just about died. I didn't know what to do, so I didn't say a word. Silence. Eventually, we just kept on talking and I was able to change the subject and we got through the game.

Well, later the next day I found out that the Blues man- agement had called a team meeting over those comments and the sh-- really hit the fan. Everything started to unravel with the Blues and unfortunately, this was seen as the catalyst. They had been to the conference finals the previous season and the pressure was on for them to get back, despite the fact that their No. 1 goalie from the year before, Roman Turek, was now with Calgary and had been replaced with Johnson. Once I found out about what happened in the locker room I knew this wasn't just going to blow over, so I called their general manager, Larry Pleau, to explain what had transpired and to apologize.

I told him that some things were said to me in confi- dence that were certainly never intended to be delivered on the air. I told him it was a mistake on my part because I never specifically told Gary that this was confidential info - off the record stuff - and not to mention it. I assumed he knew, but he didn't, so I had to accept responsibility for this. The Blues were in quite an upheaval - a time of discord. When harmony is damaged, group successes become more elusive.

The next time I saw the Blues was a few weeks later in Detroit. They had made it past Chicago in the first round of the playoffs and were working on a best-of-seven series against the Red Wings. After the game I spotted one of the Blues' top players, Scott Mellanby, as he was leaving the locker room and headed for the team bus. Scott was not only one of the brightest, most articulate players in the league, he was also a ferocious competitor.

I caught up to him and said, "Scott, I wanted to talk to you about what we said on the air in St. Louis about your goal-tending. I just want you to know that I never intended for that to come out and didn't mean to say anything that would put you guys in a bad position." He waited for me to finish and with an aggressive look said, "Well, you certainly f---in' did!" When I explained how it came down and that it had been a snafu between Gary and me, he told me he was glad I told him and walked away. Needless to say, St. Louis wound up losing the series and I could only imagine how torn apart their locker room was. I felt just awful.

I will never know if I was blackballed by any guys after that, but I probably was. Players don't forget stuff like that, when they get burned by reporters. I know I didn't. I felt bad for Brent Johnson, who was the one who had to be hurt the most by the whole thing. I hoped the incident hadn't shaken the kid's confidence and because he played nine more years in the NHL after that season, it probably didn't.

I knew the second those words came out that it would disrupt the harmony and rhythm of that locker room, and it was my screw-up, not Gary's. It's a privilege to be in the locker room and down on the bench with the players, no question. As a former player I am afforded access, both literally and fig-uratively, that other reporters don't get. I've earned that because I played the game. Oftentimes the players will tell me things that are off the record, in confidence, that you have to keep in the vault. No matter how much you want to break a news story or scoop someone, you have to maintain your journalistic integrity.

Other times players will just tell you things, like maybe that so-and-so is injured, or that so-and-so isn't liked by his teammates. You have to be careful not to slip and say anything though, and risk breaching their trust. Sometimes it's hard to remember what's on and off the record, night in and night out, it really is. I learned a pretty valuable life lesson that night though. Gary was a former prosecuting attorney in the U.S. Army and has never played an NHL game or spent any time suiting up in the locker room. How in the hell was I going to expect him to just know what was on or off the record? I couldn't blame him, I could only blame myself for not being crystal clear on something that was so important. I had to get out on that tight rope and just own up to it, for better or for worse, and that was what I did. My credibility was more important to me than anything else and I had to go into damage control. Trust...years to build up...seconds to destroy. My dad's words echoed in my head, "Do what's right. Do what's right."

To this day, I've never said a thing about it to Gary. I didn't want him to lose any sleep over something he had accidently stumbled into and wasn't responsible for.

20) BRANCHING OUT ONTO THE TIGHTROPE...

In 2003 I wound up doing a series of TV commercials for Bud Light and they were really a lot of fun. Bud Light was the No. 1 selling beer in the country at the time and they had a reputation for having really cutting edge, funny commercials. Well, the premise for the commercials was based on these four 20-something mullet-wearing hockey rubes who wore their NHL jerseys every day and lived in this fictitious town somewhere up north, called "Hockey Falls." In one of the spots, my favorite, the four of them are choosing sides for their street hockey teams. In "their" delusional world, they still think that they have a shot at hoisting the Stanley Cup one day. So they are standing on one side, and facing them is myself, Brian Engblom, Phil Esposito and Barry Melrose — all former players-turned announcers. So these knuckle-heads are standing there, talking with each other about who they want to pick — sort of sizing us up and weighing each of our pros and cons. They are debating back and forth and the dialogue shifts to the two captains who are choosing up sides.

The guy in the Bruins jersey says "What about Espo?" "Espo," the guy in the Blues jersey says "He hasn't played in like 50 years!" So the guy in the Bruins jersey says "Engblom's pretty decent." To which the guy in the Blues jersey blurts out, "He's a puck hog!" The guy in the Bruins jersey then says, "What about Clement?" This time the guy in the Blues jersey just smiles and then, together in unison, they all chant, "Clement, Clement, hands of cement!" Then they all start laughing like crazy. I just stand there shaking my head in disapproval, not saying a word. The guy in the Bruins jersey then says, "OK, take Melrose" To which the guy in the Blues jersey says real firmly, "Melrose thinks he's still coaching... And this is MY team!" Espo, getting antsy, then barks back "Boys, while we're young!" The guy in the Blues jersey finally makes his decision and reluctantly blurts out, "OK... Melrose." Barry smiles and cheers, sort of rubbing it in, and starts to jog over to his new team. As he's going past me I punch him and say real angry and depressed, "Come on... NOT Melrose!"

It's pretty hilarious, you have to YouTube it. Just classic stuff. I still get stopped by people to this day that smile and say to me, "Clement, Clement, hands of cement!" What's so funny about that line though is that I was the one who actually came up with it. We were shooting the commercial in LA and the day was getting long. The original line was, "Clement, nah, he can't play defense!" I said to the director, "Could we change that line because in reality that was the only thing I actually could do when I played." Luckily he was cool with it, "OK, what do you want them to say then?" I thought about it for a few seconds and said, "You know, when people ask my name I say Clement, as in rhymes with cement. What about something to do with hands of cement?" From there, the guys just ad-libbed it and it stuck.

Honestly, it was some of the greatest fun I've ever had shooting those commercials. To spend a whole day with Barry and Brian and Phil, it was wonderful. And these four mullet-head actors, they were hilarious, and always in character. They were from Vancouver and couldn't have been any nicer. Budweiser was family run in those days. August Busch IV was the president of the brewery at that time and they just did things right - with "values" coming before profit. As a matter of fact, it was not uncommon for their ad agency to create a million dollar commercial only to have Anheuser Busch say, "No. This isn't in step with our values," and throw it on the scrap heap. Brand managers like Tim Murphy and Phil Ware are still friends of mine. What a pleasure to be a part of all of that. We did those spots for several years and they were really popular because they were so quirky — the fans truly loved them.

****

The next year I called my agent and had him inquire about any broadcasting opportunities that might be available at the 2004 Summer Games in Athens, Greece. I had really enjoyed getting the opportunity to broadcast hockey at the 2002 Winter Games in Salt Lake City and I thought it might be fun to try something different. He made some calls to NBC and told me to submit my bio for consideration. A few months went by and I didn't hear anything. The Olympics were only six months away at this point and I figured they must've passed me over. Then, one day out of the blue, I get this e-mail from NBC announcing the lineup of announcers for the Summer Games. I looked at it and way down at the bottom I read: "Expert analyst for Badminton and Table Tennis: Bill Clement."

As it turned out, I had forgotten about this little blurb I had put in my bio about me being the Western Quebec High School Badminton Champion. I mean here I was, the champion of this obscure sport that nobody ever heard of in this tiny six-school conference in the middle of nowhere Quebec, and now all of a sudden I am this "world expert." How crazy is that? I really didn't know anything about badminton. I was just a good athlete in a rural area who had quick reflexes and could smash a birdie. At any rate I suppose NBC figured, heck, if I was an expert in Badminton then I must be an expert in ping-pong too. Wrong! A seven year old could beat me.

I thought about it and said to myself, "Why in the heck do I want to do this? I don't need this and I'm scared to death already. Nor do I feel like climbing that far out on THIS tightrope at this stage of my career." So I got on the phone and called my agent. I told him that there was no way I could pull this off. He just laughed and encouraged me to go for it. He reminded me how young-at-heart I was and about how much fun I could have if I was able to pull it off. I thought about it for a while and figured that since I preach to others about getting out on the tightrope and trying new things, this would certainly be a new challenge for me to conquer. Ok, I was in. And oh by the way, for the record it's table tennis... NOT ping-pong. Don't ask.

With that, I immersed myself into learning everything I could about Badminton and table tennis. Wow, what an unbelievable learning curve that was. It was just incredibly intense preparation for several months straight. Looking back, it was one of the most demanding things I have ever done. I had to gain a knowledge base of how the games worked, what the shots were, what the strategies were — and how to recognize them when I would see them. Who were the dominant countries and the best players - the favorites? What are the rules and how does badminton differ from table tennis?

As I began studying video that NBC had sent over to me, I started the process of surrounding myself with current and former players (if only by phone) to help me up the learning curve. I had to become a human sponge. It was quite exhausting but I figured if I was going to be advertised as an expert, then I needed to become an expert. I kept thinking about the gorge that represents our insecurities and our fears and the things that are going to push back and ultimately work against our performance success — and I was feeling all of those things. I felt that preparation would lead me across the tightrope though. As always, it would be my salvation.

Something else was in play as I prepared. Once I agreed to go to Athens, part of my personal philosophy kicked in and once again it was something that my dad had influenced. He always seemed driven to go the extra mile and to exceed expectations. That was how he lived, whether it was as someone's employee or in a customer service sense.

Shortly after I met Cissie and I created my own charter - kind of an agreement with myself. I called it, My Commitment.

MY COMMITMENT

1) I will be honest and sincere with my audience and listeners.

2) I will not allow my ego or my temper to overrule my head in a decision.

3) I am a leader! My positive attitude during difficult times will reflect this. If my attitude slips I am a role model for no one.

4) I will try to be gentle, objective, and fair with Cissie and the kids.

5) When someone engages my services I will always give them more than they pay for.

6) I'm not the toughest guy in the world...but I'll never quit!

While I have fallen from the tightrope on some of these, No. 5 is not one of them. I can look in the mirror and say that I have ALWAYS endeavored to give people more than they pay for. This, to me, is the essence of "value" and also of customer service. The starting point for giving more and exceeding expectations is doing what you say your going to do. So as I planned for Athens, I pondered the extensive preparation and how I would approach it all.

****

How many people do you know who always follow through with a commitment? I mean truly follow through? Especially with the little things.

"You will have it by Friday."
"I will be there Thursday."
"We'll repair it on Wednesday."
"I'll meet you on Tuesday."
"I'll call you Monday."
"I'll get this taken care of."

It sounds simple enough, doesn't it? Doing what you say you're going to? To me, this is the greatest "lost principle" of success. It is vital, yet because it is such a simple business principal it is often overlooked during strategic planning sessions. For a friend of mine named Nancy Meginniss, it was never overlooked.

Neither Nancy, nor her husband, Jim, were raised with a silver spoon in their mouth. They grew up in hard-working families in Philadelphia and typical of the thousands of families who comprised the local work force, nothing was ever handed to them. What they got, they earned. Early in their marriage the size of their combined paychecks was never an issue. Even though much of Jim's salary as a high school teacher was going towards the support of his three children from his first marriage, Nancy was pulling in the gaudy sum of $32,000 annually. This was the 80's and at the time, Nancy and Jim were comfortable.

There was very little glamour in working as an outside direct sales rep for a small company that manufactured printed circuit boards. Oh, it helped Nancy's ego to be able to tell people that the printed circuit boards were vital to C-130 airplanes, Apache helicopters, and B-1 bombers getting off the ground. Or that mammogram machines and other medical equipment couldn't function without printed circuit boards. But that was as glamorous as it got. The day-to-day sales slugfests were more about diving into the trenches and less about putting on make-up.

Nancy and Jim wanted a family of their own and in 1986 Nancy became pregnant with their first son, Michael. Being a fiercely loyal employee, she delayed her maternity leave as long as possible. Finally it was time. During the first few days of leave, Nancy simply relaxed and it felt good. She was, however, a worker and knew in her heart that she would be back pedaling her wares once Michael was born.

One day she began rolling some numbers around in her head. The first set of numbers centered on the cost of raising children. Jim and Nancy wanted to have at least two kids and as typically nurturing parents, hoped to provide them with a comfortable quality of life. The second set of numbers dealt with her work.

The company she worked for was bringing in gross revenues of $4 million annually and Nancy calculated that she was responsible for $1.5 million of the total. She realized that the other three salespeople and the sales manager were responsible for the remaining $2.5 million in revenue – about $625,000 each – less than half of the revenue Nancy was driving. She also knew that an independent sales rep could command a commission of 7%, which on $1.5 million in sales could easily eclipse her salary of $32,000. Of course the downside of being an independent rep was all too obvious. Independent reps work on commission only – no guaranteed salary.

In the days leading up to the birth of their son, Nancy contemplated the notion of going independent. A voice in her head kept screaming, "Are you crazy? You're about to increase your expenses with a child arriving and you're going to give up a guaranteed salary? Don't step out on that tightrope!"

Yet a second voice quietly whispered, "Go ahead. It's all right. You have what it takes to make it to the other side." Then one day her phone rang. The competition definitely knew the name Nancy Meginniss. More times than they wanted to admit, Nancy had established accounts going nose to nose with their best reps. Bill owned a company that competed in the printed circuit board market with the company Nancy worked for. When Nancy picked up the phone she hardly expected to hear the voice of an established competitor. After an exchange of pleasantries, Bill offered her a job doing exactly what she was presently doing. He would give her a 33% raise and a full benefit package. It was an intriguing proposition. Nancy said she would let him know by weeks end.

That night the Meginniss' had much to discuss. Nancy had a good job to which she could return. She had also done the math and assessed the scary elements of becoming an independent rep and now, here was Bill offering her another scenario. Nancy decided she could not accept his offer – at least not in its present incarnation. Nancy's company had been very good to her and she would not jump ship to a higher bidder. In addition, they also realized that Bill might represent a very timely opportunity.

The next day, Nancy called Bill and thanked him for his generous offer and let him know she couldn't go to work for him as a salaried employee. She couldn't do that to the company that gave her a start in the business. Then, she took step one in implementing the plan she and Jim had come up with. Nancy asked Bill if he would let her represent his company's printed circuit boards, as an independent rep at 7%

commission. With little hesitation, Bill agreed.

The next step in the plan was lining up customers to buy Bill's boards. Nancy would call her largest current client and see if he would be willing to begin buying his circuit boards from Bill if she was the person still supplying the service. Nancy and Jim struggled with this decision because it seemed to contradict the values that went into the decision not to join Bill full-time. But they ultimately concluded that as long as Nancy was in the "printed circuit board sales" business, she would end up competing nose to nose with her present employer anyway. Competing was one thing, jumping ship was another.

Her largest client was Rodney and his company assembled circuit boards. The boards Nancy sold were actually bare boards that house the hundreds of small components which comprise the completed circuit board. Rodney was a tough guy. Born and raised on the wrong side of the tracks, he was self-made with a PhD from the school of hard knocks. He threw his weight around and was hardly reluctant to lace a verbal rampage with a stream of obscenities.

As Nancy dialed Rodney's number, she remembered how he had intimidated her the first few times she had called on him six years earlier. With no one else but Nancy outside his office seeking an audience with him, Rodney would let her sit for 45 minutes before meeting with her. He often began their meetings spewing an obscenity-laced diatribe about the poor productivity level of one of his cursed employees.

Sure enough, Rodney said yes. Nancy now had her first principal, Bill, and her first client, Rodney. Rodney also agreed to let Nancy sell for him. He needed end-users of the completed circuit boards. The main reason they both agreed to Nancy's proposition was their knowledge that when Nancy Meginniss made a commitment, she always delivered. No matter how demanding a customer was, if she said it would happen, it did.

Because of this commitment, she always exceeded expectations and gave her customers more than they paid for. If it meant sitting up all night with Jim at the kitchen table covered with hundreds of circuit boards, tweaking a tiny flaw so they could be delivered the next day – on time – she would do it. If it meant driving in her car to find the truck that had broken down, picking up the boards she had sold that were due to be delivered that day, and seeing them to their final destination — she would do it.

Prosperity seemed to follow Nancy Meginniss, or at least that's what onlookers thought who weren't familiar with the effort she always made. More accurately Nancy created her own prosperity. Sure the work was taxing, but never to the point that she failed to keep a commitment. More than once, she saw printed circuits boards sitting at Bill's manufacturing facility in north New Jersey, waiting to be delivered to the client she had sold them to in Newark, Delaware. Bill had committed to a completion date when Nancy had come in with the order but since it was after-hours on Thursday there was no way they would be on the assembly line of the company in Delaware, which assembled tote machines for racetracks, by 7:00am Friday. Nevertheless, they were expected by then. Why? Because Nancy Meginniss had said they would be there.

Nancy would load the boards into her car and make the three hour drive to Delaware. She didn't miss deadlines. She even borrowed trucks when her car was too small to hold the payload. She often drove the trucks herself to ensure "on time" delivery of product. On many nights from Michael's infancy until he was three, he gnawed his way through chicken nuggets in the back seat as Jim and Nancy delivered product on time. It didn't matter that Nancy wasn't responsible for de-livery – she was an independent rep – but it was she who wrote the order and to her that meant that her name was in-volved in the commitment to deliver. It was not unusual for the Meginniss' to arrive at a client's locked up facility before sun-rise and either roust the security guard or simply gain entrance with the first employee to arrive, just so they could have prod-uct next to the assembly line when it went into action – as promised.

She once said to me when I asked her to reflect on her

great success, "I can't offer anyone anything but service…but I will give them service." Nancy Meginniss built equity with her customers through the power of commitment and the simple principal of doing what you say you're going to do.

Meanwhile, I was committed to giving NBC more than they paid for at the Olympics so that's how I approached it. In the end, I was able to pull it off. I looked like a college kid running from event to event, with my big bag full of notes and binders and videotapes. Just to learn the pronunciations of all the Asian players, yikes, that was a full time job in itself.

I will never forget one of the female names was "Suk-On-Mi." Pronounced Sook-On-Me. Another player was "Leen-Dong." Honest truth. These were Asian names - what should we have expected? Our female producer, Amy, had a great sense of humor and had some fun with us the day of our first broadcast featuring Leen-Dong. About 45 seconds before we went live to air, Amy stuck her head in our booth. She gets real serious and says to us "Look, I know you've been struggling with the whole Leen-Dong situation, so I just want you guys to know that I looked into it and found out that you can also use her Mandarin name as well. It's "Slim Penis." It took my broadcast partner, Don Chevrier, and I about three minutes to stop laughing - which meant that for the first couple of minutes on the air we sounded like we were choking on something.

During our Athens run I also knew I would be doing a solo performance. Late in the Games we knew there was a conflict between table tennis and badminton where important matches would be on at the same time. Our producers decided to let Don Chevrier handle table tennis with our researcher and former Olympian, Sean O'Neill sitting in for me. I would then handle the women's doubles badminton gold medal match…by myself.

All week I prayed for it not to be China vs. China. My prayers weren't answered. The names were very close and

I'll be damned if I couldn't tell the players apart. Same haircuts, same size, you name it. I fought hard against a panic attack prior to starting and the tightrope began swinging back and forth under me. I felt as though I was going to teeter off into the gorge at any moment. I mean I had no idea how I was going to determine who was whom - a major "accuracy issue" when calling an event of this caliber on a national stage. For me it was like calling a hockey game with no numbers on the players' backs.

Luckily, right before the match started I noticed that one of the women had a knee brace on, so I was able to positively identify her. As for the other team, I just had to hope and pray I could differentiate them somehow, because they looked like twins out there. Then I had an epiphany that really settled me down. If I didn't know who the players were...neither did anybody else. I decided to sell it with confidence.

Somehow I managed, but even to this day I have no idea how. As for the call, I let a lot of the sounds of the game carry the match. Less was more in this situation. I was not going to fear "dead-air" or silence. I was going to embrace it. I learned that about the speaking business also - that silence is as powerful, if not more powerful than the spoken word when used properly. In the end, I think I did OK. One thing I know I got right for sure, China won gold and China won silver — I knew I couldn't screw that part up!

In addition to badminton and table tennis, I also wound up doing play-by-play for the modern pentathlon. To be honest, I didn't even know what the hell modern pentathlon was before the Olympics that year. But I had to become an "expert" in that too. Go figure. It turned out it was athletes competing in five events in one day: running, swimming, fencing, pistol shooting, and horse jumping. The event was invented for the 1912 Olympics and was meant to simulate the experience of a 19th century cavalry soldier behind enemy lines. To survive he often had to ride an unfamiliar horse, fight with pistol and sword, swim and run. Without a doubt these men and women were tremendous athletes and great competitors. I was awed by them, I really was.

In the end, Athens proved to be a marvelous experience. Sure, I had to develop a knowledge base in seven new and different disciplines, but it proved to be one of the most incredible adventures I have ever been on. The only downside was that I couldn't bring Cissie with me. I knew that I was going to be working nonstop over there. I wish she could have come though because I saw some absolutely breathtaking things. Jogging up to the Acropolis with producer Jim Walton — what an unbelievable experience that was.

When I returned home from Greece that summer I was looking forward to diving into the new NHL season. Unfortunately, however, that was not going to happen. In 2004 the NHL's collective bargaining agreement expired between the owners and players and a labor war ensued. The owners locked the players out and the entire 2004-05 season was ultimately cancelled. It was sad on so many levels, but there was absolutely nothing I could do about it. Luckily, ESPN honored my contract that year despite the lockout, which was pretty incredible. I felt so blessed not to have the financial hardship that so many other hockey people had, that I became preoccupied with giving to others. In fact, I felt compelled to help as many people as I could that year.

I had often been asked for advice or guidance over the years and I never had as much time as I wanted or needed, so I decided to reach out to some of those people to see what I could do to help them. I was in a privileged position to be able to assist some people, whether it was with my time or money or knowledge or whatever. Some people wanted to get into speaking, others broadcasting, while others just needed some life coaching or were going through a tough time. Maybe that meant sending them a letter of encouragement, or visiting with them over the phone to help them develop a career plan. My hope was that if I could provide them with a boost of confidence and a suggested direction, then hopefully they would be willing to step out on the tightrope, regardless of what was pushing back against them from down in the gorge. I had no agenda, I just wanted to be there for friends and acquaintances who needed me.

Having no specific career direction leads to people being stuck in neutral more than anything. I have lost count of the times that I have been asked for career advice only to have the person unable to answer my question back, "Where exactly do you want to end up?" When this happens my response is always the same. "I'm sorry, I can't help you. I can't assist in charting a course to a destination that is vague or undefined. Write it down, very specifically, then we'll talk." Changes in expectations or circumstances may lead to directional changes along the way - we all have to call audibles at times - but having that well-defined light constantly flickering on the horizon representing your target, is paramount.

Over the years, Cissie has talked to me more than once about my working with people, some of whom I didn't know very well. She's a saint in so many ways, especially for putting up with me the way she does. My ego and my mouth often leave her frustrated. She's always very protective of me too. So, when she would see people who she perceived as taking advantage of me, or of my time, she would ask me, "Why do you do that? How can you give that away? You should be charging people for your advice and for your consulting. Don't they know how busy you are?" She wanted to stand up for me and protect me. I always appreciated it but my response to her then is the same that it is today — "This is who I am and this is what I do and I can never stop helping people."

In addition to giving back to my friends and colleagues, I also wanted to give back to the person who brought me into this world, my mom. So in November of that lock-out year, Cissie and I took mom to Scotland. She was 86 and could still travel. What an incredible time we had. Then in January we surprised her by taking her to the Manele Bay resort on the island of Lana'i, in Hawaii. I drove up to Canada to pick her up and then we flew out of Philadelphia together. She would later refer to Manele Bay as her "favorite spot on Earth." No question, it's a spectacular place. Bill Gates, of Microsoft fame, even got married on the golf course there. We looked at the lock-out year as an opportunity — and we definitely made the most of it.

I also continued to hone my craft as a speaker during this time, constantly working on my material and keynote speeches, presenting wherever I could in order to practice and refine. I found that every time I spoke at a conference or to a large group, other speaking opportunities would arise from that. There's an old saying in the speaking business: "The more you speak... the more you speak." It's so true.

Interestingly, during this transition several people asked me if I was interested in getting into coaching or becoming a general manager. Not to say I wasn't interested, because I was - but I didn't want that type of lifestyle. The quality of life that I had at this point, along with my desire to provide a stationary environment and raise a family with roots in one place — no way did I want to give that up. When you get into sports management you become a nomad, often moving every few years. No thanks. Plus, there was such a big learning curve in getting into that side of the business. I would have had to become an assistant coach and grind it out for a while before even being considered as a head coach. Then, once you're a head coach, you have no job security whatsoever. You can make a lot of money, but you don't have much of a life. You are gone all the time and you bring the work home with you too, you can never escape it. Plus, you are fair game and "constant game" for the media. As soon as your team takes a turn for the worse, the fans often turn on you too. Quite frankly, I've never felt my skin was tough enough for that kind of life and I decided that I never wanted to put my family through all of that. It's just too much - for them...and me.

****

By the time things finally got resolved between the NHL and the players union, all hell had broken loose. As it turned out, the NHL decided to part ways with ESPN and instead form a joint partnership with the Outdoor Life Network (OLN was owned by Comcast) and NBC. When I found out this deal went down I was in shock. I mean I had been with ESPN on and off for 18 years and I found out about it right alongside everybody else, by watching the news and reading about it on the internet. I immediately called my agent and he started working the phones. Luckily, I wasn't a free agent for long because I was immediately picked up by OLN and NBC, which was a huge relief. It also presented another tightrope - for the first time in my career, I would be a host, not an analyst or play-by-play guy. I had never hosted before.

OLN, which was later renamed as Versus (and is now part of NBC Sports), would do the bulk of the games while NBC did a game of the week on Saturday or Sunday, along with the Stanley Cup Finals. Versus wasn't as well known as ESPN so I knew that I was going to be a part of growing something from the ground up and that excited me.

In February of my first season as a host, I headed overseas to work as the hockey studio host for NBC at the 2006 Winter Olympics in Torino, Italy. I was going to be covering both the men's and the women's teams and was running non-stop from the moment I got over there. I worked alongside former NHLer, Ray Ferraro, doing the men's hockey competition, and Olympic gold medalist, Cammi Granato, for the women's. As it turned out, Ray and Cammi were a relatively new item at that point and they wound up getting married shortly thereafter. They are both just tremendous people. Working with Cammi was such a joy. I have so much respect for her. She was a former gold medalist as a player but brand new to broadcasting, so she was looking for direction. I really enjoyed mentoring her and sharing the tricks of the trade with her. It was on-the-job training for her because it was grueling work, but she did a marvelous job.

Ray, meanwhile, was everything I could ask for in a partner. He was a 17-year NHL veteran and a real pro's-pro. He too was relatively new to broadcasting but what a hard worker he was. I could trust him immediately. I would lead him all over the place, unscripted, and he would come up with meaningful, interesting stuff, every single time. He was so smart, so insightful, and so articulate. Whatever I needed him to do out there, he did it, and he did it really well. He was such a freaking warrior and he was certainly not afraid to speak his mind either. In fact, he created a bit of controversy for himself after the U.S. women's team got knocked out of the gold medal game when he publicly criticized Team USA's Coach Ben Smith for failing to bring what he felt were the best American players to the Games. It was a fair criticism I felt, but because Cammi had been one of those cuts, along with several other veterans in favor of younger, faster players, he took some heat.

What I remember most about those Olympics was the fact that we had some rather unusual programming circumstances. Our studio was actually a little basement room in the bottom of one of the two rinks they had there. It was extremely hot and really cramped, just a demanding work environment. It was intimate and we found ways to keep morale high - the on-air people, the researchers, the camera people, stage manager, everybody. We spent every waking moment down there, just hours upon hours, broadcasting, waiting, watching games, and then broadcasting some more. The circumstances had no chance of working without a dedicated crew.

For the amount of time we were on the air, we had very few pre-packaged features or programming to fill up time with either. This was guerilla broadcasting at it's finest. Seat of your pants kind of stuff. So we were grabbing guests out in the hall and dragging them into our little lair - it was crazy. We became so close so quickly though, we were a family by the time the Winter Games concluded two weeks later. Sometimes that's how chemistry is built, when everybody has to come together outside of their comfort zones to focus on a single cause, or mission. And as most closely knit teams do, we helped one another stay balanced on the tightrope. When Cammi, Ray and I presented gifts to our dungeon-mates on the last day, most said it was a first for them - getting a thank-you gift from the talent. They deserved it.

On the ice the hockey was decent but it didn't turn out like we had hoped. In the men's competition Sweden wound up beating Finland for the gold medal while the U.S. and Canada both got eliminated early — which definitely affected the ratings back home. As for the women, Canada beat Sweden for the gold, while the U.S. defeated Finland for bronze. Overall, it was another meaningful experience and I greatly appreciated the opportunity to be part of such an amazing global event. Again, any time you can be a part of something as momentous and impactful as the Olympics, it's pretty awe-inspiring.

21) FALLING INTO THE GORGE, AND THEN CLIMBING MY WAY BACK OUT...

Back home we finished out the 2006 regular season, which saw the Carolina Hurricanes win the Stanley Cup in a seven game thriller. My table-mates at Versus, Keith Jones and Brian Engblom, were driven to excel as were my NBC partners, Ray Ferraro and Eddie Olczyk.

The following season we were treated to another marvelous Stanley Cup Final in which the Anaheim Ducks beat the Ottawa Senators to become the Cinderella story of hockey. It was a fantastic series and my new studio-mate at NBC, Brett Hull, was a hoot to work with. I never knew what was going to come out of his mouth.

I was all set to enjoy my summer but just a few weeks later my life got turned upside down and I suddenly found myself plummeting into another gorge. In late June I got a call from NBC saying that the NHL studio at 30 Rock was being discontinued, which meant I was now out of the job that I had been doing with them for two years. I was disappointed but quickly resolved to make the best of the news and move forward.

Meanwhile, my contract at Versus was up but I had no reason to think I wouldn't be renewed. That changed when I got a call out of the blue the following week from a fellow broadcaster. He told me that he had just gotten a call from Marty Ehrlich, the guy who was running the programming at Versus at the time, asking him if he would be interested in MY job. I was in shock. I just thanked him and told him how much I appreciated him coming to me like that, because he certainly didn't have to. He said the same scenario had happened to him twice before and that nobody ever told him what was going on behind his back. Because of that, he vowed to never let it happen to a fellow colleague if he knew about it ahead of time. I was grateful for the heads-up, but nervous as hell about what was going on behind the scenes.

I called my agent and suggested we get started immediately on negotiating a new contract with Versus for the following season. I was making big money with Versus and figured that there would probably be a pay cut heading my way IF we could even get a deal done. Early the following week my agent calls me and says that they came back with an offer of a 40% pay cut. He said they needed to know whether or not I was going to accept the offer by 5:00 PM on Wednesday. We figured OK, this is standard procedure. We were in dialogue with them over the next couple of days and let them know we were working on a counter-proposal. We said we would have our counter offer to them either Wednesday night or first thing Thursday morning. We were trying to find some creative ways to modify my salary in order to make it a win-win for both of us. We dug in on the proposal and by late Wednesday afternoon we were close to finalizing it.

At 5:03 PM I received an e-mail telling me I had missed the 5:00 PM deadline and that my services were no longer required at Versus. Because I had failed to accept the offer by five o'clock, they were terminating negotiations. It was unbelievable.

Later that evening, they had already spread the word throughout the ranks of all of the broadcasters who I had worked with — including Keith Jones and Brian Engblom — that I would not be back with Versus.

Of all the times I reacted the wrong way in my life and after all I had learned from each and every experience, I was about to set a new low. I panicked and fired off an angry email to Versus and copied just about anyone I thought could influence the situation. This amounted to me doing a swan dive off the tightrope...without anyone's help. Behavioral consistency and emotional sovereignty were nowhere to be found

The next day, after I had cooled down and realized that I now appeared to be mostly unemployed, I called the president of Versus. He knew that I had worked hard for him for past two years and that my reviews were always good. I asked if he would be willing to let me accept their original offer, as-is. He said no. When I asked why they had ended it like this he said that they hadn't wanted the negotiations to drag on any longer. Really? We had been in negotiations for two weeks, it was July, and the season didn't start until October.

I realized there had been a plan all along to replace me and boy did I walk straight into it. Hell, I not only walked straight into it, I tried to douse the flames that were surrounding me with gasoline. How smart was I? Just like that, in a matter of two weeks, I lost 90% of my income. My words to myself from 20 years earlier when I started my speaking career echoed in my head: "The world of television is very subjective. If the wrong executive doesn't like my work, I can be replaced at any time."

I am constantly reminded, as I was that day, that 10% of our lives is determined by things that happen to us. The other 90% of our lives is decided by how we react to it. We have no control over the 10% and complete control over the 90%.

I remember hanging up the phone and feeling like I had been punched in the stomach because I could hardly breathe. Ironically, that very afternoon Cissie and I were scheduled to leave on our first European vacation. We had been looking forward to it for months and now the timing couldn't have been any worse. I was a mess. There I was, sitting in the airport lounge at JFK, completely upside down emotionally. I couldn't believe what was happening. It was the exact same way I felt when I realized my restaurant was going belly-up in Atlanta and that I would have to file bankruptcy. I wasn't just worried, I was really scared.

My wife looked at me and said "Sweetheart, let's just go home." I thought for a moment then said, "No, it's not going to get any better at home. I need to try to pull back and figure out what the hell just happened and why it happened. Then I need to figure out what we're going to do next." Thanks to an Ambien sleeping pill I was able to get a few hours of sleep on the flight, but when I woke up I was full of anxiety.

We spent 10 days touring Amsterdam, Prague and Copenhagen, before meeting our kids in Iceland. They were teenagers at the time and we had them fly over to meet us at our last stop. It was a stressful, yet amazing trip, and I did a lot of soul searching while we were there — especially walking through the city streets at four in the morning, unable to sleep. So many stories raced through my head and I tried to dig into my memory bank for examples of adversity that other people had coped with.

My mental rolodex stopped in Kalamazoo, Michigan, where early in my speaking career I delivered a keynote address to a group of young leaders at the University of Western Michigan. I was the first, in a series of speakers, which included Jane Elliott and Robert Kennedy, Jr. A student named Kristin Boyd who was president of the Keystone Leadership Program was assigned to be my driver and guide. She smiled easily and laughter was something she seemed very comfortable with. Her demeanor was consistently positive and her attitude was uplifting. A classic energy source. Before the sun rose in Amsterdam one morning, I thought back to her story.

A career as a gymnast seemed preordained for Kristin. When her dad put up the swing set in the back yard, she climbed to the top of the set even before swinging on it. These were monkey bars - her own version of a jungle gym - not a swing set.

Living close to Lansing, Michigan, the Boyds had a number of options when it came to providing athletic opportunities for their kids. They provided a loving environment for Kristin and her older brother and did well enough financially that they could afford extracurricular activities.

When Kristin was two and a half, Gayle and Ken enrolled her in a beginners gymnastics class. Pretty basic stuff, but at two and a half, she wasn't quite ready to begin practicing a dismount from the pommel horse. Forward summersaults were so exciting anyway - backwards summersaults, even more thrilling. Kristin couldn't get enough and loved every minute of it.

By the time she started elementary school, she was attending a summer camp at the local high school and her love for gymnastics was second to none. Every day she could hardly wait to get to camp and her proficiency was steadily growing. Because of her advanced skill level, it wasn't long before she was placed in the high school group. At age nine, she would be working out and competing with 15, 16 and 17 year-olds. Kristin Boyd wasn't just good…she was a natural. In fourth grade she enrolled in an elite gymnastics club where the curriculum was very demanding - the atmosphere, extremely competitive. She was years removed from the swing set in her back yard, yet she still exhibited the same passion for jumping and flipping and balancing and tumbling.

Just after Christmas in sixth grade, Kristin missed a week of classes with strep throat then began suffering pain in one of her ears. Another trip to the doctor's office revealed an ear infection. She missed another week of school and another week of gymnastics. She enjoyed school and was coping with a fair amount of pain, but her real aching feeling came from being separated from her uneven parallel bars and her floor exercises. Those were her favorites.

Instead of returning to health, one infection followed the other. Her immune system seemed suddenly unable to fight off unwanted intruders. Her gymnastics training became sporadic and only on the precious few days between infections, could Kristin make it to the gym.

By late February, after almost two months of fighting infections, Kristin noticed that her legs were losing strength. Each day they lost a little more and within a few weeks, she couldn't walk up a flight of stairs. At home she would crawl on her hands and knees to get up to her bedroom. To come down, she would sit down and bump, bump, bump her way to the bottom. In public she needed railings on both sides of the stairs so she could use her arm strength to help her legs.

Kristin now also needed an inordinate amount of sleep. On days when she felt strong enough to go to school she would come home and immediately crash until dinner time, then go right back to bed after she ate. Gymnastics practices and meets stopped all together. She had only made a couple of appearances in the past few months anyway. The sport she practiced four to five hours a day, five days a week – had now become an impossibility.

Doctors' appointments were the most regular activity for the Boyd family and test results became a broken record, over and over again. "We're sorry, but we don't know what this is", "Your tests came back negative, we're not sure what to do." Since the Boyds were running out of options, they had little choice but to go for broke. Surely the experts at the Mayo Clinic would be able to help.

It wasn't the diagnosis they were looking for. It wasn't even a precise diagnosis. The Mayo Clinic doctors determined that it was a virus. They thought it was in the Epstein-Barr family and that it seemed to be related to Mononucleosis, but they weren't sure. They said that since it was a virus, there was no known cure and that in time, hopefully the body would fight it off and the symptoms would disappear. How much time it would take, they didn't know. No name, no outward symptoms, no time frame for recovery, and no cure. At least it didn't seem to be life-threatening.

The start of the next school year meant comparing summer adventures with old friends and making new acquaintances. For Kristin, it also meant rolling out the same answers to the same questions. "No, I'm not really feeling any stronger." "No, we still don't know exactly what it is." "No, we really don't know when I'll start feeling any better."

In an attempt to offset a complete loss of musculature in her legs, doctors had prescribed a physical therapy program for Kristin. Ignoring her constant fatigue, she diligently worked at her program, persevering as she had done with gymnastics training. Little did she realize that another setback lay ahead.

No one knew that Kristin Boyd had one knee cap that wasn't aligned properly. The bones in her left knee simply hadn't formed correctly. As a result her left knee cap didn't track normally. Unknowingly, the physical therapists had Kristin following a regimen of exercises that was in complete contradiction with what her knee wanted to do. Her knee cap was being forced to create a new track for itself. When the pain became severe, Kristin revisited her doctor.

This time, there was at least a diagnosis. That was the good news. They knew what was causing the pain, so physical therapy was immediately halted. The bad news was that Kristin would be on crutches for two months.

On the one-year anniversary of the onset of her symptoms, Kristin was still crawling up stairs at home. More months flew by, but then there seemed to be some changes. They were small – so small that she didn't want to get her hopes up - but she was pretty sure that she could feel the strength slowly returning to her legs. As this was happening she seemed to think there was an uptick in her energy level. Could it all really be true? Each day, her strength and stamina took baby steps and as the improvements accumulated, Kristin knew this wasn't in her head. Real things – real positives were happening.

One day as she walked out the front door, heading down the street to a friend's house, Kristin Boyd realized it had been 18 months since she had felt like herself – had felt normal. So many things in her life had changed and she had yet to reach her 12th birthday. As she ambled along she broke into a slow jog. The significance of what she was doing took a moment to sink in and when it did, she began to smile.

It didn't take long before she turned her attention toward making an appearance at her gymnastics club to resume her first love. Standing under the uneven parallel bars, she stretched her arms towards the higher bar. Her fingers wrapped around the bar when her feet were still solidly planted on the floor. This was the bar she had always jumped to grab to start her routine. No longer the gymnastically ideal four-foot-eleven, she was now pushing five-eight.

Because of the virus, it would take her a long time to get her strength back and she was also now vertically challenged due to her growth spurt. In eighth grade Kristin began accepting reality – that she could no longer be a gymnast.

Anne Wicks was also too tall to be a gymnast. Volleyball was Anne's game. Since Kristin wouldn't be involved in gymnastics this summer she had plenty of time to travel with her family to some of her cousin's volleyball games. Anne was three years older and Kristin really looked up to her. How graceful yet aggressive she was. What courage she showed diving to the floor to dig out balls. The crazed look in her eyes when she went up for the spike, and the human wall she erected defensively that seemed to say, "How dare anyone invade my team's side of the court." It all looked really exciting. If it couldn't be gymnastics, then why not volleyball? Kristin would only be a freshman, but now she had size. That had to count for something.

While the goal was clear, the results fell short. When the names of the girls who made the team were posted, Kristin's wasn't among them. Oh, the determination had been there, and it was packaged with the right attitude — the skill level just wasn't there yet. It was a lofty goal anyway. Fifty girls tried out and only 14 were kept.

That night Kristin posed a question to her parents. What would they think of her becoming the team manager? It would give her a chance to stay involved and the opportunity to continue developing her skills on practice days if a regular didn't show up. Typical of the support Ken and Gayle Boyd had always provided, they told Kristin it sounded like a terrific idea.

She might have only been the manager, but the fact she wore a jersey made her feel like she was part of the team. So what if her number was double zero? That didn't bother her. And anyway, when a player would forget their jersey and shorts at home on game day, Kristin would give up hers, and double zero would make it into the game which made her smile.

After her freshman year Kristin played club volleyball in the summer and began racking up "real" playing time. She was flattered at the beginning of the summer season when some of her teammates refused to believe that she was just a freshman and that she hadn't yet played high school volleyball. As the summer wound down and the school year approached,

Kristin knew she had improved her game. Everything was better – spiking, serving, digging out balls. Getting cut in your freshman year probably should have been expected. Making it as a sophomore would be better in the long run anyway. Three years of high school competition would be sensational.

When the list was posted following tryouts, Kristin hoped that she had just skimmed over the names too quickly. She even said a split second prayer as she went back to the top of the page to look again. Slowly she scanned from name to name to name. When she got to the bottom of the list of 14, she realized there had been no mistake. She hadn't made the team.

When I met Kristin in Michigan and she told me her story, I recognized that she was an energy source. Her attitude and her "always hopeful" approach were really windows into her spirit of determination. So what an average person would have done after a second rejection, didn't concern Kristin Boyd and I wasn't surprised. The fact that the majority of humans would have walked away from volleyball at that point seemed unimportant. You see, in Kristin's mind, there was always hope. And because there was always hope, there was always a way. She would go back and play the role of team manager one more time.

Fulfilling every obligation in the "team manager" job description was important to her. Actually it wasn't so much a job description as it was a list of odd jobs. Help out with drills and warm-ups, fill out the line-up card, keep stats during games, and keep track of balls at away games and tournaments. Her double zero jersey was numerically appropriate in describing her direct contribution to the outcome of games, but she enjoyed wearing it.

To Kristin Boyd, eleventh grade had nothing to do with the fact she had failed to make the school team in ninth and tenth grade. It simply meant another opportunity to try out. On the day of the tryouts, dressed and ready to go, she crossed paths with a girl who had played on the team for the past two years.

"You here to manage again?", the girl asked.

"Only if I don't make the team," Kristin replied.

"Yeah, right." the girl droned as she walked away. Kristin Boyd's resolve never wavered.

When the list was posted, Kristin prepared for the worst. Her name hadn't been there twice – a third time wouldn't kill her. She held her breath and read the list. Before long she had wondered if she was seeing a mistake, but this time for a different reason. She stared at the list, focusing and refocusing. Could this really be happening or were her eyes deceiving her? As it began to sink in, Kristin broke into a smile. On her third try she had made the high school volleyball team. This year, double zero would be a player.

Kristin Boyd made the high school team in both her junior and senior years. She didn't play as much as some of the girls, but her story isn't really about playing time. It is about passion, enthusiasm and dreams. It is about attitude, adversity and love. It is also about redefining goals moving through life. Most of all, it is about perseverance – that powerful quality that lives inside us all…as long as we never give up hope.

****

That morning as I walked I thought long and hard about the difficulties and hardships so many people have to endure. There is a story in every family, on every street in every town. Compared to most real-life obstacles, my situation was laughable. By the time the sun came up I was done feeling sorry for myself and I vowed to move forward positively when I returned home. I made a promise to myself that no matter what happened, I was going to take the high road. If anyone opened the door for me to say something negative, I wasn't going to step through. I was going to be an energy source and not an energy vampire.

The biggest commitment I made to myself involved "giving." I decided that when we got home I was going to give more. I committed to giving more of everything - to charity and to others, especially financially. To many, this would seem counter-intuitive. You lose most of your income and decide to give more money away? Well to me the rewards from giving would act as a life-preserver while I built things back up - and there was no doubt in my mind that if I did this, good things would start to happen. I just sensed this was part of the road to rebuilding - to help others and to keep giving back.

When I got home I sat down and put pencil to paper. No. 1, I was solvent. I had put quite a bit of money away and had a very positive net worth. Of course I had overhead now, including three kids to take care of, but thankfully I had never lived beyond my means. No. 2, unlike my restaurant collapse right out of the NHL, I at least knew at this stage of my life that I had skills and talents that were recognizable to other people that I could monetize. I didn't have that when my restaurant went under and I had to start over as a starving actor. No. 3, I had a loving family that supported me, unconditionally. That was big. They were behind me and believed in me. I needed that.

I started making phone calls to see where I could work, where I could give, and who I could help. I was determined to be thorough, creative and relentless in order to create a new beginning for myself and my family. There were some people who extended their hands to me, like John Shannon and Gregg Baldinger at the NHL, who gave me the opportunity to host "The Commissioner's Show" with Gary Bettman, as well as NHL Live. Joe Thistel at XM Radio said that I could continue doing my radio broadcasts with them, which was something I had started doing earlier and really enjoyed. Rogers Sports Net, in Canada, put me to work doing some broadcasting work for them, which was great. Then, the Flyers and Comcast SportsNet said that I could fill in for Keith Jones as their TV color analyst when he was off on certain nights.

That one made me smile because Keith was one of my broadcast partners in-studio at Versus and he would miss Flyers games to do the Versus games when they conflicted. He hadn't been on Versus' original list of players they were going to audition and because I believed in him as a broadcaster and a person, I was able to get him his audition. Now, ironically, I would become his replacement doing Flyers games on nights he was doing Versus games. My partners were (and still are) Jim Jackson and Steve Coates. High quality humans, without a doubt.

It's funny, but it had all come full circle. Six weeks after plunging into the gorge, I had not only climbed back out, but had also followed through on the promise I had made years earlier to always step back out onto the tightrope. Things were coming together for me and I was beginning to breathe again. It felt really good.

****

Within a year I was completely back on my feet again. I had carved out multiple incomes from all of these endeavors. Things were good at home, we were happy and we were healthy.

My daughter Savannah graduated in 2007 with high honors from high school, The Hun School, a private school in

With broadcast partner Jim Jackson of
Comcast SportsNet, calling a Flyers game.

Princeton, NJ. In the little area where we live there is a wonderful school system and it comes highly recommended. Well, Savannah came to Cissie and me when she was finishing sixth grade and asked if she could attend private school. We asked her why and it was for all the right reasons. She felt lost sometimes in the larger classrooms and she wanted to get a good education. So, she commuted all the way through high school 45 minutes each way to Princeton. Today she is pursuing her acting career in New York, which is her passion. She's wonderful, just a really neat person.

Meanwhile, my son Chase would go on to graduate from nearby New Hope-Solebury High School in 2008. He was a star goalie on the soccer team and played a big part in leading his team to the state championship game his junior year. They wound up losing that game to Seton Academy out of Pittsburgh, 2-1, but it was such an unbelievable experience for him. For me too, to see my son playing for a championship in a sport other than hockey was so neat. It was also nerve-wracking. Any parent that has a goalie knows what I'm talking about. I was invested in that team too, big time, because I had coached 10 of the kids on the roster from my days coaching local travel soccer.

Our township didn't have a coach for Chase's age group at the time so I volunteered, even though I knew less than nothing about soccer. I immersed myself in the sport though - reading books, watching video tapes, spending time with "soccer people" — basically doing whatever I could to be the best coach I could for those kids. As long as I could stay ahead of my players on the learning curve I figured I would be all right. I was quickly reminded that coaching was way more involved than just spectating.

When you're coaching little people it's about helping them do as much as they can to succeed and my goal was to develop players and develop people. I felt it was my job to make sure that those two were intertwined. Development was going to be the key for me, no question, because I knew that if that happened properly then the winning would follow. I asked each player to come to me if he wasn't happy with his situation on our team and said I would do my best to help him. If the players weren't enjoying the experience, then I was failing.

I remember coaching my very first league game with my group of 10 year-olds. We had practiced for about a month leading up to it and we wound up losing. Honestly, I was pretty distraught over it. Afterward I remember walking back to the car with my clip board and my big bag of soccer balls, observing my players still milling around the soccer complex. Something profound hit me. In fact, it was meaningful enough that I would later write an article about it for a local publication. The title is "It's Not About You," and it was written straight from the heart.

"IT'S NOT ABOUT YOU"

The following was written out of the pride I take in being a Solebury resident and out of the great respect I have for the children, coaches and parents in our youth soccer program. It was also written after observing the youth soccer programs of other areas. Most of all, this was written in the hope that our township will continue to have the respect of neighboring townships and that in some small way, we will make a difference.

Two years ago I knew nothing about soccer, let alone coaching it. I'm not even sure I knew how to be a supportive parent for my own soccer-playing children. Since then I have learned a lot about what it takes to be a role model and a "true" supportive parent. Who have I learned from? A small group of the most wonderful teachers I have ever had — the nine and ten year olds who have played for me. If only we could put ourselves into the bodies and minds of our young soccer-playing sons and daughters. On some teams we would be asking questions such as, "Why do so many people yell at me when I have the ball?" "Why is my coach so angry, especially when we lose?" "Why is my dad screaming at the referee?" and "Why is winning the most important thing to adults?" If our kids could pass along words of wisdom, they might say, "You don't have to get so worked up dad. After all it's only a game.

And remember...I'm the one playing. It's not about you."

As parents, we live for our children. We want the best for them. We want them to be happy, well-adjusted, successful creatures. Most of all we want to protect them...especially from failure. These are natural and noble intentions — the result of our appropriate instincts. Yet when we connect these protective instincts to our actions, sometimes along the way the connection ends up short-circuiting. The result is, that rather than living "for" our little players, we end up living "through" them. Suddenly it becomes about "us" and our emotions, and not "them" and their development.

My education on this subject began five minutes after coaching my very first game...which we lost. I was rather despondent but put on a happy face for my players. We had played well enough to win; we just couldn't finish around the net. As I trudged away from the field, I began noticing my players. Some were laughing and horsing around on the playground. Others were giggling and yelling at those on the playground while ordering hot-dogs. Still others tugged at their parents' arms, begging for permission to invite some pals over to play. Then it hit me. Here it was five minutes after the game, and the only people who remembered the game or the score were me and some of the adults! Here I was, after my first game as a coach, licking my wounds and caring a great deal about something my players had already left behind. At that moment I realized the game had become about MY emotions and not about monitoring the emotions of my players, who didn't seem to need any comforting anyway. It had become about me.

As I walked, I imagined my son whispering, trying to comfort me, "It's OK dad. It's not about you." And it wasn't. It was about beautiful, impressionable, innocent children who simply wanted me to provide direction and structure.

Over the next few months I read as many coaching articles as I could and gathered a checklist of "Do's and Don'ts" from them, predicated on the words which still echoed daily in my head, "IT'S - NOT - ABOUT - YOU."

MY CHECK LIST

1) Never embarrass a player, especially in front of his or her peers.

2) Remember, my actions will speak louder than my words.

3) Be playful. Have as much fun as possible

4) My players will frustrate me. Try not to let it show.

5) Never yell at a referee nor allow my players to.

6) Try to avoid negative words such as, DON'T, CAN'T, and SHOULDN'T.

7) Be patient, but never at the expense of team discipline and structure.

8) When a player makes a mistake, rush to nurture not to criticize.

9) Have as much respect for my players as I expect them to have for me.

10)The game exists for the enjoyment and development of our young athletes.

11) It is often difficult, if not emotionally impossible to separate ourselves from the endeavors of our children. What can help us all avoid crossing that line of over-involvement is continuing to hear the soothing voices of our children whispering, "It's not about you."

It wasn't about me, it was about THEIR experiences and about THEIR development both as players and as young men. I realized that I had been blessed with this wonderful opportunity to help shape a small piece of their lives and I wanted to make the most of that opportunity.

Yet after the epiphanies I experienced just about every week, I also made mistakes. Our kids started as a Division 4 team and within three years had climbed to Division 1, so the games were really competitive. During a week of practices before a big weekend game we spent a lot of time working on defensive coverage on corner kicks. With a minute to go in the game, the score was tied and our opponents were awarded a corner kick. No problem. We were ready for this.

The play unfolded and I looked on in disbelief as my two best players botched their coverage and yielded a goal.

How could this have happened? When the game ended I was amped up and called the team together. Parents were milling around as well when I said to the team, "We worked all week on coverage and two players blew it! Who were they?" Zach and Charlie slowly raised their hands. "That's right. You guys think about that on the way home."

I knew as the words left my mouth that I was making a mistake - that I was crashing off the tightrope and contradicting my best intentions and the lessons I had learned from different coaches in my career. At that moment, emotional sovereignty had disappeared and my behavior was anything but consistent with the values I espoused.

The next day before practice Zach's dad asked if he could speak to me and we walked away from the field. "I'm really disappointed in you," he began. "You embarrassed the boys in front of everybody and it was uncalled for." He lectured me for about a minute and when he finished I responded. "You're right and I can't argue with anything you've said. I appreciate your concern for the boys and I will be apologizing to them both today," which I did.

All I could do was drag myself out of the gorge, wipe the slate as clean as possible, then start again. That day after practice I recall thinking back to a story a southern blues singer named Jerome Olds had told me. He said his grandmother had once counseled him that whenever he hurt someone he should think of it as driving a nail into a tree and that if he apologized, he should think of it as pulling the nail out. Jerome got the meaning immediately and understood that apologizing would right the wrong. Then his grandma finished the story by saying, "Always remember this - after you pull the nail out, the hole is still in the tree."

Looking back, I did more things right than wrong and I'm so glad that I made up my mind to try to "develop" players and people. I had seen it done the wrong way too many times - always coaching to win - so I was going to be committed to working on the fundamentals and on our boys' development. By doing this, I was actually working on my own development as well.

Sure enough, with that approach and attitude, the winning followed. Make no mistake, I cared about winning and losing — that was how I had measured so much of my life as a professional athlete, so there were times when I was conflicted. I just wanted to make sure that when we won, we did it the RIGHT way. That was the key. I wanted these kids to learn how to play the game the right way, with respect, with hard work, and with integrity. After each win I would walk down our handshake line as we approached the other team and quietly say to each player, "Be humble in victory."

I didn't know anything about soccer when I started, but I knew a lot about life and about togetherness. So we would practice on the big field and then one day a week in my back yard. We live on a five and a half acre lot, so we have a ton of room back there. I carved out a field, with lines and everything, and we would get out there and get after it. The players all brought their bathing suits so after practice the team would all jump in the pool while I threw hot dogs on the grill. I was, and still am, convinced that part of winning comes from trusting one another and from sharing good times away from the field. That was one of the secrets to building this successful program and I was happy to play a part in leaving a legacy about what really is important when you're running a youth athletics program.

I have always loved watching Chase play. His first go at college didn't work out the way he planned so he wound up spending a year in Guatemala and Peru, volunteering and teaching kids in the slums.

When Chase returned he enrolled at local Delaware Valley College, a Division III school with a soccer program. At age 22 it gave our family another chance to see him play and to watch him make First Team All-American. We're really proud of him.

22) THE THIRD PERIOD

By 2008 I was plugging along, making a great living, and trying to stay true to my mission — to be a giver not a taker — and to help as many people as I could. Karma. I have always felt strongly that you will receive, only as long as you give.

That summer I wound up working the Beijing Summer Olympic Games. Apparently I had done a good enough job at the Summer Games in Athens back in 2004 that NBC decided to bring me back. What was interesting about this time around though, was that I never even went to China. Nope. You see, while most of the marquis sports are covered live and on site, the lesser known sports, like the ones I did play-by-play for — table tennis, badminton, and modern day pentathlon — were all done "remotely." About half of the announcers went to Beijing but when it was time for me to announce an event or a match, I would walk from my hotel over to the NBC Studios at 30 Rock in Manhattan and sit down in one of our 10 sound-proof broadcast booths that were set up on the floor of the "Saturday Night Live" set. How crazy was that? The viewers at home never had a clue. Some of the events were on tape and when we got there they were already edited, so we would just do the highlight packages. Other times though, we'd have to be there in the middle of the night to do live events. We'd watch the live video feed and just pretend like we were right there next to athletes and the fans. It was a trip... without even having to take one.

Something else took up a portion of my life that year as well - something I will never forget. I decided to do some very meaningful charity work and as a result of that, I was able to fulfill a dream of mine: I got to have the Stanley Cup for a day. What a thrill that was. You see, I never got to have my "day with the Cup" when I won back-to-back Cups with the Flyers. That custom wasn't instituted by the NHL until the mid-90's.

246

I knew that if I could get the Cup at my event, it would just be huge. With it, I was able to set up the fundraiser that ultimately raised over $65,000 for a couple of charities that are near and dear to me. Amazing. People love the Cup. I'm still so thankful that when I asked Commissioner Bettman for permission to have Stanley for a day, he granted me that wish. It was a classy move.

So I built this big charity fundraiser around Stanley and what a fantastically amazing experience that was - to witness firsthand the power that the Stanley Cup has. To see the response in those people's eyes was something I will never forget. Everybody there was so excited and happy and friendly and positive and thankful. I was blown away. We had over 4,000 fans show up that day to see Stanley and pose for pictures with him.

From the time I put my original committee together, three months of my life seemed to disappear. Committee meetings, sub-committee reports, finding sponsors, advertising and promoting, the whole nine yards. A large undertaking that was so worthwhile and rewarding and it was a smashing success. I don't think I've ever seen that many smiling people.

Afterward I invited all the committee members and their families over to our house to thank them, and we put Stanley up on the island in our kitchen. I bought a case of champagne and we hung out drinking out of the Cup all night. How amazing. I learned about all the little rules regarding the Cup that evening from Mike Bolt, who works for the Hockey Hall of Fame as one of the "Cup Keepers." He is the guy who travels with Stanley to each Cup winner's hometown and spends 24 hours with them. That's one of the wonderful traditions that goes along with winning it today. You get it for a day to celebrate and party like a rock star. Wherever you live in the world, from Moose Jaw to Moscow, you get it for a day. Just a unique perk that leaves indelible memories.

Mike was Stanley's chaperone and he was there to make sure nobody hoisted him who wasn't supposed to. The Hall of Fame is very serious about it and they won't let just anybody grab it. No way! So, to drink out if it, as I learned, the person who holds the Cup has to have their name on it. Yes, when you win it a guy actually hand-engraves your name onto the side of it. How cool is that, by the way? Well, I actually got tendinitis in my arm from pouring so much champagne into people's mouths out of that thing! I mean it weighs 35 pounds...empty. There's a whole pomp and circumstance to it and such a universal reverence for it too. It's extraordinary.

Players are very superstitious around it too. In fact, they will never touch it unless they've won it. The superstition is that if you touch it before you won it, you will never win it. Some guys won't even be in the same room with the Cup if they haven't won it. Part of it is out of respect but most of it is fear that the superstition is true. What a blessing to have won it twice. Whenever I think about that I still get goose bumps. It's the most storied trophy in all of sports, no question, and certainly the toughest to win. I'm also really glad it's a cup. It's really hard to drink out of a plaque.

The crazy thing about the whole charity event was that it almost never happened. You see, the Cup was supposed to be flown into Philly from Toronto the Friday night before the event, but a huge weather front that brought rain and fog shut down the Philadelphia airport. I started having thoughts of having to cancel the entire celebration, it was so stressful. But how the hell were we going to turn thousands of people away at the door? I didn't even want to think about it.

We had been on our way to the airport twice only to find out that every flight was being cancelled. My dear friends, Johnathan Gingras and Jay Altmeyer (both of whom were on my committee) and our world class limo driver, Kevin Dupell, all started brainstorming when we got back to our house. How could we get Stanley to Philly by 9:00 am the next morning? What were we going to do? We all stood in my driveway searching for a solution. Kevin got a Toronto limo company on the phone to see if they would send a car to pick up Mike Bolt and the Cup and head south. I called Mike to see what he thought of the idea. He wasn't keen on it. He has an incredibly positive attitude but had red-eyed from Vancouver to Toronto the night before and had spent all day in the Toronto airport waiting for the weather to break. This was the WRONG time to be asking him if he felt like going for a 10 hour spin in the back seat of a car. I remembered that it's not what you say or ask, it's how and when. The timing sucked for Mike but I had a hunch he would agree if it was the only way. I said, "Well, I understand. Could you just think about it for a bit and I will call you back?"

Meanwhile, Jay had called a friend of his in Toronto named Joe Duplentis who happened to be a PGA caddy. We caught a huge break. It being winter, caddies were in their off-season and within 20 minutes, Joe had picked up a buddy in his SUV to be his co-pilot and was on his way to pick up Mike and the Cup. What an amazing gesture of kindness. I called Mike to give him the news and as I expected, he had wrapped his head around the idea.

At 4:00 am, Saturday morning, the knock came at our door. Stanley had arrived. The guys got a couple of hours sleep and then off we went to make people smile and raise money for charity. What an event. That day I developed a true feeling and understanding of what the Cup really stands for. It has such a unique, unifying quality. It has this power to some-how evoke an incredible charitable response from people from all walks of life. The lore of the Cup just brings it out of people. It's magical. I dare to think that if you were somehow able to plunk it down in the middle of a war zone, so long as both sides knew what it was and what it stood for, that everybody might stop fighting out of respect for it.

****

Incredibly, I got to be with Stanley again in the fall of 2010, but this time Mike Bolt came in (on a plane this time) with Stanley for a Flyers Alumni sponsored charity event that we were host-ing. Afterward everybody took off, so I asked Mike if he wanted to hang out. He likes having a beer as much as I do and he said sure. So we took Stanley in the back of my car over to this little Irish pub just south of the airport in Philly. The whole place just froze when we walked in. We set the Cup up on a table and let people take pictures with it while we had a couple of Irish beers. It was our gift to them and, boy, did they ever appreciate it. To see the impact that the Stanley Cup has on people is profound to me and it is unlike any other trophy in sports. It's so totally unique and powerful and yet it is simply an inanimate object. I just love it.

****

No sooner had we tallied the proceeds from my 2009 Cup fundraiser than the phone rang. It was a man who was the founder and CEO of Simply Beautiful Smiles, a group of 10 dental practices in both Pennsylvania and South Jersey. Dr. Louis D'Angelo wanted to hire me as a company spokesman. Dr. D and his wife, Paige, who is the head of operations for the company, have dedicated themselves to creating the "ultimate patient experience" in each office.

Originally we did some commercials and other video pieces for their website and I also did some speaking work for their various personnel groups. Our relationship just grew from there and now I also serve as their vice president of marketing. I do employee development work with them, especially the leadership team - Key Administrators. It's wonderful and I love every minute of it. I've been able to really dive deep with many of them. They are such wonderful people and the work is SO rewarding and satisfying to me.

For many of them, I have become a life coach helping them work through difficult areas. Getting a chance to work with Simply Beautiful's people on a consistent long-term basis has really reaffirmed my passion for being a trainer and motivational speaker, specializing in leadership and human development. I can work with them and coach them on everyday problems, then work to create strategies. It's so rewarding to be able to help people figure things out then provide them with the tools to move forward and grow.

I really feel connected to them and recently was told by

one Key Administrator when a tightrope presented itself, that she would say to herself, "What would be Bill's advice right now?" She even wrote down an affirmation on behavior and emotional control that I suggested and put it on the steering wheel in her car so that on her way to work, she could prepare for some of her tightropes.

I've developed a customized set of modules for my different development topics and it's allowed me to do some really profound things. At one meeting I had everybody define their tightropes. Then I asked them to each share their resistors and talk about what it was that was holding them back from being more successful. One of the Key Administrators called me afterward and told me that he had been "outed" by what I had done. He admitted that he probably could have stayed in his position for a number of years and said, "I was content to be average, and to fly under the radar. But I know that I can't do that now because I'm being forced to do the things that I thought I couldn't do - and to identify them, and to prioritize them, and to make sure that they are at the top of my list to get out and do every week. What's my tightrope-of-the-week going to be? That's the question I have to ask myself every day and it feels really good to be attacking and not always retreating."

My goal is never to expose anyone, but to help them expose their own areas that need strengthening. I had gotten through to them and they had bought-in, so many were making positive changes. I work with them on their leadership styles too and about how they interact with other people in terms of leadership. You see, leadership in my opinion is all about the power of influence. Yes, it's strategizing and making decisions for the group as a whole, but so much of leadership is in our powers to influence other people — to create buy-in and get them to contribute more positive energy, to be more productive and to jump on board as a team. That's what it's all about. When you can exert positive influence, people will actually follow you out onto the tightrope - then begin stepping out on their own - and the power to create this influence requires no job title at all. It's an amazing thing.

So many people have trouble getting out onto the tightrope, even when they see performance success on the other side. And why wouldn't they? It is instinctive to avoid potential pain until we realize that there is NO OTHER WAY. The first step is identifying what's down in the gorge pushing against them. Those demons can take on many forms but one of the most common things I run into that holds people back is communication, or lack thereof. It's the reluctance to, and avoidance of having those "difficult conversations."

****

Almost every day I am reminded of two "truths". First - opportunities exist everywhere as long as we are open to recognizing them. Second - commonality of values can create vice-like bonds.

Kent Lufkin is the president of 3rd Fed, a community bank headquartered in Bucks County, PA where we live. The better I've gotten to know Kent, the more I like him. He isn't pretentious – very down to earth. He grew up in the community bank world, not with the big players, which explains why he is strongly influenced by a sense of "community".

I often think back to the first time my Dad took me to our bank in Thurso, Quebec and introduced me to the manager along with the concept of saving. Just as my bank manager from that point on was accessible to me, Kent is accessible to every depositor and loan customer. Many even have his cell phone number.

Kent's high "customer touch" priority is what sets 3rd Fed apart from the big banks and direct community involvement is expected from the entire staff. All bank officers are required to go into the community multiple times every month to participate in, and support, business associations, charitable organizations and community groups. Since 3rd Fed has only 18 branches, people think of them as their "hometown bank" delivering a level of customer service second to none.

Being president of a bank of any size is a terrific business achievement but Kent doesn't take himself too seriously. Oh, he believes in professionalism but also wants to have fun growing the bank. This means sometimes being "unbank-like". 3rd Fed's colors are bright, lime green and they even have a mascot named "3rd Fred". Yes...he's green.

In 2013, Kent had hired me to speak to a business association he belonged to then again to his officers at 3rd Fed. In between, he had attended another function where I delivered a keynote.

After my speech to the bank's officers, Kent and I chatted over a couple of beers. I asked him if he had ever considered having a spokesman. We also compared values and discovered we were a lot alike. We worked out a personal services agreement and I now proudly represent 3rd Fed as their Community Ambassador in our area.

I've done so many interesting things in my life, which always seems to be changing and evolving. I've gone through some challenging times but the last few years have been extremely rewarding as I seem to be constantly stepping out onto new tightropes and reinventing myself. I'm still so optimistic and positive about what lies ahead. I believe my optimism comes from still being able to help people and to give to others.

A number of years ago I was walking by the TV in our bedroom after showering one morning and out of the corner of my eye, I saw an interview taking place with Senior PGA Tour golfer, Chi Chi Rodriguez. He's very flamboyant, really a flashy guy and a wonderful man. At one point in the interview, he was asked where his philanthropy came from - his giving. It was pointed out to him that he was a very generous man, who funded a home for disadvantaged children in California, as well as one in his homeland of Puerto Rico.

Without hesitation, Chi Chi said, "It comes from my father." His dad worked as a laborer and cattle handler for only a few dollars a week. Chi Chi welled up with tears in his eyes as he began telling the story of growing up with his five brothers and sisters in their tiny house in Puerto Rico. Their back yard was so small they were only able to grow one bunch of bananas. They would harvest them when they were green, then steam them to ripen them when they were ready for their family treat.

He told the story of the first night they got electricity in their home. They didn't have lights everywhere - they couldn't afford them - but they had a little lamp in the living room. The whole family was huddled around this marvelous little beacon of light and at one point, Chi Chi said that he and his dad both thought they heard something out by their back porch. His dad left and Chi Chi followed him.

They stepped out onto the porch which was barely big enough for two of them and for the first time ever were able to turn on the little outside light that had been installed. Right away they saw what looked like a man hiding under the side of the house. Chi Chi said his dad yelled out, "Who is that? Come out from under there!" A man came out and they immediately recognized him as their next door neighbor and he had a big machete in his hand. Chi Chi and his dad both realized what the man had come for. He had come to steal their bananas.

Chi Chi's dad got down off the steps, went over to the man and said, "Give me the knife." Chi Chi Rodriguez' life passed before him. He wondered if his dad was going to take this knife and chop the man up into little pieces. The demand was repeated, "Give me the knife," and eventually the man handed it over. Chi Chi's dad calmly walked to the bunch of bananas and cut off the bottom half and took it to the man. "I know you've come for these", he said. "You may take them. But I have something to ask of you. The next time you come to my home, I want you to enter through the front door. You may take whatever you need for your family...as long as you leave enough for my family."

Hearing that story had a big impact on me. As much as I wanted to help people and to give, there were days I'd say to myself, "I'm not sure I have any more to give or even enough today. I'm not sure I can help." Well, I don't say that any longer. In late 2011 I set a goal. Not a business goal or an income goal. I wanted to deliver 1,000 gestures of help or giving within one year. Incredibly, as soon as I set the goal, opportunities began presenting themselves. I thought – this is fantastic! It didn't take me long to realize that these opportunities hadn't just materialized, they had always been there. I finished with 826 and can honestly say I never enjoyed a failure more.

****

I LOVE where I am, as a broadcaster, as a performer, and especially as a human development speaker and coach, helping people change their lives. Whether it's an audience of 200 or 2,000, it is a profound experience and so meaningful. I feel I'm doing the best work I've ever done in my life right now, possibly because I am in a constant quest of ways to improve. As I reflect back, there's no question I've been blessed - without a doubt - both with opportunities to succeed and with setbacks which have led to personal tightropes to walk. And yes, I have fallen into the gorge more than once - and most often because of my own mistakes.

Facing adversity is difficult. No one achieves great success in life without coming upon it and staring it directly in the face. That's why so few people are as successful as they want to be - because of how they react when their eyes recognize what's in front of them. Instinctively, most people look for an easier way across the gorge - a path of less resistance. They will hike for miles to the left then miles to the right looking for a bridge, but eventually they come to the troubling conclusion that there isn't one. Some people walk away altogether, while others just sit and wait for a bridge to materialize — which almost never happens. Others will muster enough courage to at least step out onto the tightrope before scurrying to safety.

In the gorge lurks our resistors — the fear, the anxiety, things we just don't enjoy doing or lack confidence in. These are the things that push back against success and 80% of them are internal, or inside forces. It's easy to be paralyzed by our own resistors even though we can see success on the other side of the gorge. Invariably we notice that there is a tightrope stretched across and what does the tightrope represent? It represents our persistence, our courage and the willingness to at least attempt something we're not sure we can do. It represents our inner strength - a strength that each of us has that often remains untapped. There is no greater feeling than being able to shout to yourself, "I got on the tightrope today!" " Yes! Another tightrope accomplished today!"

We all come to gorges at various points in our lives. And sometimes they are plentiful enough to make us lose count. I know I have. There were gorges for me when I didn't know where my career was going. There were gorges for me when I was a player and I was being intimidated out on the ice by someone who wanted to beat me up. There were gorges for me when coaches decided to bench me or when general managers decided to trade me. I've had gorges in my previous marriages, as well as valleys in my current marriage. We all come to gorges that we must cross - somehow, someway.

Step out onto your tightrope. It doesn't matter if you make it to the other side. It doesn't matter if you fall into the gorge. Your strength will grow because you were willing to attempt to do the thing you weren't sure you could - the thing you weren't comfortable with. Most who try make it to the other side. Those who won't step out will never know.

Life is short and you can't look back, nor can you look down. Look ahead. Sure, there will be fears and anxieties along the way. Follow your heart and you will get there. If you believe you have the courage, you will find it. It lives in us all. Success awaits you on the other side, so long as you vow to work hard and live your life to the fullest. Be a giver, treat people with respect, love your kids, embrace your career, have fun. Remember, the world doesn't care how many times you get knocked down, only how many times you get back up. We are all EveryDay Leaders. Some of us just don't know it yet.

Thank you for letting me share my story with you. I hope you've had half as much fun reading about my continuing journey as I have had telling it. See you on the other side of the gorge. Cheers!

ABOUT THE AUTHOR

Bill Clement is a former National Hockey League center who played 11 years in the NHL, winning two Stanley Cups with the Philadelphia Flyers, and has been the face and the voice of televised hockey since 1986. He is also a successful communications coach, entrepreneur, actor and speaker.

For 15 years, Bill was the lead game-analyst for ESPN's extensive schedule of National Hockey Night telecasts. He can currently be seen on Comcast SportsNet Philadelphia broadcasting Flyers games. Clement has worked every Stanley Cup Final telecast since 1986. From 1999-2005 he did play-by-play for ESPN's Great Outdoor games and in 2004 & 2005 was the host of ESPN's Bassmaster Classic. In addition to serving as Studio Host for the "NHL on NBC" and for "Hockey Central" on Versus Network for two years, his voice continues to be an integral part of EA Sports' NHL video game as well. Further, Bill has been an integral part of the televising of five Olympiads.

Bill has won a Cable ACE Award as the best analyst in any sport and in a 1996 reader survey conducted by The Hockey News he was voted "Favorite Hockey Personality on TV." His acting credits include work on the ABC daytime drama "All My Children" and more than 250 television ads for clients such as Chevrolet, Deep Woods Off and NAPA Auto Parts. In early 1990, Bill entered the world of human development presentations and now makes corporate and association presentations on an international basis.

Bill is a native of Thurso, Quebec, the same Canadian town that produced Hall of Famer, Guy Lafleur, and both have streets in their hometown named after them. Bill is married with four children and currently lives in Bucks County, Pennsylvania.

(www.BillClementSpeaking.com)